# A Year OF FAVOR

365 Inspirational Devotionals Celebrating
God's Unstoppable Goodness.

## BENECIA PONDER

**Visionary Leader of Inspirational Devotionals**

**A YEAR OF FAVOR**
**365 Inspirational Devotionals Celebrating God's Unstoppable Goodness**
Published by ILLUMINATION PRESS
Atlanta, GA

ISBN: 978-1-950681-78-5 (paperback)
ISBN: 978-1-950681-76-1 (ebook)
Collaboration Organized by Benecia Ponder
Cover and Interior Design by August Pride, LLC

QUANTITY PURCHASES: Schools, churches, professional groups, clubs, and other organizations may qualify for special terms when ordering quantities of this title. For information, email to inspire@inspirationalauthors.com.

# An Invitation to Share Your Story

Do you feel called to write your story?

Your story is powerful. It carries hope, healing, and transformation that someone in the world desperately needs.

If you've ever felt called to share your experiences, but didn't know where to start, this is your moment.

I invite you to claim your free gift: The Inspirational Story Blueprint!

This simple, yet powerful resource includes:

- A Step-by-Step Action Guide to help you write your story with clarity and purpose.

- A 15-Minute Audio Training to inspire and support you as you bring your story to life.

- Practical Prompts and Exercises to uncover your most impactful message.

Whether you dream of writing a devotional, starting a book, or sharing your testimony, this blueprint will give you the tools to begin.

Your story matters. Let's share it with the world.

**Claim your free gift today.**

inspirationalauthorsclub.com/blueprint/

## Meet Benecia Ponder

### Visionary Leader of Inspirational Devotionals

Benecia Ponder, a Book Writing and Publishing Coach, empowers faith-driven leaders to craft impactful, bestselling books. With over a decade of experience, her mission is to inspire hope and transformation through the universal power of storytelling.

Need help writing, editing, publishing, or leveraging your book? Check out

# InspirationalAuthors.com

# Dear Reader,

Welcome to A Year of Favor—a journey that promises to transform the way you perceive and experience God's abundant goodness in your life. As you hold this book in your hands, know that it is more than just a collection of devotions. It is a beacon, a guiding light designed to illuminate the path of divine favor that God so lovingly weaves into our daily lives.

I'm Benecia Ponder, and as the Visionary Leader of Inspirational Devotionals, my heart is filled with excitement and purpose to share this incredible journey with you. I believe that God's favor is not a distant hope; it is a present reality, a gift that each one of us can unwrap every single day. This book is crafted to inspire you to recognize and celebrate that favor, to see it in the small moments and the grand, in the expected and the surprising.

A Year of Favor unfolds over 52 weeks, each week offering a new theme that delves deep into the facets of God's favor. It begins with a powerful FAVOR point, an affirmation rooted in scripture, setting the stage for your week. You will find yourself inspired by personal stories of triumph, grace, and divine intervention, stories that mirror the potential for similar experiences in your own life. And on the seventh day, you are given space to reflect and write your own Favor story, connecting your journey to the ever-present thread of God's love and favor.

My hope is that as you journey through this book, you will find courage to step boldly into God's promises, trust in His provisions, and live joyfully under His grace. May these devotions ignite a flame of hope and anticipation in your heart, leading you to share your testimony and inspire others with the goodness you've encountered.

Embrace each day with expectation, dear reader, for the time of the Lord's favor is now. Let's walk this path together, discovering His wonders anew, one day at a time.

With love and blessings,

*Benecia*

# Table of Contents

**Week 1: A Favor of New Beginnings** ................................................ 01
   Your New Beginning ................................................ 02
   A Real Yes! Dr. Nina Addison ................................................ 03
   You Will Begin Again Dr. Theresa Billingsley ................................................ 04
   Playing Safe Abruptly Ended Dr. Katherine E. James ................................................ 05
   Me First Sibyl F. Cole ................................................ 06
   I Do Rochelle D. Jacobs ................................................ 07
   Celebrating The Favor of New Beginnings ................................................ 08

**Week 2: The Favor of Grace** ................................................ 09
   God's Grace Is Sufficient ................................................ 10
   Grace In The Tears Makini Theresa L. Harvey ................................................ 11
   Messy Diaper Bonita L. Williams ................................................ 12
   Grace In Grief L. Marie ................................................ 13
   Grace In The Dark Benecia Ponder ................................................ 14
   Always Enough Sheryl Simms ................................................ 15
   Celebrating The Favor of Grace ................................................ 16

**Week 3: The Favor of Forgiveness** ................................................ 17
   Forgiveness Sets You Free ................................................ 18
   A Path to Healing Lori Miller ................................................ 19
   The Forgiveness Factor Dr. Theresa Billingsley ................................................ 20
   Remember with Mercy Rochelle D. Jacobs ................................................ 21
   Unstrapped Stacey Collins ................................................ 22
   I Must Forgive Makini Theresa L. Harvey ................................................ 23
   Celebrating The Favor of Forgiveness ................................................ 24

**Week 4: The Favor of Love** ................................................ 25
   Abundant Love ................................................ 26
   Unconditional Love Dr. Theresa Billingsley ................................................ 27
   Love Kept Us Sheryl Simms ................................................ 28
   For The Love Of... Rochelle D. Jacobs ................................................ 29
   Extraordinary Love Stacey Collins ................................................ 30
   Jesus Loves You Too Bonita L. Williams ................................................ 31
   Celebrating The Favor of Love ................................................ 32

**Week 5: The Favor of Purpose** ................................................ 33
   Living with Purpose ................................................ 34
   Finding True Purpose Autumn Anesi ................................................ 35
   Purposefully Evolving Dr. Katherine E. James ................................................ 36
   Purpose Beyond Position Alethia Saunders ................................................ 37
   A Vow That Saved Lives Benecia Ponder ................................................ 38
   Purpose Unfolds Stacey Collins ................................................ 39
   Celebrating The Favor of Purpose ................................................ 40

**Week 6: The Favor of Faith** ................................................................ **41**
   **The Faith Factor** ...................................................................... **42**
   **Ruby Stevens** Sibyl F. Cole .....................................................43
   **Believe** Sheryl Simms ................................................................44
   **Faith Fills Fridges** Stacey Collins ..........................................45
   **Closed Doors Can Open** Dr. Nina Addison ..........................46
   **A Crucible of Faith** Beverley Anderson ..................................47
   **Celebrating The Favor of Faith** ........................................... **48**

**Week 7: A Favor of Wisdom** ............................................................ **49**
   **Divine Guidance** ..................................................................... **50**
   **Be Coachable** Melanie Winters ..............................................51
   **The Secret Ingredient** Benecia Ponder ................................52
   **Job Hunt** Sibyl F. Cole ..............................................................53
   **Guided By Wisdom** Alethia Saunders ....................................54
   **God's Whisper** Sheryl Simms .................................................55
   **Celebrating The Favor of Wisdom** ...................................... **56**

**Week 8: The Favor of Joy** ................................................................. **57**
   **God's Great Joy** ...................................................................... **58**
   **Kill Joy** Rochelle D. Jacobs ......................................................59
   **Have Fun** Benecia Ponder .......................................................60
   **The Agony of Joy** Dr. Theresa Billingsley ..............................61
   **Joy of the Lord** Sueyuna Dorsey-Duthie ............................. **62**
   **Charlie** L. Marie .......................................................................63
   **Celebrating The Favor of Joy** .............................................. **64**

**Week 9: The Favor of Peace** ............................................................ **65**
   **Divine Calm** ............................................................................ **66**
   **The Authority of Peace** Dr. Theresa Billingsley ....................67
   **Know God Know Peace** Rochelle D. Jacobs .........................68
   **Peace In The Storm** Adrienne Y. Murphy...............................69
   **Choosing Calm Over Conflict** Sheryl Simms .......................70
   **Be Still** Beverley Anderson.......................................................71
   **Celebrating The Favor of Peace** ......................................... **72**

**Week 10: The Favor of Provision** ................................................... **73**
   **Divine Supply** ......................................................................... **74**
   **$2 for 2 Weeks** Karen McKinney Holley ...............................75
   **Faithful Journey** Benecia Ponder ..........................................76
   **Grandpa Eli** Sibyl F. Cole.........................................................77
   **Grow in Gratitude** Dr. Theresa Billingsley............................78
   **Don't Underestimate God** Benecia Ponder .........................79
   **Celebrating The Favor of Provision** ................................... **80**

**Week 11: The Favor of Healing** ....................................................................... 81
    Healing Promised ........................................................................... 82
    Healing Steps Sheryl Simms .........................................................83
    Cancer Battle Sibyl F. Cole ..........................................................84
    Healing Pains Rochelle D. Jacobs ...............................................85
    Soul Freedom Dr. Katherine E. James...........................................86
    Mirror of His Heart Stacey Collins...............................................87
    Celebrating The Favor of Healing ................................................ 88

**Week 12: The Favor of Community** ............................................................ 89
    Collective Strength .......................................................................... 90
    Piece of Cake Stacey Collins .......................................................91
    Unity in Diversity Benecia Ponder ..............................................92
    Iron Sharpens Iron Rochelle D. Jacobs .......................................93
    Faithful Friends Alethia Saunders ...............................................94
    From Eleven to Heaven Dr. Katherine E. James ..........................95
    Celebrating The Favor of Community ......................................... 96

**Week 13: A Favor of Strength** ..................................................................... 97
    Divine Empowerment ..................................................................... 98
    Losing Chari Sibyl F. Cole ..........................................................99
    ReNEWed Strength Dr. Theresa Billingsley ...............................100
    Finding My Strength Adrienne Y. Murphy ..................................101
    His Strength In Me Benecia Ponder .............................................102
    Defeating Downward Dog L. Marie .............................................103
    Celebrating The Favor of Strength ............................................. 104

**Week 14: The Favor of Patience** ................................................................. 105
    Trust in God's Timing....................................................................... 106
    When God Opens The Door Alethia Saunders .............................107
    AKA Journey Sibyl F. Cole ..........................................................108
    Time Heals Sheryl Simms ............................................................109
    Delay not Denial Bonita L. Williams ......................................... 110
    Incubation L. Marie .....................................................................111
    Celebrating The Favor of Patience ............................................. 112

**Week 15: The Favor of Humility** ................................................................. 113
    Lifted by Grace ............................................................................. 114
    The Power of Humility Alethia Saunders ...................................115
    Apologies Build Bridges Melanie Winters .................................116
    Kitchen Lesson Ashley Jenkins ...................................................117
    God's Plan, Your Peace Veronica Washington ...........................118
    "Help" Sheryl Simms ...................................................................119
    Celebrating The Favor of Humility ........................................... 120

**Week 16: The Favor of Salvation** ..................................................... **121**
   The Greatest Gift ..................................................................... **122**
   Fearfully and Wonderfully Made Dr. Nina Addison ........................123
   New Life In Christ Makini Theresa L. Harvey .......................... **124**
   Way. Truth. Life. Carol Holesak ...........................................125
   Paid In Full Vanessa Fortenberry ........................................ **126**
   Recovery L. Marie ..............................................................127
   Celebrating The Favor of Salvation ....................................... **128**

**Week 17: The Favor of Rest** ....................................................... **129**
   Peaceful Renewal .................................................................. **130**
   The Weary Soul Alethia Saunders ......................................131
   Life Needs an "Off" Switch Elvetra Cossie ......................132
   Let God Drive Ebony M. Cottman ..................................133
   Hands Off Bonita L. Williams ...................................... **134**
   Just Be L. Marie ...............................................................135
   Celebrating The Favor of Rest .............................................. **136**

**Week 18: The Favor of Generosity** .............................................. **137**
   Seeds of Blessing ............................................................. **138**
   Helping Hand Dr. Joyce S. Mallory ................................139
   Compassion Came Knocking Ebonie T. Pritchett ....................140
   A Heart of Generosity Dr. Theresa Billingsley ......................141
   Walmart Customer Sibyl F. Cole ...................................142
   The Joy of Giving Jacqueline James ...............................143
   Celebrating The Favor of Generosity ................................... **144**

**Week 19: A Favor of Trust** ........................................................ **145**
   Heartfelt Trust ................................................................. **146**
   Drop The Weight Kimberly Brown ................................147
   Holiday Visit Sibyl F. Cole ..............................................148
   Do I Trust Him? Mary Haney Underwood .....................149
   It Hurts So Bad Bonita L. Williams................................150
   Trust and Obey Carol Holesak.........................................151
   Celebrating The Favor of Trust ............................................ **152**

**Week 20: The Favor of Courage** ................................................. **153**
   Brave Steps ...................................................................... **154**
   Courage in the Saddle Benecia Ponder ...........................155
   Pray Big Rosie Davis .......................................................156
   Reptile Expo Sibyl F. Cole ..............................................157
   Warrior Rise Up Stacey Collins ......................................158
   Stepping Out On Faith Dr. Nina Addison .......................159
   Celebrating The Favor of Courage ....................................... **160**

Week 21: The Favor of Compassion ................................................................ 161
  Open Hearts ................................................................................................ 162
  A Divine Nudge Lori Miller .................................................................... 163
  Cemetery Visit Sibyl F. Cole ................................................................... 164
  Been There, Done That! Elvetra Cossie ................................................. 165
  Finding Strength Together Melanie Winters .......................................... 166
  Pray it Forward! Dr. Theresa Billingsley .............................................. 167
  Celebrating The Favor of Compassion .................................................. 168
Week 22: The Favor of Renewal ................................................................... 169
  New Strength ............................................................................................. 170
  Alive Again Dr. Joyce S. Mallory ........................................................... 171
  God Has An Eraser Bonita L. Williams .................................................. 172
  My Caterpillar Moment Veronica Washington ...................................... 173
  Simple Serenityrve L. Marie .................................................................... 174
  Nap Time Benecia Ponder ....................................................................... 175
  Celebrating The Favor of Renewal ......................................................... 176
Week 23: The Favor of Disappointment ..................................................... 177
  Hidden Blessings ...................................................................................... 178
  See The Bigger Picture Amanda Blake ................................................... 179
  The Performance Plan Alethia Saunders ............................................... 180
  From Setback to Purpose Melanie Winters ............................................ 181
  Love and Waffles Veronica Washington ................................................. 182
  The Gift of Rejection L. Marie ................................................................ 183
  Celebrating The Favor of Disappointment ............................................ 184
Week 24: The Favor of Surrender ................................................................. 185
  Letting Go for Greater Gain .................................................................... 186
  Beyond the Yield Stacey Collins .............................................................. 187
  Finding Courage in Faith Lori Miller ..................................................... 188
  Soulful Surrender Rochelle D. Jacobs .................................................... 189
  Gears of Surrender Felicia Pichon .......................................................... 190
  Not My Will Dr. Nina Addison ................................................................ 191
  Celebrating The Favor of Surrender ....................................................... 192
Week 25: A Favor of Vision ........................................................................... 193
  Seeing Beyond the Now ........................................................................... 194
  First Great Grand Dr. Joyce S. Mallory .................................................. 195
  Life More Abundant Carol Holesak ........................................................ 196
  Di-Vision Breaks Confidence Dr. Theresa Billingsley ......................... 197
  See Yourself Benecia Ponder .................................................................. 198
  The Gift of Wisdom Dr. Vanessa D. English .......................................... 199
  Celebrating The Favor of Vision ............................................................. 200

**Week 26: The Favor of Friendship** .................................................................. **201**
   The Gift of True Companionship ................................................................ **202**
   The Hens Sibyl F. Cole ..................................................................................203
   Soulful Sisters Benecia Ponder ................................................................204
   I Call You Friend Carol Holesak .............................................................. **205**
   A True Friend, Indeed Makini Theresa L. Harvey .............................206
   My Truest Friend Bonita L. Williams .....................................................207
   Celebrating The Favor of Friendship ..................................................... **208**

**Week 27: The Favor of Simplicity** ............................................................. **209**
   Finding More in Less ................................................................................ **210**
   Rich In Spirit Alethia Saunders ...............................................................211
   Confessions of a Hoarder Veronica Washington ................................212
   The Small Stuff Melanie Winters ............................................................213
   Slowing Down Gracefully Sheryl Simms ...............................................214
   No Wi-Fi Ashley Jenkins ........................................................................ **215**
   Celebrating The Favor of Simplicity ..................................................... **216**

**Week 28: The Favor of Resilience** ............................................................. **217**
   Strength in Trials .................................................................................... **218**
   Redeemed in Resilience Rochelle D. Jacobs ........................................219
   More Than Able Benecia Ponder ...........................................................220
   Dare to Be Different Dr. Nina Addison ...............................................221
   Broken But Not Defeated Alethia Saunders ........................................222
   1,513 Days Jacqueline James ................................................................ **223**
   Celebrating The Favor of Resilience ...................................................... **224**

**Week 29: The Favor of Reset** .................................................................... **225**
   Fresh Horizons ........................................................................................ **226**
   Break It Off Karen McKinney Holley .....................................................227
   The Reset Button Bonita L. Williams ....................................................228
   Leaning on Faith Alethia Saunders ........................................................229
   Turnaround Time Benecia Ponder .........................................................230
   God Provided That Day Hazel L. Grant .................................................231
   Celebrating The Favor of Reset .............................................................. **232**

**Week 30: The Favor of Integrity** ............................................................... **233**
   Walk Upright ............................................................................................ **234**
   Ripple Effect Miya Mills ...........................................................................235
   No Shortcuts Sheryl Simms .....................................................................236
   When The Doors Close Alethia Saunders ..............................................237
   The Lost Ring L. Marie .............................................................................238
   Price of Integrity Benecia Ponder ..........................................................239
   Celebrating The Favor of Integrity ........................................................ **240**

Week 31: A Favor of Connection .................................................................... 241
    Stay Plugged In ...................................................................................... 242
    Divine Connections Exist Dr. Nina Addison ....................................................243
    Writing Class Sibyl F. Cole ..........................................................................244
    Premeditated Provision Dr. Theresa Billingsley ...............................................245
    Amazing Touch Cynthia Beckles ...................................................................246
    Relationship Over Religion Bonita L. Williams ..................................................247
    Celebrating The Favor of Connection ........................................................ 248

Week 32: The Favor of Learning Through Failure ......................................... 249
    Rise Again ......................................................................................... 250
    Despair Meets Transformation Dr. Katherine E. James ....................................251
    From Failure to Favor Dr. Theresa Billingsley .................................................252
    Falling Forward Alethia Saunders .................................................................253
    Good from Bad Karen McKinney Holley .........................................................254
    Frozen Moment Benecia Ponder ..................................................................255
    Celebrating The Favor of Learning Through Failure ..................................... 256

Week 33: The Favor of Sharing Your Story ...................................................... 257
    Testimony of Favor ............................................................................ 258
    Turning Trauma into Testimony Rochelle D. Jacobs ........................................259
    Is Silence Golden? Dr. Theresa Billingsley .....................................................260
    Messy but Beautiful Miya Mills ...................................................................261
    My Imperfect Loaf Veronica Washington .......................................................262
    Not Alone Anymore Amanda Blake ...............................................................263
    Celebrating The Favor of Sharing Your Story ............................................. 264

Week 34: The Favor of Abundance .................................................................. 265
    Overflowing Blessings ........................................................................ 266
    Blessings Keep Flowing Adrienne Y. Murphy ..................................................267
    More Than Enough Janice White ..................................................................268
    Abundance Is My Birthright Dr. Katherine E. James .........................................269
    Ours For The Asking Bonita L. Williams .........................................................270
    Beyond Words Ebonie T. Pritchett ...............................................................271
    Celebrating The Favor of Abundance ....................................................... 272

Week 35: The Favor of Dreaming ..................................................................... 273
    Inspired Visions................................................................................ 274
    Sacred Collaboration Dr. Katherine E. James .................................................275
    Dreams Come Home Stacey Collins ...............................................................276
    When Dreams Build Bridges Alethia Saunders .................................................277
    Beneath the Weeds Kim Porter ....................................................................278
    Never Too Late Veronica Washington ............................................................279
    Celebrating The Favor of Dreaming ......................................................... 280

**Week 36: The Favor of Transformation** ............................................................. **281**
New Creation ............................................................................................. **282**
Dancing to a Different Beat Alethia Saunders ...............................................283
Transformed by the Master Vanessa Fortenberry ...................................... **284**
Spiritual Exercise Bonita L. Williams ..................................................... **285**
A Mended Heart Dr. Nina Addison .............................................................286
God Did It Veronica Washington .................................................................287
Celebrating The Favor of Transformation ............................................... **288**

**Week 37: A Favor of Worship** ............................................................................ **289**
Joyful Presence ........................................................................................ **290**
Heaven's Symphony Stacey Collins ............................................................291
The Blessing of Worship Dr. Nina Addison .............................................292
Worship Over Worry Bonita L. Williams .................................................293
Great is Thy Faithfulness L. Marie ...........................................................294
God Is My Healer Makini Theresa L. Harvey .........................................295
Celebrating The Favor of Worship ............................................................ **296**

**Week 38: The Favor of Redemption** ................................................................. **297**
Forgiven and Restored ............................................................................. **298**
A Mother's Redemption Mary Riley ..........................................................299
Do You Trust Jesus? Dr. Theresa Billingsley ...........................................300
In Spite of Stupid Kim Porter ...................................................................301
Taking Ownership Benecia Ponder............................................................302
Beyond the Wound Ebonie T. Pritchett .....................................................303
Celebrating The Favor of Redemption ..................................................... **304**

**Week 39: The Favor of Balance** ........................................................................ **305**
Harmony in Every Season ........................................................................ **306**
Balanced By Grace Alethia Saunders .........................................................307
Seasons of Balance Janice White ...............................................................308
Journey to Wholeness Beverley Anderson .................................................309
One Hat at a Time Bonita L. Williams .......................................................310
Finding Balance Sheryl Simm ...................................................................311
Celebrating The Favor of Balance ............................................................ **312**

**Week 40: The Favor of Growth** ........................................................................ **313**
Fruitful Faith ........................................................................................... **314**
Becoming Through Being Dr. Katherine E. James ....................................315
From Insecurity to Blessings Alethia Saunders...........................................316
Goals: Mine or God's? Karen McKinney Holley ...................................... **317**
Lessons in the Valley Felicia Pichon .........................................................318
Faith Over Feelings Bonita L. Williams .................................................. **319**
Celebrating The Favor of Growth .............................................................. **320**

Week 41: The Favor of Revelation ..................................................... 321
    Divine Insights ............................................................................. 322
    Trash or Treasure Sibyl F. Cole ..................................................323
    Uniquely Gifted Alethia Saunders ...............................................324
    A Real Relationship Dr. Nina Addison .......................................325
    God's Will Karen McKinney Holley ............................................ 326
    God Says I Am Bonita L. Williams ..............................................327
    Celebrating The Favor of Revelation .......................................... 328
Week 42: The Favor of Change ....................................................... 329
    Steadfast Presence ....................................................................... 330
    The Risk Revolution Dr. Katherine E. James ..............................331
    Embracing The New Janice White ...............................................332
    Be The Change Alethia Saunders ................................................333
    I Get To Bonita L. Williams ........................................................334
    I Need Exact Change Dr. Theresa Billingsley ............................335
    Celebrating The Favor of Change ............................................... 336
Week 43: A Favor of Anointing ....................................................... 337
    Divine Empowerment .................................................................. 338
    My Anointed Differencem Dr. Nina Addison ..............................339
    God Qualified Benecia Ponder ...................................................340
    Assignments Bonita L. Williams .................................................341
    Aligning with God's Purpose Beverley Anderson .......................342
    Anointed to Inspire Benecia Ponder ...........................................343
    Celebrating The Favor of Anointing ........................................... 344
Week 44: The Favor of Identity ....................................................... 345
    True Self ...................................................................................... 346
    Through The Creator's Eyes Benecia Ponder ..............................347
    Journey Back to Me Dr. Katherine E. James ...............................348
    Truth Shatters Lies Stacey Collins ..............................................349
    God is my Husband Makini Theresa L. Harvey ..........................350
    The Courage to Shine Benecia Ponder ........................................351
    Celebrating The Favor of Identity ............................................... 352
Week 45: The Favor of Hope ........................................................... 353
    Enduring Assurance ..................................................................... 354
    A Whisper of Hope Lori Miller ...................................................355
    Divine Timing Ebonie T. Pritchett .............................................356
    Finding True Love Adrienne Y. Murphy ......................................357
    Hope Through Tears Stacey Collins .............................................358
    When Hope Returns Alethia Saunders .........................................359
    Celebrating The Favor of Hope ................................................... 360

**Week 46: The Favor of Mindfulness** ............................................ 361
   Present Awareness ............................................................ 362
   Everyday Sacred Moments Sheryl Simms ........................................363
   Stay In The Moment Ishaq Edwards ..........................................364
   Silent Hearts Hear God Bonita L. Williams ................................... 365
   Hearing God's Voice Cody Persell ........................................... 366
   Listening for God's Whisper Rochelle D. Jacobs ..............................367
   Celebrating The Favor of Mindfulness ....................................... 368

**Week 47: The Favor of Confidence** ........................................... 369
   Unshakeable Trust ............................................................ 370
   From Fear to Faith Alethia Saunders .........................................371
   Not a Copy Benecia Ponder ...................................................372
   Trust Without Answers Felicia Pichon ........................................373
   Out of the Valley Bonita L. Williams .........................................374
   Never Hopeless Dr. Vanessa D. English ........................................375
   Celebrating The Favor of Confidence ......................................... 376

**Week48: The Favor of Direction** ............................................. 377
   Guided Steps ................................................................ 378
   At Your Age Dr. Joyce S. Mallory ............................................379
   From Resistance to Blessing Alethia Saunders ................................380
   The Right Way Dr. Nina Addison ..............................................381
   HOW Bonita L. Williams ......................................................382
   Called to Thrive Felicia Pichon .............................................383
   Celebrating The Favor of Direction .......................................... 384

**Week 49: A Favor of Breakthrough** ........................................... 385
   Divine Openings ............................................................. 386
   Broke Down to Breakthrough Rochelle D. Jacobs ..............................387
   Breaking Free Alethia Saunders ..............................................388
   Break Through Those Walls Dr. Theresa Billingsley ..........................389
   Brokenness Produces Breakthroughs Vanessa Fortenberry .....................390
   God Provides Veronica Washington ...........................................391
   Celebrating The Favor of Breakthrough ....................................... 392

**Week 50: The Favor of Mercy** ............................................... 393
   Renewed Grace .............................................................. 394
   Divine Do-Overs Benecia Ponder .............................................395
   Rearview Reflections Cynthia Beckles ........................................396
   Hidden Faith Vanessa Fortenberry ........................................... 397
   Not What I Deserve L. Marie .................................................398
   Teaching Me Mercy Veronica Washington ......................................399
   Celebrating The Favor of Mercy .............................................. 400

**Week 51: The Favor of Encouragement** ........................................................ **401**

    **Uplifting Words** .................................................................... **402**

    **When Words Save** Alethia Saunders ............................................ 403

    **Speak Life** Benecia Ponder ...................................................... 404

    **The Power of 5 AM** Dr. Katherine E. James ................................ **405**

    **Be Blessed, Encourage People** Makini Theresa L. Harvey ............ **406**

    **Doubt Didn't Win** Amber Rainsberry ........................................ 407

    **Celebrating The Favor of Encouragement** ................................ **408**

**Week 52: The Favor of Celebration** ............................................................ **409**

    **Joyful Praise** .......................................................................... **410**

    **Redeemed in Resilience** Rochelle D. Jacobs ............................. 411

    **60 Gifts of Love** Dr. Katherine E. James ................................... 412

    **90th Birthday** Sibyl F. Cole ..................................................... 413

    **Celebrating Christ In Me** Makini Theresa L. Harvey ................. **414**

    **God's Love in Every Hug** Alethia Saunders .............................. 415

    **Celebrating The Favor of Celebration** .................................... **416**

**Gratitude and Hallelujah** Bonita L. Williams ............................................. 417

**Author Bios** ............................................................................................... **419**

# THE FAVOR OF New Beginnings

New beginnings are a divine gift, a clear expression of God's favor in our lives

# Your New Beginning

### Isaiah 43:19 (NIV)

See, I am doing a new thing! Now it springs up; do you not perceive it? I am making a way in the wilderness and streams in the wasteland.

...

As we embark on this journey into A Year of Favor, it's a beautiful opportunity to embrace the fresh start God is orchestrating for us.

Each new beginning is not just a change; it is a divine expression of God's favor and grace. Think about how the seasons transition seamlessly, each with its own beauty and purpose. Similarly, God invites us into new phases of life, filled with potential and hope.

Isaiah 43:19 reminds us that God is always at work, creating paths where there seemed to be none and bringing life to barren places. This scripture assures us that new things are springing up, and they are not just distant hopes but present realities.

Embracing new beginnings might feel intimidating. The unknown can stir up fear and uncertainty. Yet, God's favor assures us that these changes are for our good and His glory. It's also a chance to witness God's faithfulness in unprecedented ways. Whether it's a new job, moving to a different city, or embarking on a personal transformation, these beginnings are packed with God's promise and presence.

Imagine the possibilities God is laying before you. Each step into the unknown is a step into a story only He can write.

This week as we celebrate the Favor of New Beginnings, reflect on the new beginnings God is unfolding in your life. Embrace them with confidence and faith, knowing that His favor is guiding you every step of the way. Let go of the past and step boldly into the future God has prepared for you.

...

### Lord,

Thank You for the gift of new beginnings. Help me to trust in Your plans and embrace the changes You bring into my life with confidence and joy. May I always be aware of Your guiding presence.

Amen.

...

# A Real Yes!

Dr. Nina Addison

...

## 1 Peter 1:3 (AMP)

Blessed [gratefully praised and adored] be the God and Father of our Lord Jesus Christ, who according to His abundant and boundless mercy has caused us to be born again [that is, to be reborn from above—spiritually transformed, renewed, and set apart for His purpose] to an ever-living hope and confident assurance through the resurrection of Jesus Christ from the dead.

...

It was November 21, 2010, when I finally gave God a real yes. For 21 years, I had gone to church. I was a very active member, but I didn't live right. I reached a point in my life where enough was enough. I went on a 40-day fast, seeking a new beginning with God. I had a sister in Christ fast with me, and we would pray together every morning at 5 a.m.

On the 40th day of the fast, God spoke to me through two amazing women of God. They did not know my secret prayers, yet they gave me answers from God that I knew came from Him. He showed me His power that day. He showed me He heard my cry. What I prayed in secret, He openly rewarded.

This was my new beginning! God changed so much about me starting that day. Now, 14 years later, I am walking in favors beyond my dreams.

...

### Abba Father,

as I step into new beginnings, bless my path. Remind me of Your grace and mercy daily. Guide my choices and strengthen me for this journey.

Amen.

...

# You Will Begin Again

### Dr. Theresa Billingsley

...

### Isaiah 43:18-19 (MSG)

Forget about what happened; don't keep going over old history. Be alert, be present. I'm about to do something brand new. It's bursting out! Don't you see it?

...

I will never forget the overwhelming fear and pain that gripped my heart as I faced the prospect of divorce. It felt like a literal death, a shattering of the life I had known.

Each night, I lay awake, staring at the ceiling, consumed by uncertainty about how my children and I would survive and adjust to the new reality. Questions swirled endlessly in my mind: How would I provide for them? How could I protect them from this heartbreak?

In the turmoil, when the weight of the world seemed too heavy to bear, I felt a comforting presence. My Heavenly Father was right there, holding our hearts tenderly in His hands, shielding us from a nervous breakdown. In moments when despair threatened to consume me, He whispered peace into my soul and reminded me that we were not alone.

Miraculously, as each bill came due, it was paid. The resources we needed seemed to appear just in time. It was like a tangible testament to His unwavering provision. It was as if He had woven a safety net beneath us, ensuring that we would not fall.

Sometimes, new beginnings are born from turbulent endings. Though the journey was fraught with challenges, it became a great adventure that revealed the depth of God's faithfulness. As I navigated this new chapter, I discovered strength I never knew I had and witnessed His love manifest in ways I could have never imagined. In the end, we won—not just in survival, but in thriving with renewed hope and purpose.

...

### Dear God,

Please give me strength and guidance as I start fresh,
trusting in Your endless love and support.
Amen.

...

# Playing Safe Abruptly Ended

Dr. Katherine E. James

...

**Ecclesiastes 11:4 (ERV)**

But there are some things that you cannot be sure of. You must take a chance. If you wait for perfect weather, you will never plant your seeds. If you are afraid that every cloud will bring rain, you will never harvest your crops.

...

Sitting at my desk, minding my own business, I heard God say, "I'm gon' need you to leave."

My fear responded, "God, You know Your daughter, and You're asking me to leave my good, government-paying job where I know what to expect?"

My soul knew it was true. Abba (God) indeed knew His daughter, which is why He gave me a five-year warning.

See, what you don't know is this message came thirty years in. Not only did He say that I needed to leave, but He also gave me two further instructions and a vision. I saw something jump off a cliff and an eagle soar, followed by, "And I need you to start taking risks and breaking rules."

Now, it may be difficult to believe that Abba (God) would instruct His daughter to break rules, but if you knew the life I lived, you would understand.

Rules kept me safe. Rules helped me to be right. Rules showed me the correct path so that I could follow them.

The Creator of the Universe was done with me limiting His magnificent creation with self-imposed limitations disguised as rules to keep me safe.

Six years later, at 56 (yes, I was still scared), I retired and began a life I never imagined possible—freedom like never before. There was so much to explore and experience that Abba had in store.

Are you playing it safe and limiting your life? He has so much more for you. Answer His call and start your new adventure.

...

**Heavenly Father,**

Grant me the courage to trust Your plan, embrace new adventures, and step beyond my fears. Open my heart to Your guidance, leading me to the life You have envisioned.

Amen.

...

5

# Me First

Sibyl F. Cole

...

**Proverbs 4:23 (NIV)**
Above all else, guard your heart, for everything you do flows from it.

...

I've spent most of my adult life focusing my time and attention on others. I was the "go-to" person, always putting others' needs first. This left me feeling drained and unfulfilled, causing me to lose sight of my own dreams and ambitions.

One night, I was looking through a drawer and found an old journal. It was filled with some of my aspirations—my "bucket list"—including trips I wanted to take and skills I thought about mastering. That night was a wake-up call, and I made myself a promise: to prioritize my own happiness.

The next morning, I went for a walk in my neighborhood. Instead of just walking, I made a conscious effort to feel the sunlight on my face and listen to the sounds of nature. Inspired, I signed up for a Zumba class I'd always wanted to take. This was the beginning of a new year and new beginnings. Even if it was just for one hour a week, I was going to carve out that time for myself.

This new self-awareness was unfamiliar, but I stood firm, understanding that self-care doesn't mean selfishness. I had to prioritize my own needs for my well-being and embrace the new beginnings life had in store for me. This change in attitude didn't just transform my life; it inspired others to follow my example, recognize their own needs, and do the same.

Self-love is the foundation for loving others authentically, and it's okay to be the hero of your own story. That's a new beginning we can all embrace!

...

**Dear Lord,**
Thank You for revealing my path to self-discovery. Guide me to prioritize self-care, granting strength and courage to embrace new beginnings with love and authenticity.
Amen.

...

# I Do

Rochelle D. Jacobs

...

### Numbers 6:24-25 (AMP)

The Lord bless you, and keep you [protect you, sustain you, and guard you];
The Lord make His face shine upon you [with favor], and be gracious to you
[surrounding you with loving-kindness]

...

TThe day I said "I do," God's favor was a comfort and a reminder of His presence and goodness. For years, I walked through seasons of heartbreak, praying, "Lord, send me a man," only to be left hurt and broken by relationships I thought were "the one." Still, I clung to God's promises, trusting His plan even when it felt unclear.

One evening, after a heartfelt prayer—sobs and all—I asked, "How long, Lord? When will you send my knight in shining armor?" In the stillness, I felt a whisper in my spirit: "Wait just a little longer, Rochelle; my favor is upon you." Though I didn't fully understand, I chose to trust Him. I focused on my faith, letting God heal my broken heart.

Then, in August 2020, after Wednesday night Bible class, I met my husband. He was unlike anyone I'd known—kind, patient, and deeply committed to God. He made me laugh, prayed with me, and shared dreams rooted in faith. For the first time, I felt truly seen and cherished. It became clear: this was God's favor, a reward for trusting Him.

On January 27, 2021, as we stood before family and friends, I knew this was more than a new beginning—it was a promise fulfilled. Through my journey, God gave me not only a godly husband but also a profound reminder of His love, favor, and faithfulness.

Blessing of a godly husband but had shown me His love, favor, and faithfulness.

...

**Lord,**

Thank You for Your perfect timing and unwavering love. Help us trust Your plans and embrace Your blessings.

Amen.

...

# Celebrating The Favor of New Beginnings

*Every sunrise marks a new beginning, a fresh chance to embrace the favor God bestows upon us. With faith, step into the unknown and discover the blessings that await in this new chapter.*

**Now it's your turn to write your story of celebrating The Favor of New Beginnings.**

Reflect on a moment when you felt the excitement and promise of a new beginning. What emotions did you experience? How did you sense God's favor guiding you through this transition? Capture your thoughts on how this new start has enriched your life and deepened your faith.

_____

_____

_____

_____

_____

_____

_____

_____

_____

_____

_____

_____

_____

_____

_____

_____

_____

_____

_____

# THE FAVOR OF Grace

God's grace is more than enough for every situation.

# God's Grace Is Sufficient

...

**2 Corinthians 12:9 (NIV)**

But he said to me, 'My grace is sufficient for you, for my power is made perfect in weakness.' Therefore I will boast all the more gladly about my weaknesses, so that Christ's power may rest on me.

...

In our journey through life, we often encounter moments where our strength seems to falter. It's in these times that God's grace becomes a powerful expression of His favor. His grace is not merely a comforting thought; it is an all-encompassing reality that sustains us through every challenge.

Reflecting on 2 Corinthians 12:9, we see a profound truth: God's grace is perfectly suited for our weaknesses.

When we feel inadequate or overwhelmed, it's His strength that carries us through. Our vulnerabilities are not obstacles to God's power; rather, they are the canvas upon which His grace is beautifully displayed.

Think back to moments in your life when you faced seemingly insurmountable difficulties. How did you find the strength to persevere?

It was God's grace working quietly and powerfully. This grace is a constant, unfailing presence, offering peace and courage when we need it most.

This week as we celebrate the Favor of Grace, I encourage you to lean into God's unmerited favor. Acknowledge your weaknesses not as failures, but as opportunities for His power to shine. Allow His grace to fill the gaps in your life, transforming your struggles into testimonies of His faithful love.

...

**Gracious God,**

Thank You for Your unfailing grace that meets me in my moments of weakness. Teach me to rely on Your strength, knowing that Your power is made perfect in my vulnerabilities. May I always trust in Your sufficiency.

Amen.

...

# Grace In The Tears

Makini Theresa L. Harvey

...

### 1 Corinthians 1:4-5 (NIV)

I always thank my God for you because of his grace given you in Christ Jesus. For in him you have been enriched in every way—with all kinds of speech and with all knowledge.

...

In December 2013, I was 61 years old and homeless because I couldn't find sustainable work. Terrified, I cried, feeling ashamed and disgusted with myself. I even dared to ask God, "Why me?"

The night I arrived at the homeless shelter, I was shaking like a leaf on a winter evening. The receptionist said, "Hello, Ms. Harvey, and welcome," and led me to my bed.

The next morning, I realized the shelter was on marshland where wildlife thrived. Peaceful tears flowed as I marveled at God's love and sense of humor, putting me on His beautiful waterway.

I co-facilitated Bible studies and helped residents find jobs. My anointing is to joyfully extend God's grace.

By July 2014, my daughter helped me move to Georgia near her. As I boarded the plane at 11:59 PM, I sang "I'm on the midnight plane to Georgia" during the six-hour flight.

...

### Graceful God,

Thank You for Your mercy. Help me glorify You through trials,
and lead me to persevere in challenges. In the Name of Jesus;
Hallelujah and Amen.

...

# Messy Diaper

Bonita L. Williams

...

### Lamentations 3:22-23 (NIV)

Because of the Lord's great love we are not consumed, for his compassions never fail. They are new every morning; great is your faithfulness.

...

It's hard to believe sometimes, isn't it? That our Heavenly Father loves us as much as He does. When we look at the messes we create—our messy attitudes, actions, and thoughts—it can feel impossible to imagine He still cares.

As I reflected on how God could possibly love us in our messiness, He reminded me of something from when my oldest daughter, Benecia, was a baby. One Sunday morning, dressed in a white suit, I held her on my lap. Suddenly, I felt a warm sensation and discovered her diaper had leaked, leaving a brown stain on my pristine skirt.

My first reaction wasn't anger. I didn't think, "How could you? Don't you realize what I've done for you?" Instead, I gently cleaned her, made her comfortable, and cradled her in my arms, cherishing her just as much as before.

That moment taught me something about God's love. If I, in my human nature, could respond with such care, how much greater is His compassion for us? God doesn't enjoy the messes we make, but He never leaves us in them. He's always ready to gather us in His loving arms, clean us up, and make us new again.

That's the kind of Father He is—patient, forgiving, and overflowing with love far beyond anything we can imagine.

...

### Lord,

I thank You for Your boundless grace. Cleanse my heart, guide my steps, and help me live in the light of Your love.

Amen.

...

# Grace In Grief

L. Marie

...

**Psalms 138:8 (NIV)**
The Lord will vindicate me; your love, Lord, endures
forever– do not abandon the works of your hands.

...

Tears flowed down my cheeks like a leaky faucet, and the loss I felt was almost too much to bear.

"Be strong," they said.

"It will pass," they said.

Their words, meant to comfort, only reminded me of the emptiness inside. Days turned into weeks, and weeks into months. How long would I feel this void? When would I wake from this terrible nightmare?

The pain was nearly unbearable, but I was determined not to succumb to my grief. How could I move forward?

A friend suggested journaling as a way to relieve my pain. As I wrote each day, I discovered a new sense of hope springing up within me. Putting my feelings into words helped me process my emotions. Over time, I realized my pain was becoming less excruciating. Through writing, I began to see God's transformative favor in my experiences, uncovering purpose in my journey toward healing.

...

**Dear Lord,**
even as I experience painful situations, I realize that You have a purpose and a
plan for my life. Amen.

...

# Grace In The Dark

Benecia Ponder

...

## 2 Corinthians 12:9 (NIV)

But he said to me, 'My grace is sufficient for you, for my power is made perfect in weakness.' Therefore I will boast all the more gladly about my weaknesses, so that Christ's power may rest on me.

...

Surrounded by sticky notes and Dr. Pepper cans, I was racing to meet a grant deadline. My laptop was my only focus, each keystroke getting me closer to completion. Then, just as I was picking up speed, everything went dark.

A power outage. Really? Now?

Panic set in as I felt the weight of lost time. But as I sat in the silence, something shifted. The absence of noise was strangely calming. I glanced outside and noticed the warm glow of the setting sun—a view I'd ignored in my rush. It felt like life was urging me to pause, to breathe.

I cracked open another Dr. Pepper and let the quiet settle in.

Isn't it funny how life forces us to stop when we need it most?

My tangled thoughts began to clear, and clarity emerged from the chaos. This interruption, I realized, was a hidden blessing—a chance for my mind to reset.

When the power flickered back on hours later, I returned to work with renewed energy. The words flowed effortlessly, and the looming deadline became a challenge I was ready to conquer.

Looking back, I realized grace often comes disguised as an inconvenience. That power outage reminded me to embrace the unexpected and find blessings in what seems to go wrong. It was a lesson in patience and perspective—a nudge to slow down and appreciate life's hidden gifts.

...

### Dear Lord,

Thank You for the grace in stillness. Help me embrace unexpected pauses with patience, finding peace and inspiration in Your presence.

Amen.

...

# Always Enough

Sheryl Simms

...

**Psalm 55:22 (NIV)**
Cast your cares on the Lord and he will sustain you;
he will never let the righteous be shaken.

...

It was one of the hardest seasons of my life. My younger brother David, the light of our family, fell critically ill unexpectedly. Weeks of sleepless nights, hospital visits, and unanswered prayers left me drained and afraid. I tried to stay strong for my family, but inside, I felt lost and powerless.

One day, I wandered into the hospital chapel. There, in the stillness, I broke down, admitting to God that I couldn't control the outcome. It was then I felt a quiet, undeniable peace, as if God whispered, "You don't have to carry this alone." I realized I had been trying to fix everything myself, but this was something only God could handle. From that moment, I began to notice His grace all around me.

I saw it in David's kind nurses, in my sister leaving notes of encouragement, in the meals from neighbors we barely knew, and in David's unshakable strength, even on his worst days. Slowly, David improved. The day he walked out of the hospital, laughter in his voice and light in his eyes, I cried tears of gratitude.

Looking back, the miracle wasn't just David's healing—it was God's grace carrying us through, piece by piece, moment by moment. His gentleness reminded me that even in trying times, His love is constant, and His presence never wavers. To this day, that season reminds me—God's grace is more than enough. Always.

...

**Lord,**
Thank You for Your grace; sustain us with Your love, and
guide us through every moment with Your strength.
Amen.

...

# Celebrating The Favor of Grace

*In every moment of struggle, grace finds us, a gentle reminder that God's strength is perfected in our weakness. Trust His grace to carry you through life's challenges, renewing your spirit and filling you with peace.*

**Now it's your turn to write your story of celebrating The Favor of Grace.**

Recall a time when you were overwhelmed by life's demands yet felt an unexpected strength lift you. How did God's grace manifest in your situation? Describe the peace and power that emerged, transforming your perspective and renewing your hope. How has this experience deepened your understanding of His unfailing grace?

_____

_____

_____

_____

_____

_____

_____

_____

_____

_____

_____

_____

_____

_____

_____

_____

_____

_____

# THE
# FAVOR
## OF
# *Forgiveness*

Forgiveness is a transformative gift that invites God's grace and peace, releasing our hearts to receive His abundant favor.

# Forgiveness Sets You Free

...

### Colossians 3:13 (NIV)

Bear with each other and forgive one another if any of you has a griev-
ance against someone. Forgive as the Lord forgave you.

...

Forgiveness.

It's one of the most powerful yet challenging acts we are called to embody
as followers of Christ. As you read this, perhaps someone comes to mind—
someone who has hurt you, intentionally or unknowingly. Holding onto that
hurt can feel like carrying a heavy burden, one that weighs down your spirit
and clouds your days.

In Colossians 3:13, we are reminded to forgive as the Lord forgave us. This
is not a mere suggestion but a profound invitation to release the chains of
resentment and step into the freedom of grace.

Forgiveness is not about condoning what was done; it's about choosing to
let go and entrusting the matter to God. It's about finding the courage to
say, "I release this, and I choose peace."

I know it isn't easy. Forgiveness takes courage—the kind that doesn't happen
overnight. It's a journey, one where each step forward is a deliberate act of
faith. But remember, you are not alone. God walks beside you, offering His
strength and wisdom as you navigate this path.

Think about the freedom that awaits on the other side. Imagine the lightness
of spirit that comes from releasing the burdens of the past. This is God's
gift to you—a heart unencumbered, ready to receive His blessings anew.

As you reflect on the Favor Forgiveness this week, know that it is a choice
you make for yourself, a step toward healing and wholeness. God has
equipped you with the courage you need. It's time to embrace it and move
forward in His grace.

...

**Father,** Give me the strength to forgive as You have forgiven me. Help me
release the burdens of the past and embrace the freedom that comes from Your
grace. Thank You for walking with me on this journey of forgiveness.

Amen.

# A Path to Healing

Lori Miller

...

Ephesians 4:32 (NIV)
Be kind and compassionate to one another, forgiving each other, just as in
Christ God forgave you.

...

I struggled with pain and hurt from my past, not realizing how much holding onto it affected my life—my relationships, finances, and happiness. It often felt like life was happening to me. Even though I was no longer in the situation I had put a stop to decades ago, the emotional damage remained.

As I journeyed through healing, I was able to embrace forgiveness. Letting go was a liberating gift. It didn't mean I condoned what happened, but it set me free from its grip.

I felt compelled to write a letter of forgiveness. Writing it out and then disposing of it can help with release. This time, I felt called to send the letter to the person who hurt me. Surprisingly, I felt at peace.

Weeks later, I received a response. Hesitantly, I opened it to find him thanking me for the action I took years ago, saying, "You gave me my life. I didn't want to do what I was doing but didn't know how to stop." His words touched my soul deeply. I was learning to embrace compassion—understanding that we are all God's children and no one is born intending to hurt others. Sometimes, they get lost in their pain and darkness, perpetuating the hurt done to them.

Forgiveness allowed us to heal, showing me that God's grace is ever-present, guiding us toward compassion and understanding. It reminded me that letting go doesn't just free us—it can also be a light for others to find their way.

...

**Heavenly Father,**
Grant us the strength to forgive, embrace compassion,
and find freedom through Your boundless grace.
Amen.

...

19

# The Forgiveness Factor

## Dr. Theresa Billingsley

...

Ephesians 4:32 (AMP)
Be kind and helpful to one another, tender-hearted (compassionate, understanding),
forgiving one another (readily and freely), just as God in Christ also forgave you.

...

Have you ever found yourself sitting quietly, and suddenly, the face of someone you need to forgive pops into your mind?

This has happened to me countless times, and I've come to realize these are signs from God nudging me towards forgiveness.

Initially, I resisted. How could I possibly forgive all the abuse I endured—physical, mental, and financial? I thought forgiving meant excusing the wrongs done to me. But as these divine prompts grew stronger, I couldn't ignore them. My unforgiveness was blocking my blessings, creating a barrier between Heaven and Earth.

Forgiveness isn't about how we feel; it's a decision we make. I had to take a deep breath and let God's spirit work through me. I learned that forgiveness isn't something I could do alone; it was God's strength in me doing the forgiving.

Try this: say aloud, "I choose to forgive [name] for [what they did]. I set you free from the prison of unforgiveness. You owe me nothing. I set you free."

Forgiveness frees both you and the one who hurt you. It doesn't mean you condone their actions; it means you refuse to let unforgiveness poison your spirit.

Let go of the burden and allow freedom and blessings to flow again. Forgiveness will bring healing to your soul and body, opening the door to peace and answered prayers.

...

Dear God,
Grant me the strength to forgive those who have wronged me. Help me release this burden, embracing Your peace and grace to heal my heart.
Amen.

...

# Remember with Mercy

Rochelle D. Jacobs

...

## Ephesians 4:32 (AMP)

Be kind and helpful to one another, tender-hearted [compassionate, understanding], forgiving one another [readily and freely], just as God in Christ also forgave you.

...

Navigating forgiveness in marriage can be tough, but God's favor empowers us to extend grace, even when it's hard.

In the early years of our marriage, I cherished honesty and trust, especially after past failed relationships left me broken. But one day, I discovered my godly husband had lied about a situation involving his family. My heart ached with disappointment, feeling betrayed by the one I trusted most. For years, I wrestled with unforgiveness, unsure how we could move forward.

Eventually, I surrendered my hurt to God. As I prayed, I felt a pull toward forgiveness, even when it felt unnatural. I learned forgiveness didn't erase the pain but released bitterness, offering grace instead.

I wrote my husband a letter, pouring out my hurt and the damage his lie caused. Afterward, I burned the letter, feeling a weight lift as I embraced the freedom of true forgiveness. I approached him with honesty and a softened heart, ready to forgive and rebuild trust.

With tears in his eyes, he shared his struggles and fears. Together, we prayed for God's healing and strength. Through His favor, we found peace—not just in reconciliation, but in understanding we are called to show each other the same mercy God shows us daily.

Our journey taught us that God's favor shines brightest when we forgive, inviting His healing power into our hearts and marriage.

...

**Lord,**

Grant me the strength to forgive, embracing Your grace and mercy, so I may heal and restore love in my heart and relationships.

Amen..

...

# Unstrapped

Stacey Collins

...

**Colossians 3:13 (NIV)**
Bear with each other and forgive whatever grievances you may
have against one another. Forgive as the Lord forgave you.

...

I was a social butterfly, and now I couldn't move! Alone... isolated... silenced... imprisoned... unforgiveness became my jail. I was designed to be sensitive from birth! Hurt here...pain there...it seemed to never stop!

As time went by, I "learned" to forgive, or should I say, "went through the motions" of forgiving. Wasn't I forgiven? Shouldn't I return the favor? But somehow, I felt forgiveness came from ME. Like I, Stacey, had the power to forgive. I had the honor to wear an invisible badge that said, "I forgive."

But when a hurricane came unexpectedly... when life rocked the feeble foundation right out from under me... there I was... exposed! Words... words... words... like cannonballs... slander... betrayal... rejection... SHAME... coming straight at me! Those cannonballs went right into my heart... into my mind... waiting... ready to explode at any moment...

One day, I tried to describe how I felt. It shocked me! It was as if I was sitting in an electric chair on low voltage, anticipating that at any time someone would flip the lever and UP the current... ZAP!

It was in that moment of awakening that God whispered to my spirit, "Stacey, you aren't strapped in, stand up!" I stood up! Now I stand free, knowing His forgiveness flows through me, not from me.

...

**Heavenly Father,**
Thank You for the gift of forgiveness. May Your love flow through us, empowering us to forgive as You have forgiven.
Amen.

...

# I Must Forgive

Makini Theresa L. Harvey

...

**Matthew 6:14 (NIV)**

For if you forgive other people when they sin against you, your heavenly Father will also forgive you.

...

When I accepted Jesus as my Lord and Savior, the Holy Spirit prompted me with what I needed to do next, saying I must: stop saying ugly, vile curse words, forgive others who hurt me, and ask those I hurt to forgive me.

I asked each of my five children to forgive me for being verbally and too often physically abusive, and I thank God that each one forgave me.

At a family gathering, knowing my ex-husband would be there, God gave me an idea for the "forgiveness discussion." We went to the merry-go-round, and while twirling, I asked him to forgive me for my actions that led to the divorce and ruining our marriage. With a shocked look on his face, he reluctantly forgave me. Then I forgave him for his part in ruining our marriage and thanked him. It was one of the most healing and liberating experiences of my life.

...

**Forgiving, Merciful God,**

Thank You for forgiving me and giving me the wisdom and freedom to forgive others, in the Holy Name of Jesus Christ, hallelujah and Amen.

...

# Celebrating The Favor of Forgiveness

*Forgiveness is the key that unlocks the door to freedom and peace. By letting go of past hurts, you open your heart to God's abundant favor and healing. Embrace the power of forgiveness and experience the soothing balm of His love.*

**Now it's your turn to write your story of celebrating The Favor of Forgiveness.**

Think about a moment when you chose to forgive someone or were forgiven yourself. How did this act of grace impact your heart and relationships? Describe how forgiveness brought healing and new opportunities for growth and connection in your life. Reflect on how God's favor was evident in this journey.

_____

_____

_____

_____

_____

_____

_____

_____

_____

_____

_____

_____

_____

_____

_____

_____

# THE FAVOR OF Love

God's love empowers us to love abundantly, transforming our hearts and enriching our relationships with His favor.

# Abundant Love

...

**1 John 4:19 (NIV)**
We love because he first loved us.

...

Love is one of the most profound expressions of God's favor in our lives. It's the bedrock upon which our faith is built, and it transforms us from the inside out.

1 John 4:19 reminds us that our capacity to love originates from the divine love God has poured into our hearts. This love is not just a feeling; it's an active and powerful force that propels us to reach out to others with kindness and compassion.

Consider how God's love has shaped your life. Reflect on moments when you felt truly loved and accepted. These experiences are glimpses of God's immense love for you. His love empowers you to love abundantly, building bridges of connection and understanding in your relationships.

When we embrace this love, we are not only recipients but also conduits of His favor, able to extend grace and mercy to those around us.

This week as we celebrate the Favor of Love, intentionally focus on expressing this divine love in your interactions. Let God's love overflow, enabling you to touch the lives of those around you in meaningful ways. Whether it's through a kind word, an act of service, or simply being present, your love can be a reflection of God's favor.

Remember, loving others is not always easy. It requires patience, understanding, and sometimes sacrifice. But with God's love as your foundation, you can overcome challenges and foster relationships that reflect His grace and favor.

...

**Lord,**
Fill my heart with Your love, so I may love others deeply and sincerely. Thank You for loving me first. Help me to be a vessel of Your favor, extending love and kindness in all my relationships.
Amen.

# Unconditional Love

Dr. Theresa Billingsley

...

**John 3:16 (NLT)**
For this is how God loved the world: He gave his one and only Son, so that everyone who believes in him will not perish but have eternal life.

...

Being loved by someone you've never met can be hard to comprehend. Knowing that they are fully aware of your flaws and insecurities and still love you—without impure motives or manipulation—is rare. Especially in a world where love is often defined by acts of service or gift-giving.

It takes the love of God within us to continue loving others beyond their faults, even when we receive nothing in return. Parents are meant to be an example of God's love on earth. God is love, and He loves us unconditionally.

Sometimes, when we encounter the unconditional love of God, it overwhelms us and changes us forever. We may feel undeserving and almost want to push it away.

Love is a superpower—it transforms. God sent His love to earth through Jesus Christ, and when we receive Jesus in our hearts, His love for others is manifested through us. Just as God used Jesus' body to bring love to the world, Jesus now uses our bodies to bring love to others.

My parents were the first to show me God's unconditional love. Just as God, our Father, loves us unconditionally, my parents love me the same way, and I love my children with that same love. Let us continue to share love and impact lives for good.

...

**Lord,**
Thank You for guiding me through fear, granting strength, and leading me to
redemption. I trust in Your plan for my life.
Amen.

...

# Love Kept Us

Sheryl Simms

...

### Ecclesiastes 4:9-10 (NIV)
Two are better than one, because they have a good return for their labor: If
either of them falls down, one can help the other up.

...

Sitting on our worn-out couch, I stared at the stack of overdue bills on
the coffee table, each envelope a reminder of the financial storm we were
caught in. Our debts had grown after Mark lost his job when the company
downsized. My part-time work at the local library barely covered groceries,
let alone the mortgage.

I remember the night Mark came home, his eyes weary but determined.
"We'll figure this out," he said, though I could hear the uncertainty in his
voice. Still, he wrapped his arms around me, a gesture that spoke volumes
of our unyielding commitment to each other.

We spent evenings pouring over spreadsheets, trying to stretch every dollar.
We cut down on expenses, canceled subscriptions, and sold items we
once thought we needed. Despite the tension, we found moments of levity
in our makeshift dinners. One night, Mark surprised me with a candlelit
picnic on our living room floor, a simple meal of canned soup and crackers
transformed by his humor and love.

As we sat there, sharing stories and dreams, I realized our strength lay not
in the absence of struggle, but in how we faced it together. In those quiet,
intimate moments, I understood that love was our true wealth, binding us
closer, and guiding us through the darkest days with hope and resilience.

...

### Lord,
We thank You for the strength and unity in our relationships. May love guide us
through challenges, and may we always find hope in each other's support.

Amen.

...

# For The Love Of

Rochelle D. Jacobs

...

**Mark 12:30 (AMP)**

And you shall love the Lord your God with all your heart, and with all your soul (life), and with all your mind (thought, understanding), and with all your strength.

...

Do you love me more than…?

That question pierced my soul as I hit rock bottom. How did I end up here with this STD (sugary transmitted disease)? Help, I need a doctor, please!

As a sugar addict, I tried to numb the pain and shame of being sexually molested at twelve with sugar. Addicts seek their next fix, and for me, it was money. I had a triple-threat mindset: pink slips, payday loans, and pawn shops were my escape as I mismanaged my finances, living paycheck to paycheck. Therapy revealed that my childhood trauma was the root cause of my chaos, and I realized I couldn't meet God in revival until I met Him in my brokenness.

We all have things we're drawn to—some small, some big, and some "sweet vices." Sugar satisfies momentarily, but too much leaves us craving more, masking deeper soul hunger. Money promises freedom, but when it measures our worth, it leads to emptiness. Brokenness can feel like a permanent label, chaining us to the past.

God invites us to look beyond fleeting comforts and place our hope in His eternal love and purpose. Sugar, money, and brokenness can symbolize misplaced focus or unfulfilled needs. They reveal areas God longs to restore, showing us the deeper joy of His love and grace.

The desire for sweetness isn't a sin, but true satisfaction is found in God's presence. Money, rightly used, is a tool, not our purpose. And brokenness, while painful, can be transformed into the place where God's love shines brightest.

...

**Lord,**

Help me trust You fully, find true fulfillment in You, and let Your grace make me whole. Amen.

...

# Extraordinary Love

### Stacey Collins

...

### 1 Corinthians 13:13 (NIV)
And now these three remain: faith, hope and love. But the greatest of these is love.

...

"God, give me extraordinary love today," I prayed that morning. It was Stampede Week in our city, and the kids and I were headed downtown. It was a cold and windy day, with the city bustling with visitors. We didn't have coins to pay for parking at the C-train station or to buy our train tickets, so we had to get back in our car and drive to the store. It was hectic, and frustration was building! Riding the C-train was crowded... uncomfortable... foul language! We missed the pancake breakfast! Ugh!

We found a Stampede BBQ downtown and got the last table available to fit our group. We sat down. A lady at the table huffed loudly, swore, grabbed her duffel bag, and walked off, disdain radiating from her!

Everything in me wanted to react! But God reminded me, "Stacey, remember what you prayed this morning? Didn't you ask for extraordinary love?" I took a deep breath and prayed again...

I thought I'd missed my opportunity. She came back and sat down. I reached out my hand to take hers and said, "I just want to apologize for invading your space." She began to describe to me how hard her day was. She had recently come out of an abusive marriage. My heart felt deeply for her. Holding her hand, I said, "Do you know I prayed for extraordinary love this morning?" I then asked, "Can I pray for you?" She said "Yes." We bowed our heads and prayed.

...

### Lord,
Thank You for Your extraordinary love. Help me to share this love with others, embracing each moment as a chance to reflect Your grace.
Amen.

...

# Jesus Loves You Too

Bonita L. Williams

...

**Romans 5:8 (NLT)**
But God showed his great love for us by sending
Christ to die for us while we were still sinners.

...

Understanding that Jesus loves me was one of the hardest truths to grasp. How could an all-powerful, all-knowing God love someone like me with all my mistakes and stubbornness?

I struggled to accept God's love because I believed it depended on my actions. I thought if I was good, God would love me, and if I messed up, He would withdraw His love. However, becoming a parent taught me about unconditional love.

I love my daughters despite their actions. Similarly, God's love for us surpasses any human love. We are His chosen people (1 Peter 2:9-10; Psalm 33:12). While we were still sinners, Christ died for us (Romans 5:8), proving His love isn't based on our worthiness.

I invite you to heed Paul's advice to forget the past (Philippians 3:13). According to 1 John 1:9, if we confess our sins, God forgives and cleanses us. However, we often struggle to forgive ourselves, replaying past mistakes and doubting God's forgiveness. This mindset pleases the devil, as he wants us to rely on feelings rather than truth. But as we delve into the Bible, we learn that God loved the world so much He gave His only Son (John 3:16). God sees past our faults and meets our needs. So, next time Satan highlights your flaws, take them to the Lord and trust in His love.

...

**Lord,**
Thank You for Your boundless love and forgiveness. Help me trust in Your grace and find the strength to forgive myself, embracing the freedom only You provide.
Amen.

...

# Celebrating The Favor of Love

*God's love is a transformative force, inviting us to love deeply and genuinely. When we bask in His love, we are empowered to extend that love to others, creating a ripple effect of kindness and grace.*

**Now it's your turn to write your story of celebrating The Favor of Love.**

Reflect on a time when you felt overwhelmed by God's love, inspiring you to love others more fully. How did this experience change your relationships and outlook on life? Describe the moments where love triumphed over fear or doubt, and how God's favor became evident through these acts of love.

_____

_____

_____

_____

_____

_____

_____

_____

_____

_____

_____

_____

_____

_____

_____

_____

_____

_____

_____

_____

_____

# THE
# FAVOR
## OF
# *Purpose*

Step boldly into the purpose God has for you, finding fulfillment and favor in every endeavor.

# Living with Purpose

...

**Proverbs 19:21 (NIV)**
Many are the plans in a person's heart, but it is the Lord's purpose that prevails.

...

In life, we often find ourselves making countless plans, charting paths, and dreaming of destinations. Yet, Proverbs 19:21 reminds us of a profound truth: it is the Lord's purpose that truly prevails. This scripture encourages us to align our desires with His divine plan, understanding that His purpose is far greater than anything we could conceive.

Stepping boldly into the purpose God has for you requires courage and faith. It means trusting that His plans are for your good, even when they lead you down unexpected roads. God's purpose is a unique gift, crafted specifically for you, filled with opportunities to grow, serve, and experience profound joy.

Reflect on this: Are you holding onto plans that might not align with His purpose? What would it mean for you to embrace His calling, fully and fearlessly? As you ponder these questions, remember that God equips those He calls. He provides the strength, wisdom, and grace needed to fulfill your purpose.

This week as we celebrate the Favor of Purpose, take a moment to seek God's direction. Listen to His voice and step forward with confidence, knowing that His path is filled with divine favor. Every step you take in His purpose is a step towards a fulfilling and meaningful life.

...

**Father,**
Guide me to understand and embrace the purpose You have for my life. Help me to step boldly into Your plans, trusting in Your wisdom and grace. Thank You for the favor of walking in Your will.
Amen.

...

# Finding True Purpose

Autumn Anesi

...

**Mark 12:30 (NIV)**

Love the Lord your God with all your heart and with all your soul and with all your mind and with all your strength.

...

From a young age, I dreamed of exploring the entire world. As I grew, those dreams shifted to becoming an astronaut or a movie star. What I truly wanted was adventure, to live the greatest story, and find a purpose beyond the ordinary.

But reality often felt mundane, without the excitement I craved. Can you relate? What is our purpose in a world where the everyday seems so ordinary? I found the answer not in my passions, but beyond them.

Although I love being a business coach, that isn't my ultimate purpose. God is my purpose. To love God and to be loved by Him should be the ultimate purpose for every believer.

Nothing I do will ever be enough to fulfill me completely. True satisfaction is found only in the Lord. When you make Him your purpose, peace and joy follow naturally.

No longer do we need to strive for purpose. Everything we do can be an act of worship to the Creator. Whether mundane or exciting, if it's done for the Lord, it holds purpose and brings joy. Our tasks and roles may change, but our purpose remains constant.

Love God not to gain anything, but simply because He loves you unconditionally and completely. Embrace this truth, and let your everyday life shine with purpose and joy.

...

**Dear Lord,**

Thank You for Your unconditional love. Grant me strength to find purpose and joy in everyday life through unwavering faith in You.

Amen.

...

# Purposefully Evolving

Dr. Katherine E. James

...

## 1 Corinthians 13:13 (ESV)

So now faith, hope, and love abide, these three; but the greatest of these is love.

...

Purpose is not static; it is ever-evolving. Poppa called me to retirement to give me an opportunity to refine my purpose, and I accepted the invitation.

My purpose refinement evolution began at 57 years old and occurred over a three-year period. Biblically, the number three represents God's divine wholeness, completeness, resurrection, and harmony.

My entire existence now rests on living out this one word: "LOVE." My life's purpose is to add more love into the world, one life-giving conversation at a time. I have the privilege of employing my being—gifts, talents, skills, intuitions, resources, energy, and precious time—to fulfill my refined purpose. I LOVE THIS LIFE OF MINE. This life where I get to be myself and serve others from this place of being.

Each of us is purposed to add to Poppa's universe the unique contribution that only you and I can. It is not to ask the question, "Do I have a purpose?" or "What is my purpose?" It isn't a question at all, but a knowing that, in many ways, you are already living out your purpose. What are your themes, your patterns, your consistencies in life? As you reflect, you will discover that your purpose has continually evolved as you evolved. Purpose is not static because you are the purpose.

...

**Lord,**

Guide my evolving purpose. Fill me with love, clarity, and strength to serve others and fulfill Your plan for me.

Amen.

...

# Purpose Beyond Position

Alethia Saunders

...

**Romans 8:28 (NLT)**
And we know that God causes everything to work together for the good of those
who love God and are called according to his purpose for them.

...

I was thriving in the medical field, progressing from Access Representative to Emergency Room Supervisor, overseeing multiple departments. Although I didn't have a college degree, I was determined to excel. After countless applications, I finally secured the leadership role I had longed for. I was overjoyed, and nothing felt better than choosing the color for my new office—a moment I'd dreamed of. Yet, as I settled into my responsibilities, I came to a surprising realization: "I hate this job."

I soon understood that it wasn't the job itself but the culture that troubled me. I saw dedicated colleagues, some over 70 years of age, working tirelessly with no real relief. Their hard work went unnoticed in an environment focused on clocking hours rather than valuing people. I realized God didn't intend for His people to live this way. So, I took a leap and left, despite criticism and doubt from others.

This bold step led me to my true purpose: empowering others. It's how I became Alethia Saunders, Career Development Coach, Ghostwriter, and Voice Giver. God gave me a voice, and I'm grateful for every moment I now use it to help others find theirs.

...

**Dear God,**
Thank You for guiding me to embrace my true purpose. Grant me strength and
wisdom to empower others as You empower me.
Amen.

...

# A Vow That Saved Lives

Benecia Ponder

...

**1 Peter 4:10 (NIV)**
Each of you should use whatever gift you have received to serve others, as faithful stewards of God's grace in its various forms.

...

In 2021, my sister was diagnosed with Stage 4 metastatic breast cancer. The days we spent at the treatment center were long, filled with uncertainty.

During those weeks, I became familiar with a story that seemed to echo through the halls of the center. It was the story of its founder, a man who had watched his mother suffer through terminal cancer in a hospital that provided inadequate care. Stricken by the experience, he vowed to transform his pain into purpose, ensuring others would receive the compassion and quality of care his mother had been denied.

This man's story was not just a tale of grief; it was a beacon of hope. From doctors to cafeteria staff, everyone at the center carried his legacy, embodying his vision in their daily tasks. Each person I encountered was a living testament to the founder's mission, treating patients with a level of dedication and empathy that transcended ordinary care.

As I sat with my sister, I often reflected on the power of his story. What if he had chosen to keep his pain locked inside? Without his courage to share and act upon his experiences, the center might never have existed, and countless patients, including my sister, might not have received the exceptional care they did.

Through my sister's journey, I've realized the profound impact of using our stories to help others. Today, I am deeply grateful for those stories that possess the power to change lives, reminding us all of the favor of purpose.

...

**Lord,**
Guide my story to inspire hope and heal others, with
gratitude for Your strength and compassion.
Amen.

# *...Purpose Unfolds*

Stacey Collins

...

**Psalms 139:3 (NIV)**

You discern my going out and my lying down; you are familiar with all my ways.

...

Standing in line at the grocery store, I saw Oprah's quote: "If you follow your passions, you will find your purpose."

When I read it aloud, a man ahead of me disagreed, saying it hadn't worked for him. I responded, "Well, maybe it should say, if you follow your purpose, then you will find your passion."

I've reflected on this over the years. When a person knows their purpose, discovering their passions becomes clearer—it creates a flow of direction to take action and use one's gifts for impact. True purpose comes from God and is birthed from the WHY that motivates your spirit. What's defined in my mind and heart becomes the filter through which I react to each situation.

After experiencing trauma and unexpected transitions over the last few years, in tears, I prayed, asking the Holy Spirit, "What is next for me?" He replied, "I'll give you the KEYS." Then He spoke: "rest... trust... listen…"

For the past three years, I've tried to do just that! Rest in Him... Trust Him... and listen to His heart... This season, the Holy Spirit is saying: "write…"

I'm discovering my purpose through a deep desire to write and share my stories—healing from loss and grief, remembering life's impact, experiencing transformation. I believe our purpose lies in being all that God put within us. Through our ideas, creativity, and strategies, a mission emerges—a mission to impact the world!

So I ask you, "Is it not your purpose to _____?" Ask the Holy Spirit to fill in the blank.

...

**Lord,**

Thank You for guiding me toward my purpose. Grant me strength and clarity to fulfill it, using my gifts to impact the world. Amen.

...

# Celebrating The Favor of Purpose

*God has crafted a unique purpose for each of us, a divine path that leads to fulfillment and joy. Embrace your calling with confidence, knowing His favor guides you every step of the way, turning your efforts into meaningful impact.*

**Now it's your turn to write your story of celebrating The Favor of Purpose.**

Reflect on a moment when you felt aligned with your life's purpose. How did this clarity affect your decisions and interactions? Consider how recognizing your purpose has enriched your life and how God's favor has been evident in guiding you towards this path.

# THE FAVOR OF *Faith*

Faith unlocks the door to God's boundless favor, allowing us to see mountains move and miracles unfold.

# The Faith Factor

...

**Hebrews 11:1 (NIV)**
Now faith is confidence in what we hope for and
assurance about what we do not see.

...

Faith is a powerful catalyst that activates God's favor in our lives. It is the confidence and assurance in the unseen, as described in Hebrews 11:1.

When we embrace faith, we tap into the boundless favor of God, which can transform our circumstances and bring about the miraculous.

Think about a time in your life when faith was your anchor. Perhaps you faced a daunting challenge or an uncertain future, yet through faith, you witnessed God's miraculous provision and guidance. These moments are a testament to the incredible power of faith, which moves mountains and brings His promises to life.

Faith is not a passive belief but an active trust in God's character and promises. It calls us to step out, even when the path isn't clear, trusting that God will provide and guide us. As we lean into His promises, we open ourselves to His favor, experiencing His presence and provision in profound ways.

This week as we celebrate the Favor of Faith, I encourage you to deepen your faith journey. Reflect on God's promises, and let them fill your heart with hope and assurance. Trust that He is working behind the scenes, even when you cannot see the outcome. As you do, you will witness His favor unfold in ways that exceed your expectations.

...

Heavenly Father,
Strengthen my faith. Help me to trust in Your promises and witness Your favor in my life. Increase my confidence in the unseen, so I may experience Your miraculous provision and guidance.
Amen.

...

# Ruby Stevens

Sibyl F. Cole

...

**James 1:3 (NIV)**

For you know that the testing of your faith produces steadfastness.

...

My father grew up in a tight-knit neighborhood in a small town in North Carolina, and I remember him telling me stories about one of his neighbors, Ruby Stevens, affectionately called "Miss Ruby," who was known for her giving nature and unwavering faith. Daddy said Miss Ruby went to church every Sunday, and her presence livened up everyone around her.

One winter, a destructive snowstorm hit the town and left many families in despair. Miss Ruby remained steadfast, believing brighter days were ahead. In the storm's aftermath, Miss Ruby opened her home to those in need, offering food, shelter, and most of all, comfort.

One evening, as they gathered around a warm fire, Miss Ruby shared a story from her childhood about a time when she faced adversity, speaking of how her faith had guided her through those dark moments, reminding everyone that even in the toughest times, there's always a glimmer of hope. Her words resonated deeply, inspiring others to come together and help each other get back on their feet.

Weeks passed, and the town slowly began to rebuild. Miss Ruby's unlimited generosity had not only provided shelter but it had also fostered a sense of community and resilience. As the last remnants of the storm faded, the neighborhood realized that they had emerged stronger together, united by Miss Ruby's belief in the power of faith and love. Her unwavering spirit became a symbol of hope, reminding everyone that faith can move mountains, even in the face of adversity.

...

**Dear Lord,**

Bless me with unwavering faith and strength. Guide me to find hope in adversity and to share love with those in need.

Amen.

...

# Believe

Sheryl Simms

...

## Luke 1:45 (NIV)

Blessed is she who has believed that the Lord would fulfill his promises to her!

...

When I was 14, I told my parents I wanted a car for my 16th birthday. They said they couldn't afford it, but I was determined. I told them, "I'll get one myself." They were doubtful, but that only motivated me more.

I started researching everything about owning a car—how much it would cost, insurance, gas, and maintenance. I realized it was a lot of money, but I didn't back down. I began saving every bit of Christmas and birthday money. I also started babysitting for neighbors, even getting a part-time job at a local store on weekends and during summer breaks.

When I turned 16, I finally bought my car. Sitting in the driver's seat was the best feeling ever! It was proof that my hard work paid off. This experience taught me a lot about having faith and not giving up. It showed me that if you believe in something and work hard for it, you can make it happen, even if you can't see it right away.

This experience ingrained in me the importance of perseverance and belief in achieving goals. Many decades later, it still reminds me that while the path may be challenging, unwavering faith can lead to unimaginable results.

...

### Heavenly Father,

I am grateful for the gift of faith and confident assurance. Help me trust in my dreams and give me the strength to realize them through Your guidance.

Amen.

...

# Faith Fills Fridges

### Stacey Collins

...

### Matthew 6:26 (NIV)

Look at the birds of the air; they do not sow or reap or store away in barns, and yet your heavenly Father feeds them. Are you not much more valuable than they?

...

Our two-story acreage home was busy with nine of us to feed. We had people visiting for a few days. The ladies' prayer group met at our house that morning. We had been struggling for so long financially. I wanted to keep it quiet. "Please don't open my fridge!" I was thinking! Many weeks, it amazed me how a lady would bring a pound of butter or a block of cheese, and it would be exactly what we needed! Our children looked forward to the extra snacks they would get when they came home from school.

This day, I was cleaning the fridge, and it was EMPTY! I felt compelled to start singing the song "Praise God from whom all blessings flow," and then I said to the others, "I'm cleaning the fridge to prepare it for God to fill it." Within 10 seconds, our dog Shadow started barking. There was a truck coming up our driveway. Unbelievable! A dear friend was coming to the door holding bags of groceries. Not your ordinary food—they were from the deli. As we unpacked, we discovered the $125 roast! At first, I thought, "Why didn't they just buy from a grocery store?" I then heard God say, "Stacey, I never want you to forget that you are royalty."

Now, when our fridge gets low, I remember—daughters of the King feast at His table, and He delights in providing the finest and rare.

...

### Lord,

Thank You for Your faithful provision. Help me trust Your timing and abundance, knowing You provide beyond my needs. Strengthen my faith each day.
Amen.

...

# Closed Doors Can Open

Dr. Nina Addison

...

### Hebrews 11:1 (AMP)

Now faith is the assurance (title deed, confirmation) of things hoped for (divinely guaranteed), and the evidence of things not seen [the conviction of their reality— faith comprehends as fact what cannot be experienced by the physical senses].

...

In 2022, we were living in an area that was not the safest. I had faith that God was about to bless us with a new place to live. I applied for a mortgage loan in February 2022 but was told I needed to work on my credit. By June 2022, I was looking to rent a home and met a kind realtor. Although my application to rent a house was denied, my first lady told me I would have favor with that realtor, so I held onto my faith.

On June 25, 2022, this wonderful realtor, Chantill, asked me to speak with her lender. Remembering my first lady's words, I reached out. That was a Friday. By Sunday, I finally stopped stalling and sent all the documents the lender requested. By 9 a.m. Monday, I got a call. When I answered, I was greeted with "CONGRATULATIONS!"

I believed God and had faith greater than a mustard seed that He would come through—and HE DID JUST THAT! We found and closed on a house in just 31 days. WOW! On August 1, 2022, we began moving into our new home.

It was all because of my faith. I believed God to do the impossible. I added my works, and God manifested His promise.

...

### Dear God,

Please strengthen my faith. Help me believe in the impossible. If You said it, may my faith never waver. In Jesus' Name, may it be so.

Amen!

...

# A Crucible of Faith

Beverley Anderson

...

**Isaiah 41:10 (NIV)**

So do not fear, for I am with you; do not be dismayed, for I am your God. I will strengthen you and help you; I will uphold you with my righteous right hand.

...

Life's challenges test our spiritual resilience and faith. The year was 2004, and the joy of a long-awaited pregnancy turned into a crucible of faith. Twelve weeks into my first pregnancy, I was faced with excruciating pain and rushed to the hospital. Doctors gave me a 50% chance of survival and little hope for my unborn child.

Have you ever faced a daunting moment that left you gripped with numbness?

It was a season of profound testing, where I found myself wrestling with uncertainty—moments when the weight of my pain felt too much to bear! At that moment of despair, my husband and I turned to prayer warriors and surrendered everything to God. Three days after a major operation, I developed a pulmonary embolism due to three major blood clots in both lungs.

Despite everything, my child and I survived, and my husband and I were blessed with the smooth birth of our healthy baby boy 38 weeks later—a true miracle that reflects God's promise in Jeremiah 29:11.

This experience served as a powerful reminder of God's unwavering faithfulness and His plans to bless us, even amidst uncertainty. It inspired me to trust in His promises and have peace.

True strength comes from surrendering to God's will and embracing His plan for our lives. If you're navigating a difficult season, remember that God has an amazing plan for you—believe it!

...

**Lord,**

Help us trust your divine plans, even during life's toughest challenges

Amen.

...

47

# Celebrating The Favor of Faith

*Faith is the foundation of our relationship with God, guiding us through uncertainties and leading us into His abundant favor. As you lean into His promises, watch how faith transforms your journey, bringing peace and assurance in every step.*

**Now it's your turn to write your story of celebrating The Favor of Faith.**

Recall a time when your faith in God made a profound difference in your life. How did this faith influence your decisions and bring about unexpected blessings? Reflect on the ways God's favor became evident as you placed your faith in Him and how this experience has shaped your life.

_____

_____

_____

_____

_____

_____

_____

_____

_____

_____

_____

_____

_____

_____

_____

_____

_____

_____

# THE FAVOR OF Wisdom

Seek wisdom and walk in God's favor. Divine wisdom guides us through life's complexities, leading to favorable outcomes and peace.

# Divine Guidance

**James 1:5 (NIV)**

If any of you lacks wisdom, you should ask God, who gives generously to all without finding fault, and it will be given to you.

...

Wisdom is a precious gift from God that unlocks the door to His favor in our lives. James 1:5 encourages us to seek wisdom from God, promising that He will provide it generously. This divine wisdom is not just about knowledge; it's about having the insight to navigate life's complexities with grace and peace.

Reflect on moments when you faced difficult decisions or uncertain paths. It's likely that trusting in God's wisdom provided clarity and direction, leading to outcomes that were both favorable and filled with peace. This is the essence of walking in God's favor—allowing His wisdom to illuminate your path.

Wisdom enables us to see beyond the immediate and understand the broader picture, aligning our steps with God's plans for our lives. It equips us with the discernment to make choices that reflect His love and truth, impacting not only our lives but also those around us.

This week as we celebrate the Favor of Wisdom, actively seek God's divine guidance. Whether in small daily decisions or major life choices, invite God to steer you in the right direction. Trust that His wisdom will lead to outcomes that are not only successful but also bring peace and fulfillment.

...

**Lord,**

Grant me wisdom in all my decisions. Let Your guidance illuminate my way and bring about Your favor. Help me to trust in Your divine insight, leading to peace and favorable outcomes in every aspect of my life.

Amen.

...

# Be Coachable

Melanie Winters

...

**Proverbs 19:20 (NIV)**

Listen to advice and accept discipline, and at the end you will be counted among the wise.

...

I was buzzing with excitement as I made progress on my manuscript, so I decided to share the first two chapters with a couple of friends for their thoughts. I also sent it over to a colleague who had recently published her fifth book.

My friends were incredibly supportive, showering me with praise and telling me they couldn't wait for more. It felt amazing. But then, there was the email from my colleague. It was long, started with "This needs work," and included my manuscript marked up with red comments on almost every line.

I spent two weeks feeling crushed by that email. I couldn't escape it. Every time I sat down to write, those words loomed over me—"this needs work."

One afternoon, my husband asked how the book was coming along, and I admitted that I was losing hope. I showed him the email, expecting him to share my frustration.

"This is good advice," he said, completely surprising me. "It looks like she really took the time to help you improve."

He encouraged me to reach out to my colleague and discuss her insights. "With her help, your book will be amazing," he assured me.

Receiving critical feedback isn't easy, but I've come to realize that constructive criticism often hides valuable lessons. When I managed to set my ego aside and really listen, I found the gift of wisdom in the critique.

...

**Dear God,**

Grant me the strength to embrace feedback with humility, courage to learn and grow, and wisdom to transform criticism into a path for improvement.

Amen.

...

# The Secret Ingredient

Benecia Ponder

...

**Proverbs 4:5-7 (NIV)**

Get wisdom, get understanding; do not forget my words or turn away from them. Do not forsake wisdom, and she will protect you; love her, and she will watch over you.

...

Growing up, my grandmother's spaghetti and meatballs was the hallmark of culinary perfection. Each time she made it, I relished every bite, marveling at how something so simple could taste so divine. So, when I married someone who loved spaghetti just as much as I did, I resolved to recreate her masterpiece. Armed with careful notes from a phone call with her, I meticulously followed each step, convinced of my imminent success.

Eagerly, my husband and I dug into the dish. It looked the part, but the taste was far from the comforting flavors I remembered. Confused and disappointed, I called my grandmother, recounting my every move. She chuckled warmly and offered a few crucial pointers. Realizing I needed more than a recipe, I invited her over to guide me in person.

Having her by my side in the kitchen was a revelation. It wasn't just about the steps; it was about understanding the nuances, the love infused with every stir, and the wisdom passed down through generations. This experience taught me a vital lesson: knowledge alone isn't enough. It's wisdom that breathes life into knowledge, transforming it into something meaningful.

As believers, it's essential to seek both knowledge and wisdom. The Bible provides the steps, but God grants the wisdom to understand the heart behind them. Just as my grandmother shared her cooking secrets, so too must we seek divine insight to truly comprehend and apply the knowledge we gather. In all our getting, we must get understanding.

...

**Heavenly Father,**

Grant me the favor of wisdom and understanding. Guide my heart and mind to embrace and apply Your divine insights daily.

Amen..

...

# Job Hunt

Sibyl F. Cole

...

## Matthew 7:24 (NIV)

Everyone then who hears these words of mine and does them will be like a wise man who built his house on the rock.

...

I moved to Washington, DC, after I graduated from college to look for a job in the journalism field. This was way before the digital era: no social media, no cell phones, and computers were just becoming popular. To support myself, I worked through a temporary agency and stayed with a relative until I could get on my feet.

After several weeks, I landed a four-week administrative assistant position at a local publishing company. That assignment turned into six months, which gave me the opportunity to utilize my writing and editing skills. Eventually, I was offered a permanent position. I was excited, but something just didn't feel right.

I called my mom back home in Atlanta and asked her what I should do. She told me to "just pray about it" and seek God's wisdom.

I decided to do some research, so I contacted a friend who put me in touch with a former employee. During our conversation, he shared insights about the company's culture and challenges that came with the role. The more I listened, the more I thought the job might not be the right fit for me. With a renewed sense of clarity, I respectfully declined their offer and waited for an opportunity that felt right.

A few weeks later, I received an offer from another organization that better suited my career and personal interests. Looking back, I was grateful for the favor of God's wisdom that had guided me on the right path.

...

## Thank You, Lord,

for Your guiding wisdom and clarity. May Your light continue to lead me on the right path. Amen.

...

# Guided By Wisdom

Alethia Saunders

...

**Proverbs 19:20 (NLT)**
Get all the advice and instruction you can, so you will be wise the rest of your life.

...

"Go to therapy, Alethia!"

I hated hearing those words, especially with my name attached so directly to them. Why did I need therapy? I didn't want to talk to anyone about what was happening inside me—especially when I couldn't even explain it myself. The thought made me feel chaotic and out of control.

But one day, a group of older friends—people I trusted—sat me down for a serious conversation. This wasn't just idle advice or words I could ignore. They spoke directly to my soul, pouring life into my spirit. They helped me see the truth: this was a matter of life and death. The question was stark: "Do you want to live, or do you want to die?"

Of course, I chose life. Death was never an option for me. But I realized that wanting to live meant I had to take action. So, I registered for therapy. That decision became a turning point in my life.

Through therapy, I was diagnosed with clinical depression and anxiety. I received the medical support I desperately needed and began a steady journey toward healing and recovery. I'm forever grateful for the wisdom and love shown to me by those who cared enough to intervene. They helped me see that my life was worth saving—and now, I see it too.

...

**Dear God,**
Thank You for guiding me to wisdom and healing. Bless those who offered wise advice, leading me to life's light and strength. Keep me open to their wisdom.
Amen.

...

# God's Whisper

Sheryl Simms

...

**Proverbs 2:6 (NIV)**
For the Lord gives wisdom; from his mouth come knowledge and understanding.

...

Last summer, our little library was bustling with children eager to explore stories and feed their imaginations. One afternoon, as I tidied the shelves, I noticed one boy sitting alone. He slouched low in his chair, a book unopened on his lap. Something about his sadness tugged at my heart.

I walked over, knelt beside him, and asked, "What do you like to read?" He shrugged, avoiding my gaze. I offered a few suggestions, but nothing seemed to spark his interest. My heart whispered, Pray, Sheryl.

I paused right there – not out loud, but quietly in my heart – and asked God what this boy needed. The answer came softly but clearly. It wasn't about the book; it was about being seen.

I asked his name. "Tyler," he mumbled. Slowly, we began to talk, not about books, but about soccer, his cat, and school. His story unfolded—his parents were going through a hard divorce, and he felt stuck in the middle.

That moment wasn't about fixing things but showing love. I told him, "It's okay to feel sad, Tyler. You're not alone. God sees you, and so do I." His eyes met mine for the first time, and he gave a small smile.

That day, he left with a book about courage. But I think what stayed with him most was knowing someone cared. God's wisdom reminded me to pause and listen—really listen. Sometimes, that's the greatest gift we can offer.

...

**Lord,**
Grant me your wisdom. Guide my heart to listen, my
actions to love, and my soul to honor You.
Amen.

...

# Celebrating The Favor of Wisdom

*Wisdom illuminates the path to God's favor, guiding us through life's complexities with clarity and peace. Seek His wisdom in all decisions, knowing it leads to outcomes that align with His perfect will and abundant blessings.*

**Now it's your turn to write your story of celebrating The Favor of Wisdom.**

Reflect on a decision you made that was guided by divine wisdom. How did seeking God's counsel impact your choices and their outcomes? Describe how His wisdom has brought clarity and favor into your life, transforming challenges into opportunities for growth and understanding.

_____

_____

_____

_____

_____

_____

_____

_____

_____

_____

_____

_____

_____

_____

_____

_____

_____

# THE FAVOR OF Wisdom

Seek wisdom and walk in God's favor. Divine wisdom guides us through life's complexities, leading to favorable outcomes and peace.

# God's Great Joy

...

## Psalm 16:11 (NIV)

You make known to me the path of life; you will fill me with joy in your presence,
with eternal pleasures at your right hand.

...

Joy is more than a fleeting emotion; it is a profound gift rooted in the presence of God.

Psalm 16:11 reminds us that true joy comes from walking the path of life with God. His favor transforms our perspective, enabling us to discover joy even in life's trials and unexpected places.

Picture a time when you were confronted with a challenge—a tough day at work, a misunderstanding with a loved one, or a personal setback. It's easy to feel weighed down in these moments. Yet, when we invite God's presence into our lives, we find that His joy can illuminate even the darkest days. Suddenly, an encouraging word from a friend or a quiet moment of reflection becomes a source of unexpected joy, shifting our perspective and lightening our hearts.

This joy is not dependent on our circumstances but flows abundantly from God's favor. It lifts us, providing strength and renewing our spirit as we face life's complexities. As we embrace this divine joy, we learn to celebrate life's small victories and find contentment in our journey.

This week as we celebrate the Favor of Joy, focus on cultivating joy by seeking God's presence in each moment. Open your heart to His favor, letting His joy overflow into your interactions and experiences. As you do, you will not only enrich your own life but also spread joy to those around you.

...

### Father,

Fill my heart with Your joy. May it overflow in my life and spread to those around me. Help me to see Your favor in every moment, transforming my perspective and experiences with Your everlasting joy.

Amen.

...

# Kill Joy

Rochelle D. Jacobs

...

## Nehemiah 8:10 (KJV)
The joy of the Lord is your strength.

...

The more I live, the more I realize that life be lifing—loss, disappointment, and struggles are unending. Yet, despite life's challenges, I can count it all joy—not a joy based on my circumstances but rooted in deep faith in God's favor.

In times of marital woes, parental crises, and family struggles, I lean into God's presence to experience a joy that surpasses all understanding. It's His divine favor that carries me, lifting my spirit and renewing my hope daily.

Oh, the joy that comes from knowing God is in control, especially when life spins out of control. Like a hamster wheel spinning faster and faster, I've faced burnout from OPP syndrome: overthinking, perfectionism, and procrastination. Learning to say no and set boundaries was transformative. Sharing my story of reclaiming my destiny showed others that joy isn't just an emotion—it's a gift from God. My laughter became contagious, and my transformation illuminated the lives of women who had lost their own joy.

Jesus-Centered: True joy begins with a relationship with Christ.

Optimistic: God's favor helps us see good in every situation.

Yielding: Opening our hearts to receive His joy requires letting go of burdens.

"Joy is not the absence of trouble but the presence of God's favor in our lives, reminding us He is our strength and hope."

God's favor of joy strengthens us and encourages us to shine His light. May we seek His joy daily, knowing it's a gift that transforms lives.

...

## Heavenly Father,
Thank You for Your presence. Strengthen me to overcome struggles and fill me with Your joy. Help me share this joy, illuminating others' paths.
Amen.

...

# Have Fun

Benecia Ponder

...

## Ecclesiastes 2:24 (NIV)

A person can do nothing better than to eat and drink and find satisfaction in their own toil. This too, I see, is from the hand of God.

...

""What if it was fun?"

That's what I asked Rose during one of our author coaching sessions.

"What do you mean?" she asked, curiosity flickering.

I leaned into the camera, hoping to make my point clear. "What if, instead of approaching your writing like a dreaded chore, you made it fun and exciting?"

Rose paused, and I could see the wheels turning. She had been so excited to start her book, but lately, it felt like an endless homework assignment. Each session, her lack of progress weighed on her. I was determined to change that.

Together, we brainstormed playful strategies to bring joy to her writing routine. Rose embraced the ideas, and soon, her enthusiasm returned. Watching her progress was like witnessing a garden bloom after a long winter. Within weeks, she accomplished more than she had since starting.

At our next session, I praised her incredible progress. "Fun makes all the difference," she said, her eyes sparkling with renewed excitement.

Reflecting on her transformation, I realized how true it is—when we're called to a task, it shouldn't feel like drudgery. There's divine joy in fulfilling our purpose. As Ecclesiastes reminds us, God delights in our enjoyment of our work. When we embrace the joy, even hard tasks can become a source of inspiration and fulfillment.

...

### Heavenly Father,

Sometimes I feel tired and bored with the day-to-day tasks of my calling. I want to experience joy. Please refresh my mind and heart so that I may enjoy the work I am assigned to do. In Jesus' Name,

Amen.

...

# The Agony of Joy

Dr. Theresa Billingsley

...

**Hebrews 12:2 (TPT)**

His example is this: Because his heart was focused on the joy of knowing that you would be his, he endured the agony of the cross and conquered its humiliation, and now sits exalted at the right hand of the throne of God!

...

Who knew that the journey to joy often involves navigating through pain and suffering?

One of my greatest gifts from God, my children, came through the intense struggle of childbirth. The experience was filled with pain, yet if I had to do it all over again, I would embrace that pain joyfully. Why? Because I understand the incredible joy that comes from holding a child entrusted to me by the Most High.

Giving birth is one of the most profound challenges a woman can face. In those moments of vulnerability, you might feel stripped bare, helpless, and even humiliated. Yet, just like Christ, we find purpose in our trials. The joy of raising a child in the fear and love of the Lord far outweighs the suffering.

When we encounter difficult times, it's essential to remember that these struggles are not meant to defeat us. Instead, they prepare us for something greater. The next time you face a challenge, look for the hidden joy within it. Tell yourself, "This didn't come to kill me; it came to lead me to a greater reward." Embrace the journey, knowing that joy often blooms in the most unexpected places.

...

**Dear God,**

In my moments of pain and struggle, help me to see the joy and purpose in my journey. Strengthen my heart as I embrace the gifts you provide.

Amen.

...

# Joy of the Lord

Sueyuna Dorsey-Duthie

...

**Psalm 51:12 (NIV)**
Restore unto me the joy of thy salvation; and uphold me with thy free spirit. Then will I teach transgressors thy ways; and sinners shall be converted unto thee.

...

Speeding down Broadway, my turn as a wheel woman came to a screeching halt. I pulled over to the side of the road where, on the corner, I saw a man standing distraught. I opened the car door, hurried to the tailgate, and gathered a small bottle of water and a brown-bagged lunch.

I closed the tailgate and gingerly walked to speak with the man on the corner. He caught my eye because he looked tattered, worn, and sad. He was dirty and disheveled, and I didn't care.

I asked him gently, "Sir, has anyone ever told you that God loves you and that He has a plan for your life?"

He slowly turned his gaze toward me, his head lowered. He responded, "Miss, God hates me. That's why I am standing on this corner. He's mad at me. I have nowhere to go." I said, "Sir, God loves you. He's not mad at you."

I handed him the brown-bagged lunch and the small bottle of water. He looked long and hard at the bottle of water and said, "Miss, can you baptize me?"

I looked up at him and saw the tears of life streaming down his face.

I looked into his clouded eyes and said, "Yes, Sir, I will baptize you in the name of the Father, the Son, and the Holy Spirit."

A beaming smile of joy began to shine through his weather-worn face. I departed, and the joy of the Lord welled up inside me.

...

**Dear God Almighty,**
I thank You that I am Yours and You are mine. Give me the wisdom and commitment to live my life for Your glory, honor, and praise, in the Name of Jesus Christ; Hallelujah and Amen.

...

# Charlie

L. Marie

...

### Zephaniah 3:17 (NRSV)

The Lord, your God, is in your midst, a warrior who gives victory; he will rejoice over you with gladness, he will renew you in his love; he will exult over you with loud singing.

...

Sundays used to feel heavy. Without James by my side, the house could feel so quiet it hurt. One day, my eldest granddaughter invited me to her volunteer project at a local animal shelter. At first, I hesitated. What could a 72-year-old woman do in a place crawling with rescue critters? Still, I agreed because saying "yes" makes life interesting—or so I tell my grandkids.

When I walked in, the smell nearly sent me running. But then a scrawny little dog caught my eye. His name was Charlie, a wiry terrier mix with one ear that drooped. He was shy, almost apologetic, and it broke my heart.

For years as a nurse, I'd cared for the suffering—people fighting against their own bodies—and I had the privilege of easing their pain. Turns out, it's not so different with a dog. I went back to the shelter for the next two weeks with my granddaughter, brushing Charlie's fur and sitting quietly with him. Each time, he'd inch a little closer, just like one of my grandkids with a secret to share.

After my third visit, Charlie gave me his first wag. It was small, almost invisible, but it unlocked something deep inside me.

Joy has a funny way of sneaking in, doesn't it? Now Charlie is home with me. He's filled my quiet days with mischief, and me? I'm grateful for the noise.

...

**Lord,**
thank You for unexpected joys and new beginnings. May we always find love and healing in Your gentle blessings.
Amen.

...

# Celebrating The Favor of Joy

*Joy is a divine gift that transcends circumstances, filling our hearts with light and hope. Embrace the joy that comes from knowing God's presence, allowing it to uplift your spirit and transform your perspective each day.*

**Now it's your turn to write your story of celebrating The Favor of Joy.**

Think about a moment when you experienced profound joy, regardless of the situation you were in. How did this joy impact your heart and outlook on life? Describe how God's favor was revealed through this joy and how it has influenced your faith journey.

_____

_____

_____

_____

_____

_____

_____

_____

_____

_____

_____

_____

_____

_____

_____

_____

_____

_____

# THE FAVOR OF Peace

God's peace surpasses all understanding and brings favor. In times of chaos, His peace calms our hearts and minds, assuring us of His presence.

# Divine Calm

...

**John 14:27 (NIV)**

Peace I leave with you; my peace I give you. I do not give to you as the world
gives. Do not let your hearts be troubled and do not be afraid.

...

In the world's noise and chaos, the peace that God offers is a rare and
precious gift.

John 14:27 reminds us of the lasting peace that Christ provides, a peace
unlike any the world can offer. This divine calm transcends our understanding,
enveloping us in comfort and assurance even when everything else seems
uncertain.

Imagine standing at the shore during a storm, waves crashing relentlessly,
and yet feeling an inexplicable calm. This is the peace of God—a sanctuary
in the middle of life's tumultuous moments. Whether you are facing pressure
at work, tensions in relationships, or personal uncertainties, His peace acts
as an anchor, grounding your heart and mind.

Reflect on a time when you felt overwhelmed, yet a sense of tranquility
settled within you—perhaps through prayer, meditation, or a comforting
scripture. This is the favor of God's peace, providing clarity and courage to
face challenges with a steady heart.

This week, let's celebrate and embrace this divine gift. Start each day by
inviting God's peace into your life. When chaos threatens to unsettle you,
pause and breathe in His calm. Let His assurances transform your fears
into faith, knowing His presence is a constant source of comfort and favor.

...

**Prince of Peace,**

Calm my anxious heart. Let Your peace reign in my life, bringing comfort and favor. Help
me to rest in Your presence, trusting in Your promise to still my soul and guide my steps.
Amen.

...

# The Authority of Peace

Dr. Theresa Billingsley

...

### Mark 4:39 (NKJV)
Then He arose and rebuked the wind, and said to the sea, "Peace be still."

...

Peace isn't just the calm after a storm; it's the strength we find within it, anchored in the presence of God. Without this divine presence, relying solely on our own strength can lead to feeling overwhelmed and exhausted.

I learned this firsthand when my marriage ended. The separation left me feeling stressed and disappointed, with my emotions swirling like a raging storm.

At what felt like my breaking point, in the middle of all the chaos, I cried out, "Peace, be still. Jesus, help me!"

In that moment, everything changed. Something shifted inside me.

When life's storms hit, it's essential to turn towards God for true peace.

Think about the disciples who faced a storm while Jesus slept. People often criticize them for being scared, but they turned to Jesus, the Prince of Peace, for help. They knew they couldn't find peace on their own. Just like them, when life gets tough, we need to seek the source of peace to find comfort and strength.

...

### Dear God,
In the midst of life's storms, grant me Your peace and strength. Help me lean on You for comfort and courage, trusting Your presence to guide my way.
Amen.
...

# Know God Know Peace

Rochelle D. Jacobs

...

**Philippians 4:7 (NIV)**
And the peace of God, which transcends all understanding, will guard your
hearts and your minds in Christ Jesus.

...

Have you ever found yourself waiting and worrying about your child's safety?

My husband was out of town, deer hunting with friends, and we had both decided it was time for our son to go out and hang with his friends. As the clock ticked past his 1:00 am curfew, my heart pounded with anxiety. Despite sending texts and making calls, there was no response—just silence and racing thoughts of the worst. Minutes turned into hours, and fear drove me to self-soothe with sugary sweets. I devoured an entire sheet cake and several chocolate ice cream cups, trying to numb my worry.

In desperation, I prayed, asking God to watch over my son and bring him home safely. I clung to the promise in Philippians 4:7, seeking peace. Gradually, a calmness settled over my heart, reassuring me that God was with me, even in uncertainty. I prayed for my son's safety and God's peace, trusting that He was working even when I couldn't see it. Eventually, I drifted into a restless sleep, confident that God would care for my son.

The next morning, feeling like a beached whale from my sugar stupor, I awoke to a knock at the door. It was my son, weary but safe. As he apologized and explained, I felt immense relief and gratitude. I hugged him, silently thanking God for his safe return and for granting me peace during my troubled night.

Beloved, remember that God's favor includes His peace—a supernatural calm that steadies us in life's storms. He faithfully provides peace beyond understanding, helping us trust Him with what matters most.

...

**Lord,**
Grant me peace and trust in Your protection, knowing You watch over my loved
ones, bringing them safely home and calming my heart.
Amen.

...

# Peace In The Storm

Adrienne Y. Murphy

...

**Psalms 55:18 (NIV)**
He hath delivered my soul in peace from the battle that was against me: for there were many with me.

...

There is peace even in the midst of the storm. On August 23, 2022, my husband and soulmate of over 23 years passed away from a rare cancer. He dedicated 24 years of his life to the United States Navy and was deployed three times during his career. After his last deployment, he began experiencing itchiness in his skin. By October 2021, tumors appeared on his face and head.

Carlie was a beautiful human being—generous, loving, kind, and full of life. His smile could light up any room, and he had a heart of gold. When the tumors appeared, he was diagnosed with Cutaneous T-cell Lymphoma. Treatment started right away, but after a year and a half of chemotherapy, the disease grew more aggressive, leading to multiple hospitalizations. Carlie fought with all his strength, but he eventually suffered a stroke, a complication from his treatment, and passed away six days later.

The heartbreak from losing him is beyond words. During this difficult time, I was responsible for making decisions about his care, and God gave me the peace and strength to do what was needed.

I am grateful for the peace God granted me to face this storm. I cherish the wonderful memories of a life that many can only dream of, and for that, I am eternally thankful. God provides peace when we face the storms in our lives.

...

**Dear God,**
Thank You for Your peace in my storm. Grant me strength and grace to endure life's trials.
Amen.

...

# Choosing Calm Over Conflict

Sheryl Simms

...

**Matthew 5:9 (NIV)**
Blessed are the peacemakers, for they will be called children of God.

...

I was furious. My co-worker had just thrown me under the bus for a project he didn't finish. Now my job was on the line because of him. My mind was racing with all the ways I could get back at him.

Needing some distraction, I turned on the radio. A pastor was quoting Matthew 5:9 about peacemakers. I rolled my eyes and snapped it off. "God, I'm not in the mood for peace. I want payback. This is so unfair."

Then, out of nowhere, I remembered Jesus on the Cross. I sighed, "Alright, God, that wasn't fair either, but You turned it into something good. Help me be kind to my co-worker. Please, give me peace."

The next day, I ran into him. I took a deep breath, forced a smile, and asked how he was doing. To my surprise, he looked guilty and confessed he'd forgotten about the project. He asked if I could forgive him.

I realized then that being a peacemaker isn't about ignoring my feelings or letting others walk over me. It's about choosing calm and grace over conflict. As I decided to let go of my anger, I felt a wave of peace wash over me. It's amazing how choosing peace changes everything inside you. Peace isn't just a choice; it's a gift that transforms us when we embrace it.

...

**God,**
Guide me to show mercy in unfair times, embodying Jesus' spirit. Help me act with grace and compassion. In Jesus' name,
Amen.

...

# Be Still

Beverley Anderson

...

**Psalm 62:1 (NIV)**
Truly my soul finds rest in God; my salvation comes from him.

...

In today's fast-paced world, the demands are constant and draining, often leaving us spiritually and emotionally depleted. I vividly recall a time when my life felt like an unstoppable whirlwind. The noise was deafening, and I was caught in a relentless cycle of tasks and responsibilities. Have you ever felt like you're on a treadmill that never stops? During this chaotic period, burnout took hold of me. It was a stark wake-up call that made me realize I had been neglecting my spiritual well-being by not spending time in stillness with God. The demands of life had drowned out His voice, leaving me disconnected and exhausted. Carving out intentional time for prayer and reflection brought me peace and healing during challenging times. Like Jesus, who withdrew to connect with His Father, taking time to be still in God's presence was the best investment I ever made. It's not selfish; it's stewardship of the life God has given us. In the whirlwind of our hurried lives, it's easy to become ensnared by distraction. But when we prioritize stillness with God, we tap into the true source of our strength and blessings. Today, I invite you to embrace the gift of stillness. Let go of your burdens and surrender them to God. Make it your daily mission to seek out sacred moments; they are essential for your strength and overall flourishing in life.

...

**Lord,**
Help me be still, draw me close to You, and fill me with Your sweet Spirit.
Amen.

...

71

# Celebrating The Favor of Peace

*Peace is the calm assurance that God is in control, even in the midst of chaos. Let His peace guard your heart and mind, bringing serenity and strength to navigate life's storms with grace and confidence.*

**Now it's your turn to write your story of celebrating The Favor of Peace.**

Reflect on a time when you felt God's peace envelop you during a challenging situation. How did this peace influence your actions and perspective? Describe the ways in which God's favor became evident through the tranquility you experienced, and how it has shaped your understanding of His presence.

_____

_____

_____

_____

_____

_____

_____

_____

_____

_____

_____

_____

_____

_____

_____

_____

_____

_____

# THE
# FAVOR
## OF

# *Provision*

Trust God for provision; He never fails.
His abundant resources meet our needs
in ways we could never imagine.

# Divine Supply

...

## Philippians 4:19 (NIV)

And my God will meet all your needs according to the riches of his glory in Christ Jesus.

...

Provision is a testament to God's unwavering faithfulness, a daily reminder of His abundant grace.

Philippians 4:19 assures us that God's resources are limitless, and His desire to meet our needs is profound. When we lean into His promises, we discover a divine supply that often exceeds our expectations.

Think about a moment when you faced uncertainty—perhaps a financial strain, an unforeseen expense, or a career challenge. It's in these times that God's provision shines, transforming what seemed impossible into an extraordinary experience of His favor. Remember the relief when a solution appeared, sometimes through unexpected sources or a sudden opportunity. These are not mere coincidences but reflections of God's provision, orchestrated with His loving hands.

As we live our daily lives, it can be easy to focus on what we lack. Yet, God calls us to trust in His provision, to shift our perspective from scarcity to abundance. His blessings, whether material, emotional, or spiritual, are tailored perfectly to meet our unique needs.

This week, embrace the Favor of Provision by acknowledging the ways God has met your needs. Reflect on past instances of His faithfulness and let them fuel your trust for the future. Celebrate His generosity by sharing your blessings with others, knowing that His supply is inexhaustible and His love, unfailing.

...

### Jehovah Jireh, my Provider

Thank You for meeting my needs. Help me to trust in Your faithful provision, knowing that Your resources are endless and Your timing perfect. May I always rest in the assurance of Your care and share Your blessings with those around me.

Amen.

...

# $2 for 2 Weeks

## Karen McKinney Holley

...

### Malachi 3:10 (NIV)

"Bring the whole tithe into the storehouse, that there may be food in my house. Test me in this," says the LORD Almighty, "and see if I will not throw open the floodgates of heaven and pour out so much blessing that there will not be room enough to store it."

...

"I don't have any money," my husband said.

I answered, "I have $2.00."

He was in school, so I was the only one working. I got paid on the last day of the month, and we still had two weeks to go. Before the previous payday, our pastor had invited Rev. Dr. A. Louis Patterson, a renowned pastor from Houston, Texas, to conduct a stewardship workshop.

I had never heard stewardship explained so clearly, especially tithing, and I was deeply convicted. When I got paid, my husband and I agreed that we would tithe, and we stepped out on faith.

Now, with two children, we had $2 and the $5 in a checking account that was required to keep it open. More month than money wasn't new for us. Prior to Dr. Patterson's workshop, I had always heard tithing explained as giving 10% so that God would give me back more in return. However, Dr. Patterson explained that tithing was not about receiving more but about obedience.

I didn't start trying to figure out how to stretch $2 or look for someone to give us money. We had food in the refrigerator. I had a bus pass to get to work, and we lived on campus, so my husband just walked to his classes. There was enough gas in the car to drive to church for the next two Sundays.

When I got paid, I still had the same $2! It felt good to obey.

...

### Lord,

Thank You for Your faithful provision. Teach us to trust You fully, obey with joyful hearts, and find peace in knowing You supply all we truly need.

Amen.

...

# Faithful Journey

Benecia Ponder

...

## Isaiah 30:21 (NKJV)

Your ears shall hear a word behind you, saying, 'This is the way, walk in it.

...

For over 26 years, I've navigated life with limited vision, seeing only a few inches ahead. Yet, I've never let this challenge stop me from pursuing what I love—travel.

Traveling solo, though thrilling, can be daunting for someone like me. But in every journey, I place my trust in God, praying continuously for His protection.

This time, I embarked on a business retreat to Mexico, expecting to travel with a group. Days before the trip, I discovered our flights weren't coordinated. I faced the prospect of navigating a foreign airport alone, in a country where I didn't speak the language. While I'm seasoned in airport navigation, this was uncharted territory.

I turned to God, seeking courage, wisdom, and the resources needed for this journey. His provision was swift. At the Atlanta airport, I requested assistance from the airline, ensuring someone would meet me in Mexico to help with customs and transport to the resort. Everything fell into place seamlessly, a testament to God's ever-present care.

The retreat was enriching, and as I returned home, God's provision extended further. I traveled with a newfound friend from the retreat, easing my journey back. This experience reinforced a profound truth: God provides for all our needs, not just financially but in every aspect of life.

He cares deeply for us, attending to the intricate details of our lives. In my travels and beyond, I've witnessed His faithful provision, a reminder that we are never truly alone. God's favor is a constant, guiding light, illuminating our paths even in the darkest of times.

...

### Heavenly Father,

We thank You for Your abundant provision and guidance. Grant us wisdom and strength as we navigate life's journeys. May Your favor light our path always

Amen.

# Grandpa Eli

Sibyl F. Cole

...

### Matthew 6:26 (NIV)

Look at the birds of the air; they do not sow or read or store away in barns, and yet your heavenly Father feeds them. Are you not much more valuable than them?

...

I had a friend named Mary in high school who loved talking about growing up on her Grandpa Eli's farm in Arkansas. She said he didn't have much, but his generosity was endless. One year, there was a drought, and his crops weren't doing well. He was worried.

Mary said they were sitting on his porch one evening when a stranger walked toward them. The man introduced himself as Mr. Jackson. He explained that his car had broken down a few miles down the road and asked if he could use their phone to call a tow truck.

Grandpa Eli obliged and even offered Mr. Jackson something to eat and drink while he waited. (This was back in the days when you could still open your home to people without fearing for your life.) The tow truck came, and Mr. Jackson thanked Grandpa Eli for his kindness and hospitality, then left.

The next day, it rained for hours. Grandpa Eli's crops flourished, and he had more than enough to provide for his family. A couple of days later, Mr. Jackson returned to give Grandpa Eli a small token of gratitude.

Mary said she realized then that her grandfather had been a vessel of God's provision when he told her, "Sometimes, in our darkest moments, we are called to give. When we do this, a door will open for blessings to flow."

Grandpa Eli understood that God's provision often comes through small acts of kindness and faith, and he trusted that abundance would follow.

...

### Lord,

Thank You for Your provision. Teach us to give in trust and faith, knowing that through kindness, You pour blessings into our lives and others.

Amen.

...

# Grow in Gratitude

Dr. Theresa Billingsley

...

**1 Thessalonians 5::18 (AMP)**

In every situation (no matter what the circumstances) be thankful and continually give thanks to God; for this is the will of God for you in Christ Jesus.

...

I found myself in a tough spot, struggling to put food on the table for my family. The worry was overwhelming. I felt lost, unsure of what my next steps should be.

I was tempted to complain about how unfair it all seemed. But something nudged me to try a different path.

Instead of letting fear take over, I chose to thank God for what I did have—my family's love, a roof over our heads, our health, and above all, God's protection and provision. As I turned my focus to gratitude, the heaviness in my heart began to lift. Although I still didn't know how we would get our next meal, I felt an unexpected peace and assurance that God would provide.

In the midst of this praise, I received a surprising phone call. A friend reached out, saying their freezer was overflowing, and offered me some of their food. It was a blessing I couldn't have anticipated.

Through this experience, I learned that thankfulness can open doors for unexpected help. Even when circumstances seem dire, gratitude can lead to miraculous turnarounds.

Now, the Bible doesn't say we have to give thanks for every difficult situation, but we can find something to be thankful for in every situation.

Gratitude invites God to work in our lives, while negativity only makes the burden heavier. Remember, even in tough times, a thankful heart can change everything.

...

**Dear God,**

I am truly grateful for Your endless blessings. Help me remain thankful in every moment, trusting Your wisdom and embracing Your guidance.

Amen.

# Don't Underestimate God

Benecia Ponder

...

## John 6:9 (NIV)

Here is a boy with five small barley loaves and two small fish, but how far will they go among so many?

...

A little in Jesus' hands can feed a multitude.

I'm sure you know the story: Jesus wants to feed a crowd of 5,000. The only food for miles around is a little boy's snack of two small fish and five barley loaves. The facts say there is no way that such a meager amount of food could feed thousands of people. But it did! And there was even more left over than when they started.

Whenever I think of this story in John 6, I am reminded to never underestimate what God can do.

I know my skills, knowledge, and abilities alone are not nearly enough to do what God is calling me to do. The people I want to help need so much, and I have so little...until I put it in Jesus' hands and allow Him to use me for His glory.

Our resources and wisdom may be limited, but God's aren't. Do not underestimate what God can and wants to do through your life. He wants to use the gifts, the skills, the resources, the talents, the education, and the opportunities He has entrusted to you in a mighty way.

...

## Dear God,

Please use me. I surrender my gifts and talents to you. Multiply them to impact many lives. Amen.

...

# Celebrating The Favor of Provision

*God's provision is a testament to His faithfulness and love, meeting our needs in ways only He can. Trust in His timing and resources, knowing that each provision reflects His care and abundant favor for you.*

**Now it's your turn to write your story of celebrating The Favor of Provision.**

Think about a time when God provided for you in an unexpected way. How did this provision impact your life and faith? Describe the emotions you felt as you witnessed His care in action, and how this experience has deepened your trust in His ability to meet your needs.

_____

_____

_____

_____

_____

_____

_____

_____

_____

_____

_____

_____

_____

_____

_____

_____

_____

_____

_____

# THE FAVOR OF Healing

Healing flows from the power of God's favor. Whether physical, emotional, or spiritual, His healing touch restores us and brings wholeness..

# Healing Promised

...

## Isaiah 53:5 (NIV)

But he was pierced for our transgressions, he was crushed for our iniquities; the punishment that brought us peace was on him, and by his wounds we are healed.

...

I want to remind you today that healing is not just a possibility; it's a divine promise from our loving God. When we look at Isaiah 53:5, we see that through Christ's sacrifice, a river of healing and wholeness flows into our lives. This healing is a powerful expression of God's favor, reaching into every corner of our existence.

Maybe you're dealing with a physical ailment, or perhaps it's emotional pain that weighs heavy on your heart. Let me assure you, these challenges are not the end of your story. They are opportunities for God to show up and show out in your life in a mighty way. God is in the business of restoring what's broken and making it better than ever before.

Believe that the same power that raised Christ from the dead is at work in you. Healing is not just something we hope for in the future; it's something we can walk in right now. By embracing this divine favor, you're welcoming God's transformative power into your life.

As you meditate on the Favor of Healing this week, remember that every step toward restoration is a step into God's loving embrace. Hold your head high, knowing that His favor is upon you. Walk boldly, trusting that God's healing touch is not just possible, but promised.

...

### Father,

Thank You for the healing that flows from Your favor. Help me to see Your hand at work in every part of my life. I trust in Your divine plan and embrace the wholeness You offer. Thank You for Your grace, Your mercy, and Your never-ending love.

Amen.

...

# Healing Steps

Sheryl Simms

...

## James 5:15 (NIV)

And the prayer offered in faith will make the sick person well; the Lord will raise them up. If they have sinned, they will be forgiven.

...

I remember the night of the prayer revival vividly, a night that changed everything. The preacher's voice resonated through the room, urging us to seek healing from God, even for the pains we had come to accept. I had resigned myself to the idea that my leg would never fully recover from the car accident. Walking long distances seemed like a distant dream, and the constant ache was just part of my life. But that night, something stirred within me.

Returning home, I sat on my bed and whispered a prayer for healing. I woke up the next morning filled with an unexplainable resolve. I picked up the phone and called my doctor, requesting the physical therapy sessions I had previously declined.

My dedication in the following months was unwavering. Each stretch and exercise seemed to breathe new life into my leg, as if my prayers were echoing through every muscle and tendon.

The day I walked into my doctor's office without my cane was unforgettable. His eyes widened in disbelief as I strode confidently across the room. "This is remarkable, Sheryl," he said, shaking his head in wonder.

Reflecting on those months, I see them as a testament to the power of faith and determination. I learned to never underestimate the power of prayer and the blessings that can unfold when you have the courage to believe.

...

## Heavenly Father,

We thank You for Sheryl's miraculous healing. May her journey inspire others to seek Your grace. Strengthen our faith, and remind us of Your boundless love and power to heal.

Amen.

...

# Cancer Battle

Sibyl F. Cole

...

**Jeremiah 17:14 (NIV)**
Heal me, Lord, and I will be healed; save me and I will
be saved, for you are the one I praise.

...

In the summer of 2022, during the pandemic, my cousin, "Cuzzy," a vibrant 46-year-old mother of two, received a life-altering diagnosis: triple-negative breast cancer, one of the most aggressive forms.

The news was devastating, but she was determined to fight. With unwavering support from family and friends, she began her healing journey—surgery, chemotherapy, radiation, and countless appointments. Each step was grueling, from the physical toll of treatments to the emotional rollercoaster of uncertainty.

Cuzzy found strength in her community, joining a local support group where survivors shared stories and encouragement. These connections reminded her she wasn't alone. She also used social media to advocate for breast cancer awareness and stress the importance of early detection for both women and men.

After a year of exhausting treatments, she finally received the news: cancer-free!

The experience transformed her perspective, filling her with gratitude and a renewed appreciation for life. Her battle was marked by tears, laughter, self-discovery, and resilience. Most importantly, her faith in God never wavered.

Cuzzy's journey is a testament to the strength of the human spirit and the healing power of God's favor. Through courage, determination, and unshakable faith, she emerged victorious. God brought her through, and her story inspires others to trust in His grace and favor.

...

**Dear God,**
Thank You for Your healing favor; grant me strength, faith, and love.
Amen.

...

# Healing Pains

Rochelle D. Jacobs

...

**Psalm 147:3 (NIV)**

He heals the brokenhearted and binds up their wounds.

...

God's favor is profoundly transformative, bringing healing and restoration to the broken places in our hearts. His love and grace offer a path from pain to peace.

Reflecting on my childhood trauma—memories of fear, shame, and being sexually molested—I struggled to embrace the present or envision a hopeful future. In therapy, I felt compelled to surrender my pain to God. Psalm 147:3 reminded me of His healing power: "He heals the brokenhearted and binds up their wounds."

This verse resonated deeply, showing me that healing is a journey requiring vulnerability and openness before God. I invited Him into my pain, asking for His help to confront my past. With God's favor guiding me, I've learned to journal my thoughts and acknowledge my emotions with my therapist's support. Each step, though difficult, is infused with His grace, giving me strength to reclaim my narrative.

Healing is not forgetting; it is remembering with grace, knowing that God's favor turns our scars into testimonies of His faithfulness.

Today, I am at peace, trusting that God heals our wounds and makes us whole. As His beloved daughter, I am worthy of love and joy. The journey was uncomfortable, but God's promises and community support sustained me.

Embracing His favor, I found liberation from my past. God's favor transforms pain into a powerful testimony of His love and grace. May we trust His perfect plan for restoration.

...

**Lord in my weakness,**

Be my strength in weakness, my comfort in pain. Bring healing and peace.

Amen.

...

# Soul Freedom

### Dr. Katherine E. James

...

### 3 John 1:2 (NIV)

Dear friend, I pray that you may enjoy good health and that all may go well with you, even as your soul is getting along well.

...

Why now at 59? Was this divine timing as Poppa had planned, or did it take me this long to be ready? Why now?

I sequestered myself in a hotel room with the intention of completing 12 modules. Nowhere in my imagination was there an inkling of the level of emotional and psychological healing Poppa God was inviting me to.

I once read that a scarcity mindset is a way of thinking that's characterized by a focus on what you don't have enough of and a belief that you'll never have what you want.

In February 2020, at 59 years old, my journey of freedom from a scarcity mindset began. "There is not enough for my dreams to come true, and there is nothing I can do about it." This was the message playing in my subconscious since childhood. This was the message that curated the belief that I was limited, powerless, unsafe, and xxx. This is the message that attempted to quiet my soul's cry that continually screamed, "There is more." This is the message that ultimately yielded its vicious tentacles to Jehovah Rapha.

Praise the Lord, hallelujah, I'm free!

Emotional and psychological freedom is available for you. Matthew 7:7 says, "Ask, and it will be given to you; seek, and you will find; knock, and the door will be opened to you."

...

### Lord,

Thank You for healing and freedom. Fill me with Your grace and strength to walk boldly in Your abundance.

Amen

...

# Mirror of His Heart

Stacey Collins

...

**Isaiah 62:3 (NIV)**

You will be a crown of splendor in the LORD's hand,
a royal diadem in the hand of your God.

...

Imagine a picture....one sees paint splashed on a canvas, another sees a true piece of art. A song playing... the sound is a ringing in one's ears, or to another, a harmonious symphony.

My dream was to grow up to become the 'fairytale' beauty every little girl longs to be, rising above the 'acceptable.' But instead, I felt too short, not skinny enough, not quite pretty enough. Conversations inside my head and within my heart spoke constant negatives, an invisible veil blocking me from receiving 'I'm beautiful' through another's eyes and feeling the reflection of God's heart mirroring back His love for me. Shattered, scarred, shamed—could God love me? See me as beautiful? Could I experience pure beauty and confidence deep within my soul? 'God, where are you?' I cried out over and over again. I felt He couldn't hear me!

We don't always know the exact moment something changes. I found it to be the 'links in my healing chain.' God sent people to me. Each person brought something unique, helping me take that next step, opening my heart to another dream, another possibility, to feel hope, to believe. Through God's community, through His love, a spark flickered and flamed. The veil broke! A new knowing that God truly loves me and sees me as beautiful. I am still on that journey, learning to embrace all that He is doing in me. Healing pieced into a beautiful mosaic, shattered and sharp broken pieces of my life formed into a beautiful and confident ME. Now, when I look in the mirror of His heart, I see what He sees—His masterpiece.

...

**God,**

Thank You for Your healing love. Help me see myself as Your beautiful creation, embracing transformation and the inner beauty You bestowed.

Amen.

# Celebrating The Favor of Healing

*Healing is a testament to God's power and compassion, restoring us in body, mind, and spirit. Embrace the journey of healing, knowing that each step forward is marked by His abundant favor and transformative grace.*

**Now it's your turn to write your story of celebrating The Favor of Healing.**

Reflect on a moment when you experienced God's healing touch in your life, whether physical, emotional, or spiritual. How did this healing change your perspective and relationships? Describe the ways in which His favor was evident throughout your healing journey and how it has influenced your faith and gratitude.

_____

_____

_____

_____

_____

_____

_____

_____

_____

_____

_____

_____

_____

_____

_____

_____

_____

# THE
# FAVOR
# OF
# Community

Community strengthens us and
multiplies God's favor. In unity,
we find support, encouragement,
and collective strength.

# Collective Strength

...

## Hebrews 10:24-25 (NIV)

And let us consider how we may spur one another on toward love and good deeds, not giving up meeting together, as some are in the habit of doing, but encouraging one another—and all the more as you see the Day approaching.

...

This week, let's reflect on the incredible gift of community. Our lives are enriched and our spirits uplifted when we connect with others who share our faith and values.

Hebrews 10:24-25 reminds us of the power of gathering together, encouraging one another in love and good deeds. In community, God's favor multiplies through the strength and support we give and receive.

Community is more than attending gatherings; it's about being truly connected. When we immerse ourselves in a community of believers, we find encouragement and inspiration to pursue love and good deeds. These connections become the foundation of our spiritual lives, offering support and strength when we need it most.

As we uplift and support one another, God's love and grace flow more abundantly through us. Together, we accomplish more than we could alone, reflecting God's love in powerful ways.

This week, consider how you can contribute to and benefit from the Favor of Community. Whether through a helping hand, a smile, or a prayer, each act of kindness strengthens your community's bonds. Embrace this divine gift, and watch God's favor grow in your life and in the lives of those you touch.

...

### Lord,

Thank You for the gift of community. Help me to be an active part of it, sharing Your love and favor with others. Guide me to build connections that reflect Your grace and multiply Your blessings.

Amen.

...

# Piece of Cake

Stacey Collins

...

**Romans 12:10 (NIV)**
Be devoted to one another in love. Honor one another above yourselves.

...

Out of nowhere, I hear a woman ask, "Would you like a piece of cake?" I look up, tears filling my eyes, and whisper, "Yes, thank you." In that moment, that small piece of cake was worth a million dollars. I felt seen, heard, and welcomed. I attended a new Bible study group in a new town and only knew the leaders. The house was bustling with people everywhere, conversations and laughter all around me. I felt alone. I found a seat at the table by myself. People were mingling and enjoying each other's presence.

Growing up, I had the experience of moving often and attending a different school each year. I was very shy, insecure, awkward, alone. I don't know when things shifted, but one day a light bulb turned on. I smiled. Someone smiled back. For years, I had waited for another to make that first move, say "hi," turn and smile. But one day, I smiled, and they smiled back. A door was opened. My heart smiled.

This is community: a tapestry woven as if becoming a fabric, a cloak, a covering; to commune as one, to weave together our stories. Community is not just a group of people getting together. It's to commune, to become, to fit, find our place, find our home, and be a safe place. Who can you be that "open arms" embrace for today? Next time you step into a room, look around. Is someone alone? Who would you like to serve a "piece of cake" to?

...

**Lord,**
thank You for the blessing of community. Grant us courage to connect, share, and support one another in love, weaving our lives into a beautiful tapestry.
Amen.

...

# Unity in Diversity

Benecia Ponder

...

**1 Corinthians 1:10 (NLT)**

I appeal to you, dear brothers and sisters, by the authority of our Lord Jesus Christ, to live in harmony with each other. Let there be no divisions in the church. Rather, be of one mind, united in thought and purpose.

...

Difference is inevitable. Division is a choice.

In a world of diverse opinions, disagreement is natural and can be celebrated, not feared. We can stand firm in our beliefs without letting differences drive us apart.

I have strong opinions and never shy away from defending them. Recently, during a Bible school class, the teacher made a statement that contradicted one of my core beliefs. I raised my hand and respectfully challenged him. The debate grew intense, neither of us backing down.

After class, we hugged and laughed together, surprising those who had witnessed our spirited exchange. Someone asked, "How can you be joking after that argument?" I replied, "We don't have to agree to love each other."

Disagreement doesn't require disrespect. We can engage in passionate discussions while honoring each other as God's cherished creations.

This experience reminded me that while differences are unavoidable, division is not. When we approach disagreements with love and respect, they can deepen our understanding and strengthen our connections.

...

**Heavenly Father,**

Guide my heart to embrace differences with love and understanding. May I always seek unity and reflect Your grace in every encounter.

Amen.

...

# Iron Sharpens Iron

Rochelle D. Jacobs

...

**Proverbs 27:17 (ERV)**
As one piece of iron sharpens another, so friends keep each other sharp.

...

Pre-COVID, I struggled with focus and accountability, feeling isolated as I navigated personal and professional challenges. Proverbs 27:17 reminded me, "Iron sharpens iron," revealing the power of community.

Investing in the book anthology When Destiny Needs An Intervention brought me into a sisterhood of "Destiny Diamonds." Surrounded by like-minded women, we shared our stories to reclaim power, foster support, and celebrate each other's victories. We embraced vulnerability and honored every journey, creating a space for growth and empowerment.

Through the H3W Mastermind group, I found accountability that aligned my goals with my vision. Weekly gatherings provided a safe space to set intentions, track progress, and encourage one another. Ecclesiastes 4:9 (AMP) says, "Two are better than one because they have a more satisfying return for their labor." This truth resonated deeply as I experienced the profound favor of a community that challenged and supported me.

The collective wisdom of these groups renewed my sense of purpose, ignited creativity, and inspired me to push beyond limits. My sisters in Christ continue to cheer me on in my journey toward Unleashed Destiny.

Community is God's gift, where dreams become stronger and intentions clearer through shared experiences and accountability. The bonds I formed with the Destiny Diamonds and H3W Mastermind group filled my journey with joy and encouragement. Let us cherish the communities that inspire, hold us accountable, and propel us toward our God-given destiny.

...

**Lord,**
Thank You for community. Guide us with shared strength and support toward Your plan.
Amen.

...

# Faithful Friends

Alethia Saunders

...

**Hebrews 10:24-25 (NIV)**

And let us consider how we may spur one another on toward love and good deeds, not giving up meeting together, as some are in the habit of doing, but encouraging one another—and all the more as you see the Day approaching.

...

My father made a comment to me the other day. It went something like, "I'm glad you are around the people you are around. I feel like you are actually your real self now."

It kind of stuck with me because I never knew he noticed who I was around. As I reflected on his words, I realized they were true.

When I surrounded myself with individuals who had a profound respect for God and the Universe, I experienced more peace. Having the right community to push me to be better and walk in God's purpose helped me excel and provided me with a safe haven.

I wouldn't trade this feeling for the world.

Choosing to surround myself with goal-getters, disciples of Christ, leaders, and humble spirits helps me also reflect those same qualities. You are only as strong as the people you surround yourself with. I love my little community. We laugh, cry, carry, and build each other up as needed. We are a fortress all by ourselves.

...

**Dear God,**

Thank You for blessing me with a supportive community. May we continue to uplift each other, grow in faith, and strengthen our bonds.

Amen.

...

# From Eleven to Heaven

Dr. Katherine E. James

...

**1 John 4:7 (NIV)**

Dear friends, let us love one another, for love comes from God.
Everyone who loves has been born of God and knows God.

...

Was it too good to be true? No. It was good and true!

Shiloh Deliverance Church began in 1989 with the Bracys—husband and wife co-pastors and their three children. My family—my husband, our 18-month-old son—and close friends joined, forming a group of eleven.

In December 2024, Shiloh Deliverance International 2.0 celebrated its 34th anniversary.

As the first official member and an early leader, I've witnessed countless stories within this church community. Shiloh was the perfect place to grow in my relationship with God and develop my calling as an associate pastor. We encouraged each other's gifts, explored our callings, and learned how to "do church" together. Like the early church, we broke bread, traveled, and raised children as one family in Christ.

Were we perfect? No. Did we make mistakes? Yes—sometimes big ones, especially during certain seasons. Yet, through it all, we remained a healthy, loving church family.

I often reflect on what made the difference. My conclusion? Love. We truly love God and each other. Love is the foundation of a thriving community.

As you connect with your community, remember: love must be abundant. Add love, and expect love to be added. It transforms relationships, strengthens bonds, and sustains the journey together.

...

**Lord,**

Thank You for the gift of community. Strengthen our bonds
with love, unity, and grace, reflecting Your favor in all we do..
Amen.

...

# Celebrating The Favor of Community

*In the embrace of community, we find strength, support, and shared joy. God's favor is magnified when we come together, lifting each other up and creating bonds that reflect His love and grace in our lives.*

**Now it's your turn to write your story of celebrating The Favor of Community.**

Think about a time when your community played a vital role in your life. How did their support and encouragement impact your journey? Reflect on the ways God's favor was manifest through these relationships and how being part of a community has enriched your faith and well-being.

_____

_____

_____

_____

_____

_____

_____

_____

_____

_____

_____

_____

_____

_____

_____

_____

_____

_____

# THE
# FAVOR
# OF
# *Strength*

God empowers us with strength for every challenge. In our weakest moments, His strength upholds us, allowing us to overcome obstacles.

# Divine Empowerment

...

**Philippians 4:13 (NIV)**
I can do all this through him who gives me strength.

...

Life often presents us with hurdles that seem insurmountable. Yet, the promise of divine strength means that we are equipped to handle whatever comes our way. God's favor doesn't just provide us with enough strength to get by; it gives us abundant strength to thrive, to overcome, and to achieve our dreams.

This is the favor of strength—a divine empowerment that lifts us beyond our natural abilities into a realm of limitless possibilities.

When we rely on God's strength, we tap into a source that never runs dry. It's a strength that renews us daily, enabling us to push beyond our limits and achieve things we never thought possible.

Whether you're facing personal challenges, professional hurdles, or emotional battles, remember that with God's strength, you can conquer them all.

This week, embrace the Favor of Strength by trusting in God's power to guide and support you. Let His strength be your foundation, anchoring you as you pursue your goals and face challenges head-on. With God by your side, there is no limit to what you can accomplish.

...

**Almighty God,**
Thank You for being my constant source of strength. Fill me with Your power to face life's challenges with courage and faith. Help me rely on Your divine empowerment every day, knowing that with You, I can overcome anything.
Amen.

...

# Losing Chari

Sibyl F. Cole

...

**Psalm 73:26 (NIV)**
My flesh and my heart may fail, but God is the
strength of my heart and my portion forever.

...

In the summer of 1993, my six-year-old daughter, Chari, was admitted to the hospital. Born with a heart defect, she had her first surgery at just three weeks old. The doctors had warned us that a follow-up surgery would eventually be necessary to update the initial work. Chari spent 72 days in the hospital, her spirit illuminating even the darkest moments. Her visitors were limited to family and her primary nurses—Susan, Markie, Liz, and Mike—who became like a second family to me. They supported us throughout her entire stay. Chari adored them, and we all marveled at her fighting spirit, which gave us hope that she would return home stronger to rejoin her sister, Ashley.

As weeks passed, her condition worsened. I watched helplessly as my brave little girl fought valiantly, her strength waning. On August 27th, 1993, I received a call at 4:20 am to return to the hospital immediately. I had gone home to check on Ashley and get some rest. By the time I arrived back at the hospital, it was too late; Chari had already taken her last breath. That moment felt surreal, as if time had stopped, leaving an unbearable void in my heart.

After her passing, I struggled with overwhelming grief and loss, relying on my faith that God would grant me the strength to carry on. Though Chari is no longer with me, her spirit lives on, guiding me through the darkness and reminding me to cherish every moment.

...

**Heavenly Father,**
In my struggles, grant me strength and peace. Guide me
with Your love, renewing my spirit through faith.
Amen.

...

# ReNEWed Strength

Dr. Theresa Billingsley

...

**Isaiah 40:31 (KJV)**
But they that wait upon the LORD shall renew their
strength; they shall mount up with wings as eagles; they shall
run, and not be weary; and they shall walk, and not faint.

...

The doorbell rang, and I hesitated before answering. Standing there was a man, a gun visible on his hip, who handed me papers and signaled for the moving truck behind him to approach.

Fear and humiliation washed over me as I realized they were here to move us out of our first family home. Strangers invaded our space, packing everything away for storage. Overcome with embarrassment and shame, I retreated upstairs, seeking refuge in the bathroom, where my tears flowed freely.

I felt like a failure, consumed by a desire to hide away from the world. But in my darkest moment, I found strength in the Lord. My mother welcomed me back home with open arms, and I thanked God for her unwavering support. Instead of succumbing to despair, I was filled with renewed strength and determination. Within three months, I had found my footing once more.

Waiting on the Lord doesn't mean standing still; it's about serving with anticipation, and believing in the promise of renewal. With faith as my anchor, I lifted my head high, ready to embrace the future with resilience and hope.

...

**Dear God,**
Please give me strength and resilience. Help me face challenges with faith,
renew my spirit and purpose, and guide me towards success and growth.
Amen.

...

# Finding My Strength

Adrienne Y. Murphy

...

**Psalms 73:26 (NIV)**
My flesh and my heart faileth: but God is the strength
of my heart, and my portion forever.

...

In the shadow of loss, I discovered an unexpected strength. Married to my soulmate for nearly twenty-four years, our life was rich with adventure, travel, and the joys of raising our blended family. But in 2021, everything changed when my husband was diagnosed with cancer, turning our world upside down.

As he underwent treatment, we cycled between hope and despair. Each new tumor and treatment tested us, yet nothing prepared me for the next chapter. Despite his physical fitness and our active lifestyle, his health declined. Through it all, we clung to our faith, trusting God as our pillar of strength.

After months of battling, my husband suffered a stroke and passed away. In that moment of profound grief, I discovered my true strength. Facing life-altering decisions, I felt the weight of the world, but the strength others saw in me wasn't my own—it was God's favor manifesting within me.

In my brokenness, God granted me the resilience to move forward. His promise to never abandon me became my anchor, guiding me through the storm. I realized His favor had equipped me with courage I didn't know I had.

This journey taught me that divine strength is our greatest ally in times of despair. It's God's unyielding presence that empowers us to rise when life feels insurmountable. Through faith, I found the favor of strength, a gift that continues to light my path forward.

...

**Heavenly Father,**
Thank You for Your strength. Grant us courage to persevere, trusting You.
Amen.

...

# His Strength In Me

Benecia Ponder

...

**Habakkuk 3:19 (ESV)**
God, the Lord, is my strength; he makes my feet like the
deer's; he makes me tread on my high places.

...

Waking up that morning, I was enveloped in an overwhelming sense of weakness and despair. Every part of me—emotionally, mentally, spiritually, and physically—felt utterly depleted. The task at hand, writing to inspire others, seemed insurmountable. How could I empower anyone else when I felt so powerless?

As I lay there, a voice of doubt crept in, whispering that I couldn't possibly find the strength to write, to inspire, to lift others. I was on the brink of surrendering to this feeling of inadequacy. But then, in the stillness of my heart, I felt a gentle reminder: the favor of God's strength.

In that moment, I realized that I didn't have to rely on my own limited power. God's strength, unyielding and steadfast, was there to lift me up. When I am weak, He is stony—solid, unwavering, and eternal. It was as if a veil had been lifted, and I could see clearly that His power, not mine, was at work within me.

With this newfound clarity, I rose to write, not with my own strength, but with the divine power that flows through me. Each word, each sentence was a testament to the transformation that faith can bring. God's strength had turned my weakness into a source of inspiration, not just for me, but for others who might feel the same.

This journey taught me that in moments of deepest weakness, God's favor envelops us, reminding us that His power is always sufficient.

...

**Heavenly Father,**
I thank You for Your unwavering strength when I am weak. Empower me daily,
guiding my steps and filling my heart with courage and faith.
Amen.

...

# Defeating Downward Dog

L. Marie

...

**2 Chronicles 15:7 (ESV)**

But you, take courage! Do not let your hands be weak, for your work shall be rewarded.

...

Right after I turned 65, my daughter convinced me to join her yoga class. "It'll be fun!" she said. I was skeptical—my idea of a workout was chasing after my grandkids, not contorting my body into something resembling a pretzel. But I showed up, mat in hand, for the beginners' class.

That's when I met my nemesis—Downward Dog. It looked easy enough until I realized my arms wobbled like a Jell-O mold at a church potluck, and my heels refused to touch the ground. Meanwhile, the instructor, a perky 20-something, floated through the poses as if she had no bones. "Breathe deeply and find your inner strength," she cooed.

I was about to surrender when I noticed my daughter smiling at me from the next mat. I couldn't be defeated. I planted my hands and pushed my hips into the air with determination rivaling a toddler reaching for the cookie jar. For three glorious seconds—THREE—I nailed it. Not only did I survive Downward Dog, but I also made it through the class. The best part was I didn't fall over once.

Walking out, sweaty but victorious, I realized that strength isn't just in muscles. It shows up when you're willing to try something new—even if it's scary or you might embarrass yourself.

Now, I'm practically a local yoga legend… in my head, anyway.

...

**Lord,**

Thank You for turning challenges into growth. Help us find strength in moments of doubt and courage to try the unexpected.

Amen.

...

# Celebrating The Favor of Strength

*Strength is found in God's unwavering support, empowering us to face challenges with courage and resilience. His favor surrounds us, turning our weaknesses into platforms for His strength to shine through and transform our lives.*

**Now it's your turn to write your story of celebrating The Favor of Strength.**

Reflect on a time when you felt strengthened by God's presence in a challenging situation. How did His strength manifest in your actions and outcomes? Describe the impact this experience had on your faith and how God's favor revealed itself through your journey of resilience and perseverance.

_____

_____

_____

_____

_____

_____

_____

_____

_____

_____

_____

_____

_____

_____

_____

_____

_____

_____

# THE FAVOR OF Patience

Patience is the pathway to God's perfect timing. Waiting on the Lord teaches us reliance and trust, bringing about His best in our lives.

# Trust in God's Timing

...

**Psalm 37:7 (NIV)**
Be still before the Lord and wait patiently for him; do not fret when people succeed in their ways, when they carry out their wicked schemes.

...

In our fast-paced world, it's easy to feel frustrated with waiting. We're used to getting what we want instantly, whether it's information, communication, or services. However, when life throws us into seasons of waiting, it can be challenging to remain patient. But it's in these moments that patience becomes a precious virtue, guiding us toward God's perfect timing.

Psalm 37:7 invites us to be still and wait patiently for the Lord. It's a gentle reminder that God's timing is never flawed, even when we don't see the full picture. While we yearn for immediate answers and quick fixes, God calls us to trust in His timeline, crafted with infinite wisdom and love.

Consider a gardener who plants seeds and waits for them to sprout. They water, nurture, and have faith that in time, the seeds will transform into a beautiful garden. Patience in this process is not passive but active and hopeful, much like how we should approach God's timing.

Embracing patience allows us to align with God's divine plan. It teaches us to lean on His strength rather than our own, finding peace in knowing His timing is best. As we cultivate patience, we open ourselves to the unexpected blessings that come with trusting His perfect plan.

This week, reflect on the Favor of Patience by inviting God's peace into your moments of waiting. Trust that He is orchestrating every detail of your life and that His plans will unfold beautifully in their own time.

...

**Patient Father,**
Thank You for teaching me the value of patience. Help me to wait on You with a trusting heart. May I find peace in Your perfect timing and embrace the growth that patience brings
Amen.

...

# When God Opens The Door

Alethia Saunders

...

## Lamentations 3:25-26 (NIV)

The Lord is good to those who wait for him, to the soul who seeks him. It is good that one should wait quietly for the salvation of the Lord.

...

I wanted that apartment so badly because I was tired of living in and out of hotels. However, due to my credit, I was getting denied for everything I applied for. It hurt my feelings, but I knew it was because of my own decisions.

When I finally received the "Not Approved" letter, I was so discouraged. I prayed for God to open a door for me and promised to do better with my finances. Living in a hotel with a dog was not sustainable, just making it day to day and barely being able to afford food.

That's when I found it—a house online that was for rent. The price was within range, and I almost thought it was a scam. I hopped in the car for the hour-long drive to see it. It was perfect: two bedrooms, two bathrooms, and enough space and a yard for my dog. I applied, prayed, and then waited.

Two days later, I received an email from the owners stating that although the other potential tenants were more qualified for the location, there was something about my spirit that they liked, and they wanted to give me an opportunity.

I cried as I thanked God for His favor. I just had to be patient and wait for His placement. Within a week, after paying the deposit, I was pulling up to my new home.

...

## Heavenly Father,

Thank You for Your favor in my life. I am grateful for Your blessings and commit to practicing patience as I navigate life's challenges. Guide my steps.

Amen.

...

# $\mathcal{AKA}$ Journey

Sibyl F. Cole

...

**Romans 12:12 (NIV)**
Be joyful in hope, patient in affliction, faithful in prayer.

...

My journey to join Alpha Kappa Alpha Sorority, Inc. began later in life. I knew this endeavor would take more than just ambition; it would require patience. Before the pandemic, I attended public events of several local chapters and was impressed by the sisterhood and commitment to service.

Becoming a member was not an overnight process, and it was especially challenging because intake was by invitation only and occurred during the pandemic. As the application period approached, self-doubt crept in. I wasn't an attorney, business owner, educator, or in the medical field. In my mind, there was nothing impressive about me; I was just ordinary. What if I wasn't "good enough?"

I dismissed the negative thoughts, submitted my paperwork, and waited. Finally, the email announcement arrived: I'd been approved as a candidate for the line of Spring 2022. I was ecstatic! All candidates participated in three-weekend sessions, virtually and in person. It was quite a learning experience, and the Zoom study sessions were informative and fun.

When 57 of us crossed over and I stood among my "sisters," my heart was full. As tears trickled down my face, I felt my mom's Heavenly presence and heard her voice whispering, "You're my legacy now, Sibyl."

This accomplishment would not have been possible without God granting me patience to wait for His perfect timing, and becoming a member of one of the oldest organizations that focuses on issues involving economics, education, social action, the environment, human rights, political activism, and equity.

...

**Heavenly Father**
Grant me patience as I await Your favor. Guide me with Your wisdom and perfect timing.
Amen.

...

# Time Heals

Sheryl Simms

...

**Colossians 3:13 (NLT)**
Make allowance for each other's faults, and forgive anyone who offends you.
Remember, the Lord forgave you, so you must forgive others.

...

When I lost Rachel's trust, it felt like a knife to my heart. She'd been my closest friend since college, but one careless word from me—repeated by someone else—broke her confidence in me. I could see the hurt in her eyes when she confronted me, and I knew I had let her down.

That night, I prayed hard, asking God for wisdom and patience. I knew restoring our friendship wouldn't happen overnight, and I had to accept that I couldn't rush Rachel's healing. The next day, I texted her, apologizing sincerely. She replied, short but civil, and I knew the road ahead would be long.

Over the next few months, I showed her my sincerity. I gave her space but stayed consistent. I listened more and spoke less, learning to guard my words. I didn't shy away from the hard conversations when she brought them up. Instead of defending myself, I admitted my fault and asked her how I could do better.

One Saturday, I invited her out for coffee. To my surprise, she agreed. Sitting across from her, I could feel the weight of our friendship still hanging in the balance. After some silence, she said, "I can see you've changed. You've been patient, and I appreciate that."

In that moment, I felt God's grace. Rachel and I aren't just friends again—we're stronger now because of what we've been through.

...

**Lord,**
Grant me patience to mend what's broken, humility to seek forgiveness, and steadfast love to prove my sincerity. Thank You for the favor of second chances.
Amen.

...

# Delay not Denial

Bonita L. Williams

...

**Micah 7:7 (NLT)**
As for me, I look to the Lord for help. I wait confidently for God to save me, and my God will certainly hear me.

...

Planning is often seen as the key to success. You've likely heard, "He who fails to plan, plans to fail." But what does God's Word say about planning?

Proverbs 16:9 reminds us, "In his heart a man plans his course, but the Lord determines his steps." While there is wisdom in planning, we must remember that God has the final say. His timing and purpose take precedence over our schedules.

Sometimes, our carefully laid plans face delays or unexpected changes. This can be discouraging, but a delay is not a denial. God, in His infinite wisdom, sees the entire picture—every detail of our lives—and works all things together for our good.

Patience requires trusting His ability to meet our needs, even when the path seems unclear or the wait feels long. If God asks us to wait, it's not to harm us, but to prepare us, protect us, or lead us to something greater.

Lean into His perfect timing and trust that His plans are always better than our own. With patience, we discover His grace in the waiting and His faithfulness in the fulfillment.

...

**Lord,**
grant me patience to trust Your perfect timing, strength to wait with faith, and peace to rest in Your unfailing grace.
Amen.

...

# Incubation

L. Marie

...

**Psalm 27:14 (CSB)**
Wait for the Lord; be strong, and let your heart be
courageous. Wait for the Lord.

...

Patience was a lesson I thought I'd mastered during my years as a nurse, but then came my granddaughter, Lucy. She was born prematurely, weighing barely over two pounds, and I'll never forget the helpless feeling of watching her fight for every breath. The NICU became our world, filled with machines, alarms, and emotions that swung from hope to despair in moments.

I remember sitting by her incubator, unable to do anything but place my hand gently on the side, praying she could somehow feel how much she was loved. Nurses would come and go, each one with their kind reassurances, and yet, it felt like time barely moved. Every small milestone was a victory—her first full feeding, her first day without oxygen.

I thought my experience would mean I'd be calm, but being on the other side was humbling. Patience, I learned, isn't passive. It's holding hope in the waiting. It's trusting that healing takes time.

Eventually, Lucy grew stronger, and that day when I finally held her in my arms, I cried like a newbie nurse on their first hard day. She's six now and full of life. Every time she races into my arms, I'm reminded of those weeks in the NICU and the beauty that patience can bring. It taught me that even when we can't see it, something wonderful can be just around the corner.

...

**Lord,**
Thank You for teaching patience and hope. May we trust in
Your perfect timing and unfailing love.
Amen.

...

# Celebrating The Favor of Patience

*Patience is the virtue that aligns us with God's perfect timing, allowing His favor to work in our lives. By waiting on Him, we find peace and assurance that His plans are always for our good and His glory.*

**Now it's your turn to write your story of celebrating The Favor of Patience.**

Think back to a time when waiting tested your patience but ultimately revealed a greater blessing. How did trusting in God's timing change the outcome and your perspective? Reflect on how patience has deepened your faith and how God's favor manifested through your willingness to wait.

_____

_____

_____

_____

_____

_____

_____

_____

_____

_____

_____

_____

_____

_____

_____

_____

_____

_____

# THE FAVOR OF *Humility*

Embracing humility allows God's grace to elevate us, creating space for His divine favor to flourish.

# Lifted by Grace

...

**James 4:10 (NIV)**
Humble yourselves before the Lord, and he will lift you up.

...

In a culture that screams for self-promotion and accolades, humility is often undervalued. However, it is precisely through humility that we access the beautiful favor of God.

James 4:10 offers us a profound truth: When we humble ourselves before God, He doesn't just notice—He lifts us up!

This isn't about shrinking back; it's about stepping into a power that's bigger than us, a divine strength that can only come from God Himself.

Humility is the secret sauce of spiritual success. It's not about losing your voice; it's about amplifying God's voice in your life.

It's recognizing that the true, lasting strength is in surrendering to His mighty plan.

When we lay down our pride, we make room for God's grace to overflow in our lives, turning ordinary into extraordinary.

Think about it: Humility transforms our hearts, opening us up to the full spectrum of God's blessings.

It's like flipping a switch that lights up the path of divine favor, guiding us to places we never thought we'd reach. With humility, we're not just waiting for God to show up—we're expecting Him to move mountains on our behalf.

So this week, embrace humility with boldness! Trust that as we lower ourselves in the presence of the Almighty, He's preparing to elevate us to new heights of joy, purpose, and influence.

...

**Merciful Savior,**
Thank You for the gift of humility. Guide me to walk humbly before You and others. Teach me to trust in Your timing and to embrace Your uplifting favor.
May my life reflect Your grace and love.
Amen.

...

# The Power of Humility

Alethia Saunders

...

**James 4:10 (NIV)**

Humble yourselves before the Lord, and he will lift you up.

...

Humility is a powerful force, one that can open doors we never thought possible. For much of my life, I wrestled with pride. I didn't want to ask for help, fearing it would make me seem weak or incapable. But there was a turning point in my life that showed me the favor of humility in a way I'll never forget.

I attended an Eric Thomas conference, fully aware of the pride I carried. As the session opened for questions, something in me urged me to speak. I knew I had to humble myself. With great vulnerability, I shared what was weighing on me personally, pouring out the struggles I had been facing. Eric Thomas, a man I greatly admired, did something that changed everything—he listened. He spoke life into me, prayed with me, and most importantly, he humbled himself to listen to my story.

His words and the prayers that followed became the catalyst for something bigger. He connected me with his team, which led to opportunities that expanded both my personal and professional life. What's more, my story was shared on his YouTube platform, reaching thousands of people. In that moment, God's favor was evident through humility.

What I learned that day is this: when we choose humility, we position ourselves for favor that can propel us into new opportunities. Humbling ourselves before God and others allows His grace and favor to flow in ways we never imagined. When we let go of pride and embrace humility, we can experience breakthroughs beyond our comprehension.

...

**Lord,**

Thank You for teaching me the power of humility. Help me release pride, seek Your grace, and walk in the favor only You can give. Amen.

...

# Apologies Build Bridges

Melanie Winters

...

**Matthew 7:12 (ESV)**

So whatever you wish that others would do to you, do also to them, for this is the
Law and the Prophets.

...

I was always in battle mode, ready to defend my ground at a moment's
notice. You know the drill—someone challenges you, and your mind gears
up with an arsenal of justifications. That was me. A constant defender of
my own truth, convinced that being right was more important than being
connected.

One day, during an unexpected argument with my husband over something
as mundane as who left the dishes unwashed, I felt that familiar urge to
jump in and justify myself. But instead, I took a deep breath, paused, and
did something completely out of character—I apologized. I didn't feel
entirely at fault, but I apologized anyway, not for the sake of being right, but
for the sake of the relationship.

That pause, that simple act of humility, changed everything. My husband's
defensive walls came tumbling down, replaced by a look of surprise and relief.
He responded with his own apology, and suddenly, we were having a real
conversation—a dialogue without the usual armor of resentment and pride.

This was my lightbulb moment: humility isn't about conceding defeat, it's
about opening a path to genuine connection. By lowering my defenses, I
discovered a strength I didn't know I had, and a deeper trust was forged.
Sometimes, the bravest thing you can do is to let go of being right and
embrace the power of humility.

...

**Lord,**

Grant me the strength to choose humility, the courage to apologize first, and the
grace to build trust and love in my relationships.

Amen.

...

# Kitchen Lesson

Ashley Jenkins

...

**Proverbs 11:2 (NIV)**
When pride comes, then comes disgrace, but with humility comes wisdom.

...

I was standing in the kitchen, glaring at the sink. The sink was glaring back, full of dirty dishes—and secrets. My dishwasher had broken two weeks ago, and I, determined to be the patron saint of self-sufficiency, declared, "I can fix this." Spoiler alert: I could not fix this.

Two YouTube tutorials and one stripped screw later, the dishwasher sat smug. I still refused to ask for help. My pride wouldn't allow it. Besides, if I couldn't handle a broken dishwasher, what else was I failing at in life?

Then, one morning during my quiet time, it hit me. God wasn't calling me to "figure it out" alone. He was calling me to community. To humility. To text my dad.

Now, y'all, my dad showed up in twenty minutes with his toolbox like some kind of blue-collar superhero. He diagnosed the problem before I could even finish apologizing for calling him. We cracked up about my "handywoman phase" as he unclogged a hose I didn't know existed. Dishwasher fixed. Dishes done. A side of father-daughter bonding thrown in for good measure.

Here's what I learned: You're not weak for asking for help. You're human. Sometimes, God works through the hands of those who love us—like dads with toolboxes or friends with wisdom. That day, my kitchen got back to normal, but so did my understanding of strength. Real strength? Asking for help when you need it.

...

**Lord,**
Thank You for teaching me humility and the courage to ask for help. Guide me to trust in Your wisdom and to lean on the support You provide.
Amen.

...

# God's Plan, Your Peace

### Veronica Washington

...

**Isaiah 55:8-9 (CSB)**

"For my thoughts are not your thoughts, and your ways are not my ways." This
is the Lord's declaration. "For as heaven is higher than earth, so my ways are
higher than your ways, and my thoughts than your thoughts."

...

My daughter, Tasha, called unexpectedly. "Ma," she said softly, "we're
moving to Atlanta. Malik got the job, and it's happening fast."

My heart sank. Tasha and my grandbabies were leaving? I put on a brave
face but felt like crying out, "Why, Lord? Why now?"

For days, I clung to frustration, thinking my upset might change things. I
prayed, but my prayers were more complaints, begging God to keep them
where I thought they belonged. Then one quiet morning, I felt God whisper,
"Do you trust Me, or are you holding onto control that was never yours?"

That question was hard to face. Slowly, I surrendered my plans to Him,
and what unfolded was beyond anything I could've imagined. In Atlanta,
Tasha's family thrived. Malik loved his new role, they found an amazing
church family, and the kids blossomed in ways I hadn't envisioned. As for
me, I found joy in visiting and experiencing their new life alongside them.

Through this, I learned the beauty of surrender. When I chose to trust, God's
plan revealed itself as far more wonderful than mine.

Maybe you're in a similar moment today. Is it time to open your hands,
release control, and see what God has in store? His plans are always better
than we can imagine.

...

**Lord,**

Help me surrender my plans, trust Your perfect will,
and find peace in the beauty of Your divine purpose.
Amen.

...

# "Help"

Sheryl Simms

...

**1 Peter 5:6-7 (NIV)**
Humble yourselves, therefore, under God's mighty hand, that he may lift you up in due time. Cast all your anxiety on him because he cares for you.

...

I've always prided myself on being independent, the one others rely on. But behind that capable exterior, I often felt overwhelmed. Between caring for my mom after surgery, running community projects, and managing my rebellious teen daughter, I could barely keep up. Yet, I refused to ask for help, believing I had to handle everything alone.

One Saturday, the stress reached a breaking point. I'd promised to host a church women's group, but nothing was ready. The house was a mess, snacks were unprepared, and my daughter refused to help. I snapped at her, and the hurt in her eyes broke me. Sitting in the chaos, I prayed, "Lord, I can't do this. I need help."

That prayer changed everything. For the first time, I reached out to the group and explained my situation. They showed up early, brought food, cleaned, and wrapped me in love. One even brought flowers. Their kindness lifted a weight I didn't realize I was carrying. Even my daughter softened, helping me clean after everyone left.

I realized my independence was rooted in pride—a fear of seeming weak. But humility isn't weakness; it's trusting God and leaning on the people He places in our lives. That night, I saw God's grace through my friends and felt His peace wash over me.

Now, I pray daily, "Lord, teach me to rely on You." True strength comes in surrender, and God's favor shines brightest when we walk humbly with Him.

...

**Lord,**
Teach me to rely on You. Grant me strength, courage to surrender, and trust.
Amen.

...

# Celebrating The Favor of Humility

*Humility opens our hearts to God's uplifting favor, inviting His strength to be perfected in our weaknesses. Embrace the grace found in humility, allowing it to guide your actions and thoughts, leading to profound peace and divine favor.*

**Now it's your turn to write your story of celebrating The Favor of Humility.**

Reflect on a situation where humility led you to unexpected favor and growth. How did this experience change your approach to challenges and relationships? Consider how embracing humility allowed God's favor to work in your life, transforming your perspective and deepening your spiritual journey.

_____

_____

_____

_____

_____

_____

_____

_____

_____

_____

_____

_____

_____

_____

_____

_____

_____

# THE FAVOR OF

## Salvation

Salvation is the greatest gift of favor, unveiling God's love and grace. It transforms lives, bringing hope and peace.

# The Greatest Gift

...

## Ephesians 2:8-9 (NIV)

For it is by grace you have been saved, through faith—and this is not from your-selves, it is the gift of God—not by works, so that no one can boast.

...

This week, we're diving into the most extraordinary gift we could ever receive—the gift of salvation.

Ephesians 2:8-9 reminds us that salvation is not something we earn through our efforts or achievements. Instead, it's a gift, a divine favor bestowed upon us by God's boundless grace and love.

Imagine receiving a gift so precious, it transforms every part of your life. That's what salvation does. It's the ultimate unveiling of God's love, a testament to His desire for us to live in freedom, joy, and purpose. It's not about what we can do for God, but what He has done for us. In giving His Son, He offers us a life free from the burdens of our past, inviting us into a relationship filled with hope and everlasting peace.

As we reflect on this incredible favor, let's hold onto the truth that we are saved by grace through faith. This understanding frees us from striving and allows us to rest in God's love, knowing that our worth is not tied to our works. Instead, we can live out our days in gratitude, letting the joy of our salvation shine through every action and word.

This week, celebrate the Favor of Salvation with hearts full of gratitude. Share the love and grace you've received with those around you, becoming a living testament to the transformative power of God's favor.

Remember, salvation is not just a gift for us to hold onto, but one to share, spreading God's love wherever we go.

...

## Redeeming Lord,

Thank You for the precious gift of salvation. Let it continually renew my heart and guide my path. May I live as a reflection of Your grace, bringing hope and peace to others.

Amen.

...

# Fearfully and Wonderfully Made

## Dr. Nina Addison

...

### Titus 3:5 (NIV)

He saved us, not because of any works of righteousness that we have done, but because of His own compassion and mercy, by the cleansing of the new birth (spiritual transformation, regeneration) and renewing by the Holy Spirit.

...

I was born with a physical difference called "club hands." This means my hands and arms did not properly develop. My thumbs didn't have bones, which led doctors to cut the skin that formed my thumbs and shift all my fingers over by one place. My arms are short and curved. However, I can do anything I need, want, or desire.

It wasn't always this way. When I was 8 years old, I got saved and began to learn what God's Word said about me. Before that, I hid my arms and felt shy about my differences. After I got saved, I began to love the God in me. He sent Jesus to die for me. He knew me before I was formed in my mother's womb. He made me fearfully and wonderfully. He's done so much for me—and for you!

Getting saved literally saved my life. Since then, I've meditated on the Word of God and have grown in my self-love. I know God created us in His image. We have favor with both God and man. All of this comes through His saving grace.

...

### Dear God,

Help me rest in Your saving grace. May I know who I am in You and fully enjoy the salvation You have granted me. May all Your words and promises toward me manifest from the spiritual to the natural. In Jesus' mighty name, Amen!

...

# New Life In Christ

Makini Theresa L. Harvey

...

**2 Corinthians 5:17 (NIV)**

Therefore if any man be in Christ, he is a new creature: old things are passed away; behold, all things are become new.

...

In 2002, I became my mother's caregiver because she was dying from hypertension. At that time, I didn't know Jesus, and as the oldest child who was always fixing issues, I believed I should be able to save her. Of course, it didn't work, and she died on December 18, 2002. My dad passed away on December 12, 2003. After moving to Seattle, Washington, my marriage ended in June 2004.

I was crushed, lost, hopeless, ashamed, guilty, defeated, alone, abandoned, depressed, and suicidal. After the divorce, I moved back to California and became homeless.

But God!

I accepted an invitation from my friends, the Taylors, to rent a room, agreeing to attend church with them.

On September 18, 2004, sitting at the Taylors' kitchen table, I surrendered my life to Jesus Christ. They had prayed for 15 years for this day!

Jesus was all I had left. I became a new woman, His child, realizing He was always there and all I ever needed.

...

**Dear Jesus Christ, my Savior,**

Thank You for loving, choosing, and rescuing me,
giving me a new life, to live like You;
Hallelujah and Amen.

...

# Way. Truth. Life.

### Carol Holesak

...

**Acts 4:12 (NIV)**
Salvation is found in no one else, for there is no other name under heaven given
to mankind by which we must be saved.

...

My life changed radically during the Christmas season of 1978 when I was 31 years old. At that time, I lived with my boyfriend, Louis, and my 8-year-old son, Erik, in Boca Raton, Florida. I was working as a hairdresser at the JC Penney Hair Salon and regularly used marijuana. Looking back, I realize I was not emotionally stable due to many traumatic experiences in my younger years.

That Christmas, I received a gift from a client—a Bible. Instead of a Starbucks card or a pretty scarf, I got this unexpected present. The client encouraged me to read the Book of John. My first thought was that I would toss it in the trash as soon as I left.

However, God had other plans, and I found myself reading the Book of John. In John 14:6, Jesus said, "I am the way, the truth, and the life. No one comes to the Father except through me." I didn't understand why these words resonated with me so profoundly; looking back, I can see it was the Holy Spirit at work.

I believed.

From that day until today, forty-six years later, my Lord and Savior have confirmed that yes, Jesus, my Messiah, is the Way, the Truth, and the Life.

...

**Lord,**
Thank You for transforming my life through Your truth and salvation. Guide me
on Your path, renewing my spirit and strengthening my faith daily.
Amen.

...

# Paid In Full

Vanessa Fortenberry

...

**John 19:30 (NIV)**
When he had received the drink, Jesus said "It is finished." With that, he bowed
his head and gave up his spirit.

...

There's a special pride in writing "Paid in Full" on a check. It represents freedom, accomplishment, and relief. Now imagine the immense joy and fulfillment Jesus felt when, as He completed His mission on Earth, He declared from the cross, "It is finished."

I remember sitting in my doctor's waiting room when a young man explained to the receptionist that he couldn't pay his co-pay. She politely suggested he reschedule, but the man pleaded, promising to pay later. The conversation caught everyone's attention.

Then, a lady stood and offered to cover his payment. An older gentleman chimed in, willing to help too. Although my funds were low, I yearned to do the same. Suddenly, the man turned to thank them and confidently said, "I can make the payment—just later today."

The doctor eventually appeared, softening her stance. "I'll allow you to pay later," she said. Relief spread across the room, and smiles followed. Her grace and the kindness of strangers reminded me of Jesus, who paid our ultimate debt on the cross. There's no "copay" required for salvation. Jesus' unselfish love and sacrifice paid it all, so we can have eternal life.

What God desires in return is simple yet profound—our surrender and devotion. As the hymn says, "Jesus paid it all, all to Him I owe."

...

**Lord,**
Thank You for Jesus' sacrifice. Help us follow His example,
serve others, and live in devotion to You.
Amen.

...

# Recovery

L. Marie

...

### Psalm 40:2-3 (CSB)
He brought me up from a desolate pit, out of the muddy clay, and set my feet on a rock, making my steps secure. He put a new song in my mouth, a hymn of praise to our God.

...

When I first met Kyle, he was a young man who'd been admitted to the hospital after a relapse. He was bruised, not just physically, but emotionally too. You could see it in his eyes. I've worked with a lot of patients battling addiction, and I'll be honest, I thought he was just another sad story.

Then one day, I heard a quiet voice coming from his room. A chaplain was talking to him about grace and second chances. I didn't expect much to change, but over the next few days, Kyle started asking me questions about forgiveness and about faith. He wasn't talking much about his pain anymore. He was asking if he could really start over.

Slowly, I saw the weight he carried begin to lift. He sat up straighter, and smiled more. When he told me he'd prayed for the first time, he looked like a kid again. I didn't have the words then, but in my heart, I knew I was witnessing something extraordinary. When Kyle left the hospital, he hugged me and said, "I finally believe I'm worth something."

That changed me. I've spent years helping to heal bodies, but watching Kyle's soul heal, I realized something deeper—God doesn't just patch you up, He makes you whole. Kyle's transformation was God reminding me that no one is too far gone. That's a truth I'll never forget.

...

**Lord,**
Thank You for Your grace that heals and renews. May we never forget Your power to make us whole.
Amen.

...

# Celebrating The Favor of Salvation

*Salvation is the greatest expression of God's love and favor, offering us eternal life and a restored relationship with Him. Rejoice in this miraculous gift, knowing you are cherished and redeemed by His grace.*

**Now it's your turn to write your story of celebrating The Favor of Salvation.**

Reflect on the moment you first understood the depth of God's salvation in your life. How did this realization transform your heart and outlook on life? Describe the ways in which this gift of salvation has influenced your faith journey and how God's favor continues to unfold in your daily walk.

# THE FAVOR OF *Rest*

Rest in God's presence and find true favor. His rest rejuvenates our weary souls, inviting us into His peace and renewal.

# Peaceful Renewal

...

## Matthew 11:28 (NIV)
Come to me, all you who are weary and burdened, and I will give you rest.

...

Life can feel overwhelming, but God offers us a promise of hope. In Matthew 11:28, Jesus invites us, saying, "Come to me, all you who are weary and burdened, and I will give you rest."

What an incredible gift! No matter how heavy your load feels, God wants to lift your burdens and fill you with His peace. This divine rest isn't just a pause—it's an invitation to experience renewal and strength that only God can provide. When you step into His presence, you align with His perfect plan and feel His love surrounding you.

Making rest a priority in your spiritual journey is an act of trust. It's about believing that God will rejuvenate your spirit and guide your steps. His favor brings clarity and peace, empowering you to live with joy and purpose.

This week, take time to slow down and embrace the rest God so graciously gives. Trust Him to carry your burdens and fill your heart with His lasting peace. Remember, God's favor is always available to refresh and uplift you.

...

### Dear God,
Thank You for the gift of rest. Help us bring our burdens to You and find peace and renewal. Teach us to value rest in our spiritual journey and trust Your loving presence. Refresh our souls and guide our paths.
Amen.

...

# The Weary Soul

Alethia Saunders

...

## 1 Peter 5:10 (NIV)

And the God of all grace, who called you to his eternal glory in Christ, after you have suffered a little while, will himself restore you and make you strong, firm and steadfast.

...

I was tired—so tired that I swallowed a half bottle of Percocet, chased it with Hennessy, and hoped for it all to end. My life felt stolen, full of pain and betrayal, and I didn't want to fight anymore. I called my mother as I drifted off, expecting it to be the last time.

But I woke up in the hospital. After clearing my system, they placed me under the Baker Act and sent me to a mental health facility. I wanted to resist, to cry out, but deep down, I knew I needed to be there.

I was tired. Bone tired. And God was asking me to rest. I had spent too long pouring out my soul for others, molding myself into something I wasn't, and it had left me empty.

At night, I could hear Him speaking—not through medication, but through stillness. I surrendered, praying day by day, until I realized I didn't want to die. I wanted to live. Slowly, I opened myself to healing—spiritually, emotionally, fully.

When I walked out into the sunlight, I wasn't the same woman. I was whole. I was ready to begin again.

...

Lord,

Thank You for granting me rest and renewal in Your presence. Help me embrace each day with gratitude, refreshed by Your unfailing love.

Amen.

...

# Life Needs an "Off" Switch

### Elvetra Cossie

...

### Isaiah 30:15 (NIV)

This is what the Sovereign Lord, the Holy One of Israel, says: "In repentance and rest is your salvation, in quietness and trust is your strength, but you would have none of it.

...

I don't know about you, but I often find myself sacrificing my rest and rejuvenation time for a desire to power through—to complete the assignment, to get to the end of the situation or circumstance. I just want to get the task done, get the house cleaned, get the house sold, get the errands done.

My brain, emotions, and sometimes my physical body will not shut off until it's DONE!

God is showing me that my desire for DONE is not His desire for my life. It's been a challenging 15 months for me since my 91-year-old mother's fall, multiple surgeries, hospital visits, nursing homes, and ultimately her death. My mind and body were constantly in the "on" position while supervising her care, working full-time, and trying to maintain my own health. My role has now transitioned from caring daughter to executor.

As you can imagine, this new role has its own set of duties and challenges that don't have an "off" switch. The Holy Spirit is reminding me to "be still." I find that even though I might desire to power through physically and emotionally, God is shutting down my plans, putting up roadblocks, and allowing me no choice but to rest.

With rest comes release, creativity, new perspectives, and peace. Of course, I still have occasions when I want to get to "done," but I am now more attuned to the Spirit saying, "Cease striving and know that I am God."

...

### Heavenly Father,

Thank You for teaching us to be still. Grant us rest,
renewal, and peace as we trust fully in Your plan.
Amen.

...

# Let God Drive

Ebony M. Cottman

...

**Proverbs 16:3 (NIV)**
Commit your work to the Lord, and your plans will be established.

...

No! I overslept and missed the 6 am prayer again. How?! I had perfected my evening routine—completed all my tasks, checked every box, went to bed by 9 pm, and fell asleep by 9:30 pm. Yet, I still overslept!

I had been striving to build a God-centered morning routine but kept falling short. Convinced the issue was with my evenings, I kept tweaking them. Back when I lived in Vegas, I joined 6 am EST prayer calls—3 am PST! It seemed impossible to wake up that early, so I prayed each night, asking God to wake me, and He did. I never missed a call.

When I moved back to Baltimore, I thought waking up for 6 am prayer would be easier. It wasn't. Despite alarms and adjustments, I kept failing. Frustrated, I asked myself, why could I wake up at 3 am in Vegas but not at 6 am here? And then it hit me—it wasn't my strength, routine, or discipline that got me up in Vegas. It was God. I prayed, surrendered, and trusted Him to help me. On the East Coast, I relied on myself instead of Him.

I realized planning can't replace prayer. Proverbs 16:3 says, "Commit your work to the Lord, and your plans will be established." I had to put God in the driver's seat, not the passenger seat. When I surrendered to Him, I ended up exactly where I needed to be. Trust Him. Rest in His strength. Let God drive.

...

**Lord,**
I surrender my plans and efforts to You. Teach me to trust Your strength, not mine. Lead me, guide me, and help me rest in You.
Amen.

...

# Hands Off

Bonita L. Williams

...

### Exodus 33:14 (ESV)
And he said, "My presence will go with you, and I will give you rest.

...

Over the years, I have experienced the grace and mercy of God. Yet, I consider myself one of His spiritually developmentally challenged children. I love Him, I trust Him, and I know He is all-powerful. But still, there are moments when I try to take things into my own hands.

God's Word tells us to be still and know that He is God. *Be still and KNOW that He is GOD.* One of my struggles has been fully acknowledging who God is and the incredible things He has done, is doing, and will do in my life. It's crucial for me to remain Christ-centered.

To help me in this, God led me to a devotional by Cynthia White. She shares an acronym for the word REST that has changed my perspective: "Release Everything, Situation Totally." When I release control and allow God to lead, I find peace and purpose, knowing I am exactly where I should be.

Each day, we must acknowledge God's presence and exercise our faith in Him. Think about it—do we question man-made things? Did you inspect the chair you sat in yesterday? Did you turn it over to check if the screws were secure? No, you simply sat down. If we can trust a chair, why is it so hard to trust God?

He's asking us to sit down, be still, and REST. Will you release it all to Him today?

...

**Lord,**
Help me release all control, rest in Your presence, and trust Your plan with faith and gratitude.
Amen.
...

134

# Just Be

L. Marie

...

...

It was one of those quiet afternoons where the world felt still, but my mind
was anything but. I was out on the porch with a mug of chamomile tea, the
kind that's supposed to be calming. The breeze was doing its job, swaying
the palm trees, and the sky was postcard-perfect. But I couldn't shake the
gnawing worry about Ella, my daughter. She'd been having a rough time at
work, and all I wanted was to make things better for her. That's what moms
do, right? We fix things.

But there I was, stuck in my thoughts, running through ideas that wouldn't
solve anything. I sighed, put my tea down, and remembered an old trick
I used to preach to my patients. "Deep breath, Marie," I told myself. And
I did. Then, instead of spiraling, I started noticing little things—the sweet
smell of tea, the birds singing like they didn't have a care in the world, the
way my chair creaked just a little as I leaned back.

Suddenly, it hit me. I didn't need a grand plan to help Ella. I just needed to
be there. Listen, without jumping in to fix her.

Funny enough, Ella called that evening. I didn't give her advice. I just listened.
By the end of the call, she sounded lighter. I felt lighter too. Sometimes the
best thing you can do is just be.

...

**Lord,**
Help me to be still, find peace in Your presence, and offer love and support with
an open heart.
Amen.

...

# Celebrating The Favor of Rest

*Rest is a divine invitation to experience God's peace and rejuvenation. In His presence, our weary souls are renewed, and we find strength to embrace life's challenges with grace and vigor. Embrace the rest He offers and let His favor refresh you.*

**Now it's your turn to write your story of celebrating The Favor of Rest.**

Think about a time when you allowed yourself to pause and rest in God's presence. How did this rest impact your energy and perspective? Reflect on the ways God's favor was revealed through moments of rest and renewal, and how they have influenced your spiritual journey and well-being.

_____

_____

_____

_____

_____

_____

_____

_____

_____

_____

_____

_____

_____

_____

_____

_____

_____

_____

_____

# THE FAVOR OF *Generosity*

Generosity plants seeds of divine favor. Through acts of giving, we extend God's love and invite His blessings into our lives.

# Seeds of Blessing

...

### 2 Corinthians 9:7 (NIV)

Each of you should give what you have decided in your heart to give, not reluctantly or under compulsion, for God loves a cheerful giver.

...

Generosity is a beautiful expression of God's favor, a channel through which His love flows into the world.

In 2 Corinthians 9:7, we are reminded to give from the heart, with joy and sincerity. This cheerful giving enriches both the giver and the receiver, creating a ripple effect of blessings.

Consider how acts of generosity have impacted your life. Whether it was a small gesture or a significant sacrifice, each act of giving carries the potential to transform situations and touch lives deeply. When we give, we reflect God's nature, allowing His love and favor to manifest through us.

Perhaps you've experienced moments when someone's generosity lifted your spirits or met a need you couldn't fulfill on your own. These moments remind us of the power and impact that generosity can have, not just materially, but spiritually and emotionally as well. The seeds of generosity we plant can grow into abundant blessings, nurturing hope and kindness in others.

This week, embrace the Favor of Generosity by actively seeking opportunities to give. Whether it's your time, resources, or encouragement, know that each gift offered with love has the power to change lives and invite God's blessings. Celebrate this divine favor by becoming a vessel of God's love and watching as those seeds of generosity flourish.

...

### Gracious Lord,

Thank You for the gift of generosity. Instill in me a generous heart that reflects Your love. Help me to give cheerfully and plant seeds of Your favor in the world. May my actions bring glory to You and touch the lives of others.

Amen.

...

# Helping Hand

Dr. Joyce S. Mallory

...

**3 John 1:5 (NIV)**

Dear friend, you are faithful in what you are doing for the brothers and sisters,
even though they are strangers to you.

...

The day was warm, and the school sat silent under the late afternoon sun. With 65-year-old walls and no central air, open windows were a necessity. The students and teachers were gone, leaving only silence. Terry, the dedicated secretary, had just left. It seemed like the perfect time to finish some work before heading home.

As I paused near the repaired stairwell door, unexpected footsteps echoed down the hallway. Who could it be? The building was supposed to be empty. From the hall emerged a figure, her clothes loose and worn. Her unsteady steps stopped at the office door. Her voice, barely above a whisper, carried a plea: "Can you help me get home and feed my kids?"

I didn't ask questions. Her eyes spoke volumes. Reaching into my jacket pocket, I handed her what money I had. She thanked me softly and disappeared into the afternoon light.

Sitting there, I questioned myself. Was I too quick to give? Did people see me as an easy ask? But deep down, I knew. Like in Mark 6, where a miracle fed thousands, small acts can feel monumental. Generosity isn't just about giving; it's about recognizing shared humanity. But for God's grace, I could be the one in need.

That quiet moment reminded me: every small act of kindness ripples outward, touching lives in unseen ways. It was a testament to the enduring power of giving.

...

**Lord,**

Grant me the heart to give freely, recognizing your grace in every exchange. May my actions reflect your boundless generosity and love.

Amen.

...

# Compassion Came Knocking

Ebonie T. Pritchett

...

**Proverbs 14:31 (NIV)**
Whoever is kind to the needy honors God

...

The Bible clearly enjoins Christians to embrace kindness and generosity—through both financial giving and the dedication of one's time and talents. Throughout my career journey, from Crisis Counselor to Program Administrator, I've remained deeply humbled by God's guidance. While I've always felt blessed to follow God's plan in my various roles, this position has profoundly touched my heart.

As I grew into my responsibilities, I felt God calling me deeper into His service. I've been blessed to provide crisis intervention and counseling services aligned with each person's individualized treatment plan. This involves supporting their daily needs—from scheduling appointments and helping them progress toward goals to encouraging daily activities. One of my greatest joys has been preparing home-cooked meals for them whenever possible.

This opportunity has opened my eyes to God's endless grace in my own life. Even during my hardest moments, He made a way where there seemed to be none. As Scripture reminds us, He is Jehovah Jireh (The Lord will Provide) in Genesis 22:14, Jehovah Rapha (The Lord who Heals) in Exodus 15:26, and El Roi (The One who sees me) in Genesis 16:13. My heart overflows with joy when celebrating holidays like Thanksgiving and Christmas with those who haven't experienced these festivities in years or have lost connection with their families.

Each day, I thank God for using me for His glory and blessing me so that I might be a blessing to others.

...

**Lord,**
Thank You for the favor of generosity, allowing us to reflect Your love and bless others with joyful hearts.
Amen.

# A Heart of Generosity

Dr. Theresa Billingsley

...

**2 Corinthians 9:7 (NLT)**
You must each decide in your heart how much to give. And don't give reluctantly
or in response to pressure.

...

One of the most beautiful qualities of my mother is her ability to recognize a need and fulfill it without being asked. Her generous spirit is a true blessing from God, and I never take it for granted. There have been countless times when I've felt overwhelmed and in need of financial support, and my mom has always been there for me.

While some might assume parental support is a given, not all parents provide help during tough times. That's why I am profoundly grateful to Jesus for blessing my mother with such a generous heart. I truly believe that God works through her, making her His hands on Earth to answer my prayers.

God often uses people to respond to our pleas, and I am thankful that my mother serves as one of my earthly angels. When Jesus uses someone to uplift our spirits and show us His love, it's vital to listen and obey. We are His representatives on Earth, and when He calls us to give, we must respond with open hearts.

We cannot be selfish, we must be selfless in order to be generous with no ulterior motives attached to the giving. I am so glad I learned this from my mother at a young age. My mother is my shero!

...

**Dear God,**
I am grateful for the generosity of those around me. Please continue to bless
them and guide us all to serve each other with love and grace.
Amen.

...

# Walmart Customer

Sibyl F. Cole

...

### Proverbs 11:25 (NIV)
Whoever brings blessings will be enriched and one who waters will kindly be watered.

...

Unexpected acts of kindness can manifest in many ways when least expected, often surprising both the giver and the receiver.

One Saturday afternoon, I was in Walmart. An elderly lady on the same aisle had a cart overflowing with fresh produce and essentials. As she reached for a box of cereal on a high shelf, she lost her balance, and her cart tipped over, spilling all her items onto the floor. Mortified, she looked around and then slowly bent down to pick them up. I rushed over to help, assuring her not to worry and that I would gather everything for her.

After her groceries were back in her cart, she thanked me and continued on her way.

I finished shopping and got in the checkout line. A young man behind me had about four items in his hands, so I let him go in front of me. After he paid, I placed my items on the conveyor belt. The clerk rang them up and gave me the total. As I went to pull out my credit card, she told me my items were already paid for.

Seeing the look on my face, she repeated herself.

"Who, how?" I asked.

The young man had paid for my items because I'd been kind enough to let him check out before me. His act of generosity was totally unexpected but very much appreciated.

Another reminder that, "Goodwill comes to those who are generous and lend freely."

...

### Heavenly Father,
Thank You for the gift of generosity. Help me share Your favor and love with others daily. Amen.

...

142

# The Joy of Giving

Jacqueline James

...

## Acts 20:35 (GNT)

I have shown you in all things that by working hard in this way we must help the weak, remembering the words that the Lord Jesus himself said, 'There is more happiness in giving than in receiving.

...

On a recent trip to South Africa, I had the privilege of visiting one of the richest and most beautiful cities in the world. At the same time, I witnessed one of the poorest and most destitute areas imaginable.

To my astonishment, the highlight of my trip took place in the heart of Soweto, the poorest district in South Africa. We visited a kindergarten/daycare center in the township. The scene was humbling. Sixty-eight children and two teachers shared a room that was approximately 12 by 12 feet. The space had no learning materials, nothing on the walls, and old rugs barely covered a dirt floor. There was no bathroom or running water. Despite these challenges, the children stood out. They were immaculately clean, neatly dressed, and full of happiness. They were obedient, loving, and vibrant. Looking at them, it struck me—they seemed to have nothing, yet, in so many ways, they had everything.

After returning home, I was inspired to do something for that classroom. I sent numerous educational materials along with two large educational rugs. These supplies arrived on my 78th birthday, and shortly after, I received photos of the children and their teachers with the gifts. Seeing their joy and gratitude made that birthday the most meaningful and rewarding one of my life.

This experience reminded me that there truly is more happiness and joy in giving than in receiving.

...

**Lord,**

Thank You for the joy of giving. Guide our hearts to serve others selflessly, sharing love and blessings with those in need. May generosity always shine through our actions.

Amen.

...

# Celebrating The Favor of Generosity

*Generosity is the heart's expression of God's abundant love, spreading joy and blessings to others. When we give freely, we align with His will, inviting His favor into our lives and creating ripples of kindness that transcend boundaries.*

**Now it's your turn to write your story of celebrating The Favor of Generosity.**

Reflect on a moment when you gave selflessly and witnessed the impact of your generosity. How did this act of giving transform your perspective and relationships? Consider how God's favor was revealed through your generosity and how it deepened your understanding of His boundless love.

_____

_____

_____

_____

_____

_____

_____

_____

_____

_____

_____

_____

_____

_____

_____

_____

_____

_____

# THE FAVOR OF *Trust*

Trust opens our eyes to God's limitless favor. Leaning not on our understanding but on His wisdom leads us to His divine plans.

# Heartfelt Trust

...

## Proverbs 3:5-6 (NIV)

Trust in the Lord with all your heart and lean not on your own understanding; in all your ways submit to him, and he will make your paths straight.

...

Have you ever faced a situation where you felt completely overwhelmed, and yet somehow, things just fell into place?

That's the beauty of trusting God.

Proverbs 3:5-6 reminds us to lean on His wisdom rather than our own. It's like having a reliable GPS for life that guides us to the best destinations.

Think back to a time when you decided to trust God with something important. Maybe it was a career decision or a personal relationship that needed guidance. When we truly place these concerns in God's hands, we often find His favor working in ways we never imagined. Sometimes, it's a gentle nudge in the right direction or an unexpected blessing that changes everything.

Trusting God isn't about sitting back and doing nothing—it's about actively choosing to believe that His plans for us are good. It's about the peace that comes when we stop trying to figure everything out on our own and instead, rely on His infinite wisdom. When we do this, we open ourselves to His divine plans that are filled with love and purpose.

This week, take a moment to really embrace the favor of trust. Hand over your worries and plans to God, and watch how He guides you through. Celebrate His faithfulness as you see His favor unfold in your life. Remember, with trust, comes clarity and a path straightened by His loving hand.

...

### Faithful God,

Today I choose to trust in You. Thank You for guiding my steps and unfolding Your favor in my life. Help me to lean on Your wisdom and submit my ways to You. I am grateful for the peace and assurance Your guidance brings.

Amen.

...

# Drop The Weight

## Kimberly Brown

...

### 1 Peter 5:7 (NIV)
Cast all your anxiety on him because he cares for you.

...

"Have you prayed about it?"

That simple question from my friend stopped me in my tracks. I had been venting for the past ten minutes about my struggle to shed those stubborn pounds. The endless cycle of diets, the gym sessions that seemed to work for everyone but me, and the frustration of seeing no results despite all my efforts had left me exhausted and disheartened.

"Pray about it?" I scoffed. "Surely God has more pressing issues than my weight loss woes."

But my friend, ever wise, replied, "There's nothing too small for God when it comes to you."

It got me thinking. How often do I overlook the power of a quiet moment, a whispered prayer, in resolving life's challenges? I realized that my journey wasn't just about losing weight—it was about gaining perspective. It was about finding balance between my body and spirit, about nurturing the soul as much as the physical self.

So, I took a deep breath and began to pray. It wasn't a formal plea but more a heartfelt conversation, an introspective journey. I asked for strength, patience, and a reminder of my worth beyond numbers on a scale.

This prayer didn't magically melt away the pounds, but it did lighten my heart. And perhaps that was the weight I needed to lose most of all.

...

### Heavenly Father,
When I am tempted to hold on to all of my worries, please help me to remember that I can come to You. Thank You that there is nothing too big or too small for You.
Amen.

...

# Holiday Visit
Sibyl F. Cole

...

## Psalm 56: 3-4 (NIV)
When I am afraid, I put my trust in you. In God, whose word I praise, in God I find trust. I shall not be afraid, what can flesh do to me?

...

The holiday season was approaching, and I was filled with dread and anxiety. My 12-year-old daughter, Ashley, wasn't looking forward to spending Thanksgiving with her father in Virginia. He and I had divorced a few years earlier, and we weren't amicable co-parents, living in different states.

My anxiety was undeniable as I wrestled with doubts. How would her father treat her? Would she be safe? As I packed her suitcase, my heart felt like a dead weight. In my quiet moments, I prayed, seeking peace. "Lord, guide us," I whispered.

Then I remembered the words of my favorite aunt, Dorothy. Auntie and Ashley shared a love of joke-telling and bonded over trading them back and forth. Auntie's words popped into my head: "Trust in the journey, even when it's hard."

The day of the trip arrived, and before Ashley boarded the plane, I hugged her tightly. "Try to have fun, and remember I love you," I said. She looked back with uncertainty, promised to call when she got there, then walked through the door.

While leaving the airport parking lot, a wave of fear washed over me. But in that moment of uncertainty, I said aloud in the car, "I trust you, Lord. You're with her."

The days passed slowly. On Thanksgiving Eve, Ashley called to let me know she was fine and having fun with her cousins. After hearing from her, I was relieved; in my heart, I knew that trusting God was a leap of faith worth taking.

...

**Lord,**
Grant me the strength to trust Your plan, embracing peace
and courage as I walk this uncertain journey.
Amen.

# Do I Trust Him?

Mary Haney Underwood

...

## Mark 9:24 (NIV)

I do believe; help my unbelief.

...

I could barely stand. My body was weak, but I was determined to see my daughter's face. I hadn't seen her since her premature birth five days earlier. With the support of my nurse, I eased out of the wheelchair. Her tiny one-pound body, surrounded by tubes, looked surreal. I gasped and fell back into my chair. How could she possibly survive? I felt angry, sad, and scared. My faith faltered.

Did I trust God with her life?

We see a similar story in Mark 9:23-24. A father seeks healing for his son in a critical situation. When he finds Jesus, he says, "But if you can do anything, have compassion on us and help us." (v 23)

Jesus responds, "'If you can'? Everything is possible for the one who believes."

Immediately, the father cries out, "I do believe; help my unbelief."

Jesus' gentle rebuke prompted a response that we can learn from: "I do believe; help my unbelief."

We are fixers. We want answers and solutions now. But often, God wants us to develop our "trust muscles" more than find quick and easy answers. His promises sustain us: "I will strengthen you; I will help you; I will hold you with my…right hand." (Isaiah 41:10b)

Yes, Lord, I do believe; help my unbelief.

Ninety-three days after her birth, my daughter came home. She suffers no ill effects from her early beginnings. God was faithful, even in my unbelief.

...

## Heavenly Father,

Strengthen my faith in times of doubt. Sustain me with Your love
and guide my heart with unwavering trust in Your power.

Amen.

...

# It Hurts So Bad

Bonita L. Williams

...

### Isaiah 43:2-3 (NIV)

When you pass through the waters, I will be with you; and when you pass through the rivers, they will not sweep over you. When you walk through the fire, you will not be burned; the flames will not set you ablaze. For I am the Lord your God, the Holy One of Israel, your Savior; I give Egypt for your ransom, Cush and Seba in your stead.

...

On the morning of my last radiation treatment, I stood in the shower, carefully cleaning the raw areas of my breast. The skin was peeling daily, and the pain was relentless. I was assured it would heal a few weeks post-treatment, but sleepless nights and constant discomfort made that hard to bear. As I pondered my situation, the Holy Spirit reminded me that my pain was incomparable to what Jesus Christ endured for my sake.

Life is filled with painful moments—losing loved ones, job loss, financial struggles, or failed relationships. These experiences hurt deeply, but we must be careful not to dwell on our agony and overlook healing. God never promised a life without pain, but He assured us of His presence through trials (Isaiah 43:10).

We must adopt the attitude Jesus had on the cross, accepting the challenges before us. Everyone faces difficulties; our role is to trust that God is at work in our lives. We need to learn to trust God in everything. Yes, the pain hurts, but we must remember we have a true healer who can take it all away.

...

### Lord,

Grant us strength to endure our trials, faith to trust in Your divine plan, and peace in knowing Your healing presence guides us through every pain.
Amen.

...

# Trust and Obey

Carol Holesak

...

**Proverb 3:5-6 (NIV)**

Trust in the Lord with all your heart, and lean not on your own understanding In all your ways, acknowledge Him and He will direct your paths.

...

After sharing my story about a Jewish girl who came to know Jesus the Messiah, I often heard, "Carol, you should write about your life."

This suggestion came up repeatedly over the years. Finally, after much prayer, on March 15, 2023, I asked, "Is this the time, Lord?"

A still, small voice whispered, "Jesus, Jesus, Jesus: The Life Journey of a Jewish Girl Who Came to Know Jesus the Messiah."

I realized that title described me perfectly. For over 30 years, whenever I stood to speak in front of women, I always began with "Jesus, Jesus, Jesus."

With a title in hand, a friend encouraged me to contact a publisher. I called and learned what publishing a book would entail. This was way out of my wheelhouse. After reviewing their information, I prayed, "Lord, if this is Your will, then You are the publisher."

The very next day, my son Erik shared his testimony and said, "My greatest passion is to share what Christ has done in my life." Hearing him say that, I knew it was time. Despite some challenges—like not being a writer, struggling with spelling, and lacking grammar skills—I trusted that this was God calling me to do what seemed impossible.

Approximately one year later, on November 13, 2024, my husband Louis and I searched "Carol Holesak" on Amazon, and there it was: Jesus, Jesus, Jesus. We looked at each other, and tears were in our eyes. Trust and obey; there is no better way.

...

**Lord,**
Guide my steps with faith, trust, and Your perfect timing as I embrace Your call despite life's challenges. In Jesus' Name,
Amen.

...

# Celebrating The Favor of Trust

*Trust is the bridge that connects us to God's unfailing promises, providing strength and direction. When we trust in Him, we open the door to His unwavering favor, allowing peace and confidence to fill our hearts and guide our paths.*

**Now it's your turn to write your story of celebrating The Favor of Trust.**

Reflect on a situation where placing your trust in God led to clarity and peace. How did trusting Him alter the outcome and your perspective? Describe the ways in which His favor became apparent through this trust and how it has influenced your journey with Him.

# THE FAVOR OF *Courage*

Courage fueled by faith opens doors to God's favor. In stepping out bravely, we discover His strength and guidance.

# Brave Steps

### Joshua 1:9 (NIV)

Have I not commanded you? Be strong and courageous. Do not be afraid; do not be discouraged, for the Lord your God will be with you wherever you go.

...

Life can sometimes feel daunting and uncertain, but God offers us a powerful promise that brings courage.

In Joshua 1:9, God commands us to be strong and courageous, reassuring us that He is always with us.

No matter what challenges lie ahead, God is there to strengthen and guide us.

Courage is not just about facing fears; it's a divine gift that God provides to empower and equip us for the journey. When we step into God's presence, we're not merely confronting obstacles—we're accessing a source of strength and determination that only He can give.

It's in these courageous moments that we find ourselves aligned with His divine purpose, feeling His strength surrounding us.

I want to encourage you to make courage an essential part of your spiritual journey. It's not just about taking risks; it's about trusting God to lead you through every challenge. When you rely on Him, you'll discover that His favor opens new doors, allowing you to live boldly and purposefully.

This week, take intentional steps to embrace the courage that God so generously provides. Trust Him to guide your path and fill your heart with His unwavering strength. Remember, God's favor is present, ready to support and elevate you as you journey forward.

...

### Mighty God,

Thank You for the courage You pour into my heart. Help me to face life's challenges with faith and strength, knowing You are always by my side. Guide my steps and open the doors to Your favor.

Amen.

...

# Courage in the Saddle

Benecia Ponder

...

**Psalm 34:4 (NLT)**

I prayed to the Lord, and he answered me. He freed me from all my fears.

...

Those who know me, know that animals terrify me. My fear of animals is so intense that being within even 100 feet of them freaks me out.

So, what made me mount this (surprisingly gentle) two-ton beast?

Something more important than my fear... my 16-year-old nephew.

Ishmael loves animals and wanted to celebrate his birthday at a horse farm. When I first learned of his plans, I decided I would go and watch everyone else ride from an appropriate distance away. But when we arrived at the farm, my nephew begged me to fully engage in the festivities by riding a horse.

He said, "Getting on a horse will be a gift to me."

To me, it sounded like, "Getting over your fear will be a gift to me."

Somehow, my desire to bring joy to my nephew became bigger than my fear. I rode China around the pasture, arms shaking, legs trembling, and heart racing, with a big smile on my face. My fear didn't go away; it was just no longer a controlling factor.

I ended up really enjoying myself, and the experience prompted so many stories to tell. I'll definitely have to share about the serendipity of a visually impaired girl riding a one-eyed horse. But for now, I just wanted to leave you with this—

The fear doesn't have to go away before you act. For way too long, I've avoided potentially life-changing experiences because I thought I had to get over my fears first. Now, I'm embracing the idea that I can feel the fear and do it anyway.

...

Lord,

Grant me the courage to face my fears, trusting in Your strength. Let my heart be steady, my spirit bold, and my actions a testament to Your unwavering love.

Amen.

# Pray Big

Rosie Davis

...

### Ephesians 3:20 (NLT)

[20] Now all glory to God, who is able, through his mighty power at work within us, to accomplish infinitely more than we might ask or think.

...

I've always believed in the power of prayer, but when it came to my own needs, I would hesitate. Growing up, I was taught that asking God for personal requests seemed selfish. But as I delved into my Bible, I didn't find any support for that belief. One verse, in particular, spoke to me: 1 Peter 5:7 - "Give all your worries and cares to God, for he cares about you."

I realized that my reluctance stemmed from a fear of being vulnerable. One morning, I decided to take a leap of faith. I poured out my concerns about my small business to God, asking not just for survival, but for growth and success.

As I prayed, a sense of peace enveloped me, and I felt inspired to take actions I had never considered before. That evening, following a friend's advice, I started a prayer journal. I wrote down my hopes, fears, needs, and every dream I presented to God.

Months passed, and one evening I flipped through the pages of my journal. I was amazed at how many of my requests had been answered. The business hadn't just flourished—it had opened doors I never dreamed possible.

This journey taught me that God welcomes our prayers, no matter how big or small. My prayer journal became a testament to His faithfulness and a reminder to keep praying boldly. I learned that courage in prayer doesn't just change situations; it transforms hearts. I know now that I'll never hold back from praying big prayers again.

...

### Lord,

Grant me the courage to bring my deepest needs before You. Help me trust Your plans and embrace the peace that comes from praying boldly and believing in Your faithfulness.
Amen.

...

# Reptile Expo

Sibyl F. Cole

...

**Psalm 27:1 (NIV)**
The Lord is my light and my salvation; whom shall I fear?

...

When I was younger, I was at my neighbor's house. Her uncle was there with his pet iguana. I had never seen anything like it, and thus began my fascination with lizards. When my son was nine years old, we bought our first bearded dragon and named him Spike, who quickly became a beloved family member. We even dressed him as Prince one year for Halloween. After ten years, Spike passed away, and we were devastated.

Repticon is a reptile expo that travels to different cities throughout the United States and stops in Georgia about four times a year. After losing Spike, we talked about getting another bearded dragon and decided to go to the expo. The atmosphere buzzed with excitement as families moved from booth to booth, looking at snakes, lizards, and turtles—oh my! There was a booth where people were being photographed with a giant python. I decided to have my picture taken, too. My son thought I'd lost my mind, but I figured, what better way to conquer my fear of snakes than to pose with one?

My heart raced throughout the entire process. I stepped up, the snake was placed on my shoulders (EEEEKKK!!!), and the picture was snapped. Before it was placed around me, I said a silent prayer, "Lord, I know you've got me," and I wasn't afraid. Did it cure my fear of snakes? Absolutely not, but it did show me that with God's help, I found the courage to face it.

...

Lord,
Guide me with Your strength and courage, as I face my
fears, knowing Your presence is always with me.
Amen.

...

# Warrior Rise Up

## Stacey Collins

...

### Deuteronomy 31:6 (NIV)

Be strong and courageous. Do not be afraid or terrified because of them, for the LORD your God goes with you.

...

What is courage? It stirs something deep within—the strength to face what threatens to break us, paralyze us, feel impossible. O mighty warrior-hero! Have you laid your battle sword down? In the grief-fog, have you forgotten who you are? Your sword dusty, your heart hurting, spirit discouraged? Can you remember how brave you really are, the moment you stopped fighting for your dreams, for those you love, for yourself?

I've walked this path through devastating loss, including four siblings and my father. Words can't describe such grief. Inspired by Queen Esther, who turned to God in fasting and prayer, placing her life in His hands, embracing identity, strategy, brilliance in the face of great danger, it was then I discovered courage burning within me. Beyond me!

With vulnerable and uncertain steps of courage, I've faced the impossible—adopted my precious son after raising four children to adults, watched my husband nearly die from COVID, moved through estranged relationships to reconciliation and some still waiting, hoping. With tears and trust, I've gotten out of bed on days where my heart whispered, 'I can't do this anymore.' Through courage, I found my voice, my influence, stepped off the bench and into purpose. I'm taking my journey of pain, my still overcoming, to bring hope and healing to others.

Today, warrior-hero, is your new beginning. Let courage arise in your heart. There's a warrior inside you waiting to emerge, dreams waiting to unfold. Pick up your sword and repeat after me: "I think I can... I think I can... I think I can...!"

...

Lord,

Thank You for the gift of courage. Grant me strength to face challenges, and may Your divine presence guide and uphold me through every trial.

Amen.

# Stepping Out On Faith

## Dr. Nina Addison

...

### Matthew 6:25 (NIV)

Therefore I tell you, stop being worried or anxious (perpetually uneasy, distracted) about your life, as to what you will eat or what you will drink; nor about your body, as to what you will wear. Is life not more than food, and the body more than clothing?

...

I remember sitting at an event that Les Brown was hosting in September 2010. I was on the edge of my seat, saying, "I belong on that stage!"

It was a feeling I could not describe. I just knew it was a feeling God gave me. I did not personally know any motivational speakers, but I immediately felt the urge in my spirit to figure out how I, too, could change lives by speaking on a stage.

I connected with Les Brown's mentee, Talayah Stovall, and asked her to take me under her wing, and she did. I knew I had to have courage. See, this was going to be something new—standing on a stage, telling people about living with a disability, sharing the mistakes I made, but doing it with courage… Whew!

But God put it in my spirit, so I said YES!

This journey took me on an incredible path. I even wrote my first book and was asked why I was sharing my personal story. I had to ignore all the negativity and do what God said with courage. Because I did, many lives continue to be changed.

...

### Daddy God,

please grant me courage and strength. May I go forth in all You empower me to do. Because You are with me, may I remember I can do all things! In Jesus' name, may it forever be.

Amen!

...

# Celebrating The Favor of Courage

*Courage is the bold step into the unknown, fueled by the assurance of God's presence and promises. Embrace the strength He provides, as His favor transforms fear into faith and uncertainty into victory.*

**Now it's your turn to write your story of celebrating The Favor of Courage.**

Recall a time when courage shaped your actions and decisions. How did trusting in God's support enable you to overcome fear or adversity? Reflect on how His favor was evident through your courageous steps, and how this experience has deepened your reliance on His strength.

_____

_____

_____

_____

_____

_____

_____

_____

_____

_____

_____

_____

_____

_____

_____

_____

_____

_____

# THE
# FAVOR
## OF
## *Compassion*

Seek wisdom and walk in God's favor. Compassion opens hearts, unlocks the soul's potential, and unveils the transformative power of God's abundant favor.

# Open Hearts

...

### Colossians 3:12 (NIV)
"Therefore, as God's chosen people, holy and dearly loved, clothe yourselves with compassion, kindness, humility, gentleness and patience.

...

IIn a hurried, self-centered world, compassion powerfully reflects God's love and favor. It's more than a feeling—it's a divine connection that channels His blessings into our lives and others'.

Think of times when compassion touched you deeply, reminding you of God's boundless love and mercy. When we act with kindness and understanding, we become vessels of His transformative power. Compassion not only blesses the receiver but also enriches the giver, creating ripples of favor for all.

God's compassion is our guide, clothing us in love, lifting us with grace, and encouraging us through His patient care. By embodying these qualities, we see the world through His eyes and realize the profound impact of simple kindness.

This week, as we celebrate the Favor of Compassion, embrace each day with a heart ready to extend God's mercy. Through a listening ear, helping hand, or kind word, your compassion can be a lifeline, reflecting His love and drawing you closer to His purpose.

...

### Compassionate Father,
I am grateful for Your endless love and mercy. Help me to clothe myself in compassion, mirroring Your heart in all I do. May my actions reflect Your favor and bring comfort to those around me.
Amen.

...

# A Divine Nudge

Lori Miller

...

**Isaiah 6:8 (NIV)**
Then I heard the voice of the Lord saying, "Whom shall I send? And who will go for us?" And I said, "Here am I. Send me!"

...

One morning, I woke up wanting nothing more than to stay in my cozy bed. I had a busy day ahead, and all I wanted was a little more sleep. But I felt a nudge in my spirit, urging me to get up and go for a walk.

I listened, got dressed, and took my dog out into the crisp morning air.

As I walked towards the river, I felt another nudge—this time to take a different path. I followed the feeling, not knowing what I might find.

In a short time, I came across a young man walking towards me. As I approached, he shared that he had nowhere to go and no way to contact anyone. He had stopped at his pastor's house for a meal, but now he was alone again.

I began telling him he was at a crossroads—a point where he could choose to continue relying on his own strength or open himself to God's guidance. I shared stories of overcoming hardships, emphasizing that every challenge is an opportunity to grow closer to God and align with His purpose.

I walked alongside him, back in the direction I had come, feeling honored to be used by God to lift his spirits. I reminded him that he was not alone, that God is always with him, guiding him. It was a powerful reminder that God often calls us out of our comfort zones to be His vessel of hope and encouragement.

...

**Lord,**
Fill our hearts with compassion to serve and uplift others. May we be vessels of Your love, spreading kindness and hope.
Amen.

...

# Cemetery Visit

Sibyl F. Cole

...

**Lamentations: 3:32 (NIV)**

Though he brings grief, he will show compassion, so great is his comforting love.

...

My mother passed away on June 1, 2021. On November 24, 2021, the day before Thanksgiving, I mustered the courage to visit the cemetery for the first time since her funeral.

It was a beautiful day; the sun was shining brightly, and there was a slight chill in the air. My heart was heavy, and I didn't feel thankful or eager for any family gathering.

As I walked to her plot, I knelt down and traced my fingers over her engraved name. I placed flowers in the attached vase and just stood there. Tears rolled down my face as I spoke to Mom, telling her how much I missed and needed her. After I thought I had cried all the tears I could, I gathered myself and walked back to my car.

While driving home, I stopped at a traffic light near a Family Dollar. Overwhelmed by my emotions, I began to cry again. A woman in the lane next to me honked her horn to get my attention. Seeing my distress, she mouthed, "Are you okay?" I nodded yes, and when the light changed, she drove off.

That night, I reflected on that brief exchange at the stoplight. That woman didn't know me, and she didn't have to check on me. But it must have been divine intervention for her to show a perfect stranger some much-needed compassion at that very moment.

...

**Dear God,**

Thank You for the unexpected compassion given by strangers. May I always recognize and share such grace, feeling your love in every moment.

Amen.

...

# Been There, Done That!

Elvetra Cossie

...

2 Corinthians 1:3-4 (NIV)

Praise be to the God and Father of our Lord Jesus Christ, the Father of compassion and the God of all comfort, who comforts us in all our troubles, so that we can comfort those in any trouble with the comfort we ourselves receive from God.

...

We don't always know where God is leading us or who He will place in our path. Recently, I went to the bank during my lunch break to open an account. The bank manager greeted me warmly, and I thought, Great! This shouldn't take long.

As we started, she apologized for her appearance, explaining she'd just returned from visiting her son's college that morning. She mentioned how tired she was and admitted she'd considered staying home.

As she shared her struggles as a mother, I noticed the frustration in her voice and on her face. I felt led to share my own experiences, fears, and victories. I told her that as a single mother and believer, the success of my children and me was only possible through God's grace.

With tears in her eyes, she called me her angel sent from God. A quick transaction turned into a 2½-hour conversation filled with compassion and praise. Not only did I open the account and find favor with the manager, but God used me to reassure a hurting mother that she was not alone.

The enemy tries to convince us that our struggles are unique, isolating us in pain. But God uses our trials to encourage others—if we take the time, are willing to be vulnerable, and share our journey.

That day, I didn't just accomplish a task; I witnessed how God can turn an ordinary moment into an extraordinary encounter.

...

**Heavenly Father,**

Thank You for using our trials to bring compassion, connection, and healing. May we always share Your grace freely.

Amen.

# Finding Strength Together

Melanie Winters

...

**Galatians 6:2 (NIV)**
Carry each other's burdens, and in this way you will fulfill the law of Christ.

...

When my father was diagnosed with a severe illness, the news hit like a storm in our small church community, where everyone knew each other by name. Our family was engulfed in a whirlwind of hospital visits and sleepless nights. But it was during these trying times that the true heart of our church community revealed itself.

Our pastor's wife, Mrs. Thompson, rallied the ladies of the church to organize a weekly meal train. Every day, a different family would bring over home-cooked meals—comfort food like casseroles and hearty soups that eased not just our hunger but also our burden. On weekends, Mr. Harris, who owned a small grocery store, would drop by with bags of fresh produce and essentials, all gifted with a warm smile and a reassuring hug.

One particularly challenging evening, the church choir surprised us with an impromptu visit. They filled our living room with harmonies of hope, their voices lifting our spirits and reminding us of the strength found in unity. I remember sitting on the couch, surrounded by familiar faces, and feeling an overwhelming sense of gratitude. Their laughter and shared stories transformed our house from a place of worry into a sanctuary of love.

This outpouring of love and support taught us the invaluable lesson of collective faith and compassion. In times of despair, it's the bonds of community that provide solace, proving that we are never truly alone.

...

**Lord,**
Thank You for the blessing of community. May we always cherish and nurture these bonds, finding strength in shared love and faith.
Amen.

...

# Pray it Forward!

Dr. Theresa Billingsley

...

## 2 Peter 3:9 (TLB)

He isn't really being slow about his promised return, even though it sometimes seems that way. But He is waiting, for the good reason that He is not willing that any should perish, and He is giving more time for sinners to repent.

...

We should all care about more than just ourselves going to Heaven. We are called to share the gospel of Jesus Christ with others in our sphere of influence, especially those whom the devil wants us to give up on. It's a battle for souls.

We cannot take our house or car with us when we transition from this earth to Heaven, but we can take souls with us if they believe in Jesus as the propitiation for their sins. Don't give up on your friends, family, and enemies. Be encouraged, no matter how it looks. Pray for their redemption. God does not want anyone separated from Him.

I have prayed for many of my family and friends to come to know Jesus. Some of them I have witnessed give their lives to Christ. Others are still in progress, and some I may never know, but God does, and I continue to pray for them.

For those who need salvation, pray Psalms 103:1-5 (among other applicable scriptures) out loud for them and call their name out loud to experience redemption. Prayer has no expiration date. Someone prayed for us, so let us pay it forward.

Just as we have been reconciled back to God through Jesus Christ, let's give others the same opportunity by sharing the gift of unconditional love—Jesus Christ. He is Love that came in the flesh.

...

### Lord,

Soften hearts and draw loved ones to You. Strengthen us to persevere in prayer, share Your love boldly, and trust Your perfect timing.

Amen.

...

# Celebrating The Favor of Compassion

*Compassion is the heartbeat of God's love, moving us to reach out with kindness and understanding. By embracing compassion, we reflect His favor, touching lives and spreading His grace in profound ways. Let your heart be a vessel of His boundless love.*

**Now it's your turn to write your story of celebrating The Favor of Compassion.**

Reflect on a time when an act of compassion made a significant difference in your life or someone else's. How did this expression of kindness impact your faith and relationships? Describe the ways God's favor was revealed through this compassion and how it continues to shape your journey.

# THE FAVOR OF *Renewal*

Embracing renewal in God's presence revitalizes our spirits, infusing us with life, hope, and abundant favor.

# New Strength

...

### 2 Corinthians 4:16 (NIV)
Therefore we do not lose heart. Though outwardly we are wasting away, yet inwardly we are being renewed day by day.

...

We've all had those moments where life feels overwhelming—juggling too much, running on empty, and struggling to keep up. It's easy to feel stretched thin, like the world is spinning too fast for us to catch our breath.

But here's the good news: God has an incredible plan to revive us. He steps in with His amazing gift of renewal, refreshing our weary souls and drenching us in His favor just when we need it most. Even when we're at the end of our rope, God is right there, ready to lift us up and infuse us with His boundless strength and love.

Think about a time when you felt renewed after a tough season—a prayer that recharged you or a quiet moment that shifted your perspective. That's God at work. He's always ready to fill us with His endless hope and remind us we're never alone.

God's renewal isn't just a temporary boost; it's a deep transformation. When we lean into His presence, He reshapes our thoughts, rejuvenates our spirits, and gives us the courage to face anything with grace and confidence.

This week, make space for God's renewal. Pause each day to soak in His presence—through prayer, time in His Word, or a quiet walk. Trust that He's working in you, restoring your strength and refreshing your soul. Step into each day with His favor and the confidence to overcome whatever lies ahead.

...

### Lord
I'm ready for Your renewal. Refresh my spirit and fill me with Your strength. Help me embrace Your favor every single day, finding joy and purpose in Your presence.
Amen.

...

# Alive Again

## Dr. Joyce S. Mallory

...

### Isaiah 54:4-5 (NLT)

Fear not; you will no longer live in shame. Don't be afraid; there is no more disgrace for you. You will no longer remember the shame of your youth and the sorrows of widowhood. For your Creator will be your husband; the Lord of Heaven's Armies is his name! He is your Redeemer, the Holy One of Israel, the God of all the earth.

...

In April, I come alive. Like a bear, I hibernate from November to April. This past winter was especially hard. My best friend and husband of 36 years passed away in October, and I withdrew from social events, enveloped by solitude.

Then, a gentle tap on my shoulder broke through the silence. "Are you okay?" my friend, the mother of the bride, asked, encouraging me back into the world.

The church was filled with the scent of fresh flowers, a vibrant contrast to the shadows I had known. This was a wedding—a celebration of life and love.

As the organist played, the bride appeared, moving gracefully down the aisle. The sunlight cast a golden glow through her veil, painting her in light. Struggling to hold back tears, I prayed, "Lord, I don't want to spoil this joy. Help me."

She looked stunning in her white gown, holding a bouquet of lilies, ivory roses, and daisies. Memories of my own wedding surfaced, and tears fell despite my efforts. A friend's comforting touch and a tissue appeared, reminders that I wasn't alone.

"Thank you, Lord, for sending comfort through these friends," I thought. Their kindness was a lifeline, guiding me from sorrow to light.

In that moment, I felt God's favor renewing my spirit, lifting me from grief toward hope and reminding me of the beauty still waiting to be embraced.

...

### Dear Lord,

thank You for Your grace and favor in renewing my spirit. May Your light guide me from grief to hope and new beginnings.

Amen.

# God Has An Eraser

Bonita L. Williams

...

### Isaiah 1:18 (NLT)

"Come now, let's settle this," says the Lord.
"Though your sins are like scarlet, I will make them as white as snow.
Though they are red like crimson, I will make them as white as wool."

...

This morning during devotion, I reread an article about a child watching an airplane write a message in the sky. When the skywriting faded, the child explained, "Maybe God had an eraser." Imagine that for a moment—God has an eraser.

The thought is comforting, isn't it? All of us have moments we regret—words spoken carelessly, thoughts we shouldn't have entertained, or mistakes we've made. These can haunt us, dragging us down and making our future seem bleak. But God's Word reassures us that He will blot out our sins.

1 John 1:9 reminds us, "If we confess our sins, He is faithful and just to forgive us and cleanse us from all unrighteousness." The problem is often not God's forgiveness, but our inability to forgive ourselves. We carry guilt, believing it makes our repentance more genuine. Yet, that guilt is a deceitful weight from the enemy, meant to keep us from fully experiencing God's grace.

Paul encourages us in Philippians 3:13-14, "Forgetting what is behind and straining toward what is ahead, I press on toward the goal to win the prize." If God has erased our sins, why hold on to them?

When the enemy condemns you, fight back with God's Word—your spiritual sword. Celebrate that your sins are forgiven through Christ, who paid your debt. hank Him for His grace and move forward in freedom.

Rejoice today, remembering the power of God's spiritual eraser.

...

### Lord,

Thank You for renewing my spirit through Your grace. Help me release the past and walk in Your forgiven, unburdened freedom.

Amen.

...

172

# My Caterpillar Moment

Veronica Washington

...

**Psalm 16:11 (NIV)**

You make known to me the path of life; you will fill me with joy in your presence, with eternal pleasures at your right hand.

...

I never thought I'd find myself in front of a classroom again, let alone surrounded by third graders with sticky fingers and chocolate-smudged faces. Yet there I was, holding a book about caterpillars, feeling both triumphant and slightly overwhelmed.

Life had been exhausting. Raising my grandkids several days a week, juggling church meetings, and helping at the food bank had left me running on fumes. My energy seemed to have packed its bags and disappeared.

It was my neighbor, Miss Loretta, who nudged me. "You need to do something for yourself," she said. At first, I dismissed it. Wasn't serving my family and church supposed to be enough? But deep down, I knew I'd been running on autopilot.

That's how I ended up volunteering for the library's reading program. Initially, it felt like just another task. But something shifted when the kids began giggling at my butterfly impressions and gasping as the caterpillar munched through leaves. Their cheers as it broke free from its cocoon were contagious.

By the end, I realized those caterpillars weren't the only ones transforming. The kids' joy reminded me of the magic in small steps. Renewal doesn't always come through sweeping changes—it's in the giggles, the wonder of a caterpillar's journey, and letting yourself bloom again

Turns out, even a seasoned grandma can have a caterpillar moment—and it's sweet to feel your wings again.

...

**Lord,**

Thank You for renewal and the joy You bring. Help me find delight in small moments and keep sparking my soul.

Amen.

...

# Simple Serenityrve

L. Marie

...

### Isaiah 58:11 (NLT)

The Lord will guide you continually, giving you water when you are dry and restoring your strength. You will be like a well-watered garden, like an ever-flowing spring.

...

This morning, I sat down at my kitchen table with a cup of tea. Earl Grey, just the way I like it—one sugar, splash of milk. The house was quiet. The sun peeked through the window, warming the top of my hand as I held the mug. I closed my eyes and just listened. To nothing, and to everything. The hum of the fridge, a bird chirping outside, and the faint creak of the old floorboards as I shifted in my seat.

It didn't happen all at once, but as I sat there, I felt this lightness come over me. It was like the tightness in my chest didn't have a reason to stay anymore. I took a deep breath, and it felt like I'd been holding it in for months.

Funny how we think we need big moments to feel renewed, but sometimes it's just a quiet morning. No TV blaring, no errands pulling you out the door, just tea, sunlight, and stillness.

I think I needed it more than I realized. My days get full—life has a way of keeping you busy—but that little pause reminded me that peace doesn't always come in loud sermons or long prayers. Sometimes, it's a simple moment with the sun warming your hand. I don't know why, but it made me feel whole all over again.

...

### Lord,

Thank You for Your quiet peace. Renew my heart and guide me in Your steadfast favor and salvation.

Amen.

...

# Nap Time

Benecia Ponder

...

**Jeremiah 31:25 (ESV)**
For I will satisfy the weary soul, and every languishing soul I will replenish.

...

I remember a season when I was running on fumes. I'd just come off a whirlwind tour of speaking, teaching, and pouring into others. It was exhilarating, fulfilling, and everything I love about what I do. But when I returned home, I convinced myself to jump straight back into work. After all, I had a big ghostwriting project with a looming deadline.

That first day back, I sat in front of my laptop, staring at the screen. My brain felt like it was moving through a thick fog. No matter how hard I tried, the words wouldn't come. I pushed myself for hours, ignoring the quiet whispers of my body telling me to rest. Finally, I gave in, thinking I'd take a short nap.

When I opened my eyes, I realized I'd slept for ten hours. Ten! At first, I panicked, but then I noticed something amazing—I felt refreshed. My mind was clear, and the ideas I'd struggled for the day before were flowing effortlessly.

God used that moment to remind me that even in the midst of doing His work, I need to pause and trust Him with my rest. Psalm 23:2-3 came alive for me that day: "He makes me lie down in green pastures, he leads me beside quiet waters, he refreshes my soul."

His favor is not just in the doing—it's in the resting, too.

Since then, I've embraced the gift of renewal, knowing that God isn't just glorified in my work but also in my willingness to be still.

...

**Lord,**
Refresh my mind, restore my soul, and renew my
strength as I trust Your favor and rest in Your grace.
Amen.

...

175

# Celebrating The Favor of Renewal

*Renewal is God's gift of fresh strength and hope, breathing new life into our weary souls. Embrace the moments of renewal, knowing they are filled with His favor, ready to transform and rejuvenate your spirit.*

**Now it's your turn to write your story of celebrating The Favor of Renewal.**

Reflect on a time when you felt renewed and reenergized in your faith journey. What circumstances led to this renewal, and how did it impact your perspective and actions? Describe how God's favor was evident in this process of renewal and how it has strengthened your relationship with Him.

_____

_____

_____

_____

_____

_____

_____

_____

_____

_____

_____

_____

_____

_____

_____

_____

_____

_____

# THE
# FAVOR
## OF
## *Disappointment*

Find God's incredible favor and hidden blessings even when disappointment strikes, revealing His greater plan and unexpected goodness in your life.

# Hidden Blessings

...

### Romans 8:28 (NIV)
And we know that in all things God works for the good of those who love him,
who have been called according to his purpose.

...

Disappointment often sneaks in when life doesn't unfold as we planned—when dreams hit a wall, carefully crafted plans unravel, and cherished hopes seem to dissolve. In those raw moments, it's easy to feel like we're standing at a precipice, wondering what's next.

But here's the truth: God's favor can weave itself into our disappointments, working in mysterious and beautiful ways. What if those closed doors and barriers aren't endings but God's way of preparing us for something greater? What if the waiting and wondering are part of a divine setup for blessings beyond what we can imagine?

When we trust God, disappointment becomes a tool for His grace. Perhaps you've faced a setback that felt insurmountable, only to find it opened the door to unexpected opportunities or lessons. That's God at work, turning loss into preparation for His favor.

Consider Joseph's story. Sold into slavery and facing years of hardship, he was ultimately positioned by God to save nations. His disappointments became stepping stones to a destiny beyond his dreams.

In our own lives, disappointment invites us to look beyond the frustration and ask God to reveal His purpose. As we trust and surrender, His favor unfolds in unimaginable ways. This week, shift your perspective. See disappointment not as a dead end but as a divine detour. Embrace the hidden blessings God is weaving into your story and trust in His goodness.

...

### Dear Heavenly Father,
help me to trust in Your plans even when I face setbacks. Turn my disappointments into opportunities for Your favor. Reveal Your goodness in all situations, and guide me to see Your hand at work in my life.
Amen.

...

# See The Bigger Picture

Amanda Blake

...

### Psalm 42:11 (ERV)

Why am I so sad? Why am I so upset? I should put my hope in God and keep praising him, my Savior and my God.

...

It was a Friday afternoon when my phone buzzed with an email notification. My heart raced as I opened it, only to find out I didn't get the job. Disappointment washed over me like a cold wave. I had pinned my hopes on this role, imagining it as my stepping stone to a better future.

As I sat staring at the rejection, my mind wandered back to similar moments of letdown. Like the time I missed my train by just a minute, which felt like the end of the world then. Yet, that delay led me to a café where I met a now-close friend, proving that not all setbacks are missteps.

Now, as I wrestled with my feelings, a thought nudged its way into my mind. What if this disappointment was paving the way for something greater?

I remembered how each seeming coincidence in my life had unfolded with a purpose I couldn't see at the time. It was as if there was a bigger picture being painted, one that needed every stroke, no matter how random it seemed.

While it was hard to see past the immediate sting of rejection, I knew that trusting in a greater plan was key. For anyone feeling defeated by life's twists and turns, take heart. There is a design beyond our understanding. Every detour has a purpose, guiding us to where we truly belong. Keep faith, for even in the chaos, God is crafting something wonderfully intentional.

...

### Lord,

Help me to trust in Your perfect plan even when life seems uncertain. Grant me patience and faith to see Your purpose in every situation.

Amen.

...

# The Performance Plan

Alethia Saunders

...

**Romans 11:33 (NIV)**

Oh, the depth of the riches of the wisdom and knowledge of God! How unsearchable his judgments, and his paths beyond tracing out!

...

I've always been a hard worker. I set a goal, and I trust that I'll reach it if I work diligently. I finally secured a job working from home, and I was thrilled to achieve this goal. It was going to help me transition into working for myself. However, I struggled to meet the required metrics, which was a hard pill to swallow since I'd never faced this issue before.

Suddenly, I found myself in meetings, getting written up, and placed on performance improvement plans—PERFORMANCE IMPROVEMENT PLANS! I knew it was only a matter of time before I was let go. I was so disappointed. It wasn't time yet. I was supposed to be locked in for six months. That was my plan. But it seemed God had other plans. There was a reason why this job wasn't working for me. So, I prayed hard about it! Then I turned in my two weeks' notice.

I still remember the first day I sat at my desk as my own employer! That was the day my life began!

...

**Dear God,**

thank You for Your unwavering protection and love. Grant me the strength to uphold integrity and deepen my faith in You.

Amen.

...

# From Setback to Purpose

Melanie Winters

...

## Psalm 32:8 (NIV)

I will instruct you and teach you in the way you should go; I will counsel you with my loving eye on you.

...

Life has a way of surprising us, doesn't it?

For thirteen years, I poured myself into a company that felt like home. The people, the projects, the purpose—it all fit so well.

Then, one ordinary day, everything changed. Downsized.

My world unraveled. "Why me? Why now?" I wrestled with doubt and uncertainty.

In the midst of the struggle, a small opportunity appeared—a chance to join a coach training program. It felt like God was whispering, "This isn't the end; it's a new beginning."

With courage, I stepped into the unknown. Each lesson, encounter, and moment in the program planted seeds that blossomed into a vibrant, purposeful business. I found not just a career but a calling.

Becoming a Christian coach allowed me to help others turn their setbacks into setups and uncover their God-given potential.

The blessings that followed exceeded my imagination. Unexpected doors opened, connections were made, and lives were transformed. And it all started because I trusted the new path God placed before me.

Life's detours are often divine designs. When one door closes, God opens a window—or even an entire sky of opportunities. Embrace the change, and you'll discover the beauty of His plan unfolding.

...

### Heavenly Father,

Thank You for guiding me through life's unexpected turns. I trust Your plan and embrace the new opportunities You place before me.

Amen.

...

# Love and Waffles

Veronica Washington

...

**2 Corinthians 4:17 (NIV)**
For our light and momentary troubles are achieving for us an eternal glory that
far outweighs them all.

...

My twenties were a glorious mix of questionable fashion choices and even more questionable dates. One night, though, still makes me laugh.

It began with Daryl, with his too-perfect hair and toothpaste-commercial smile. He was supposed to pick me up at 7. By 7:15, I thought, "Fashionably late." By 7:30, I was pacing, planning how I'd curse him out. By 7:45, it hit me—he wasn't coming.

Any sensible woman would've called it a night, but not me. I yanked off my heels, grabbed my purse, and decided I needed waffles immediately.

At the Waffle House, I slid into a sticky booth, ordered coffee and waffles, and noticed a man sitting alone at the counter. He wore a faded denim jacket and ate hash browns like he had all the time in the world.

We made eye contact, and he smiled—a real smile, not that Daryl "this-is-for-the-camera" nonsense. He introduced himself as Greg and asked if he could join me. I don't remember how we started talking, but by the time my waffles were gone, I didn't mind Daryl ghosting me.

Greg actually listened when I talked—no pretense, just real. Forty years later, he still claims he fell in love with me somewhere between the syrup and the stories.

Funny how the best things in life often come after disappointment. Thank God!

...

**Lord,**
Help me trust Your plan, turning disappointment into favor, knowing Your
goodness brings blessings beyond what I can see.
Amen.

...

# The Gift of Rejection

L. Marie

...

**Philippians 1:6 (NIV)**

Being confident of this, that he who began a good work in you will carry it on to completion until the day of Christ Jesus.

...

When I was fresh out of nursing school, I dreamed of working in a big hospital. I wanted to work in the kind of place where everyone wanted to be—fast-paced and exciting. I applied, full of hope, but after weeks of waiting, I got a letter. They turned me down. I was crushed. I cried that night, feeling like I wasn't good enough.

A few days later, my mother suggested I apply at a small clinic near our home. At first, I wasn't excited about the idea. It felt like settling. But I needed a job, so I went. The clinic was quiet, with a single doctor, a receptionist, and a lot of older patients. It was nothing like the bustling hospital I had envisioned.

My disappointment didn't last long. Working there, I got to spend real time with my patients. I learned their names, their stories, their struggles. One sweet man, Mr. Harris, brought me fresh oranges from his grove just to say thank you. It felt good to make a direct difference in people's lives.

Looking back, being rejected wasn't a failure, it was a gift. That little clinic showed me the heart of nursing—caring for people, not just treating symptoms. It was the best lesson I could've learned.

...

**Heavenly Father,**

Guide us through disappointments, revealing Your blessings and purpose. Strengthen our faith and trust in Your plan.

Amen.

...

# Celebrating The Favor of Disappointment

*In disappointment, we often find the seeds of God's greater plans. Though it may seem like a setback, each disappointment is a stepping stone to His favor, teaching us resilience and revealing blessings beyond our current understanding.*

**Now it's your turn to write your story of celebrating The Favor of Disappointment.**

Think of a time when disappointment led you to a greater blessing or lesson. How did this experience change your perspective and strengthen your faith? Reflect on how you discovered God's favor in the midst of what seemed like a setback and how it has shaped your journey.

_____

_____

_____

_____

_____

_____

_____

_____

_____

_____

_____

_____

_____

_____

_____

# THE FAVOR OF Surrender

Release your hold and embrace God's will, discovering His abundant favor that transforms and enriches your life beyond measure.

# Letting Go for Greater Gain

...

**Matthew 16:25 (NIV)**
For whoever wants to save their life will lose it, but
whoever loses their life for me will find it.

...

In a world that glorifies relentless striving and celebrates control, surrender can feel counterintuitive—even daunting. Society often applauds those who shape their futures with sheer willpower, but as followers of Christ, we're invited to live differently. Surrender isn't weakness; it's the gateway to God's immeasurable favor.

Picture surrender as stepping off the treadmill of striving and into the tranquil flow of God's grace. In letting go, we don't lose control; we gain alignment with a Creator who sees the bigger picture and blesses us beyond what we can imagine. Trusting God's will doesn't mean forfeiting our dreams—it opens us to His perfect plan.

Have you noticed how clinging to control brings stress and fear, while surrender brings peace? Releasing control allows God to work in ways that transcend our understanding. Think about moments when letting go led to unexpected blessings. Surrender isn't about losing; it's about gaining more than we could ever achieve on our own.

Reflect on areas where you're holding on too tightly. What might God be calling you to release into His capable hands? Surrender is not passive—it's an active choice to trust that God's ways are higher and His plans infinitely wiser.

This week, lean into the favor that comes with surrender. Let go of the need to control every outcome and watch as God's abundant blessings unfold.

...

**Sovereign Lord,**
I surrender my life to You. Guide me with Your wisdom and bless me with Your favor.
Teach me to trust Your plans and embrace the peace that comes from letting go.
Amen.

...

# Beyond the Yield

## Stacey Collins

...

### Leviticus 25:19 (NIV)

Then the land will yield its fruit, and you will eat your fill and live there in safety.

...

"Stacey, you must YIELD. Give up everything. Lay it ALL down!"

This was the prophetic word I received three days before my sister died. A year later, in a class, the speaker held up a sign with "Yield" written on it. My spirit stirred with deep emotions as tears fell down my cheeks. Up until then, I'd thought it meant to pause... stop... let go... The Holy Spirit began to touch me and bring healing to my broken heart as I began to understand it was also about "provision." This wasn't just about surrendering, but that God had positioned me to receive a gift—a child—one that would come through another's seed. Poignant!

"God is birthing you with deep compassion" resonated from the word I'd received. Unknown to me, He was preparing my heart before my sister went to heaven, creating space for His compassion to pour out within my heart for me to become a mom again. God was already aligning His plan through Zackery, my sister's precious baby, now my son. His name means "God has remembered." Zackery is heaven's gift to us through another's seed. I'm learning that yielding opens our hearts to receive heaven's sweetest blessings, even when they come from unexpected places. What was grief and struggle has transformed into an invitation to yield to the Holy Spirit's leading and receive. As I release and surrender, peace floods my spirit. I know that as I yield, God brings forth life even from my deepest losses.

...

### Heavenly Father,

Thank You for Your guidance and unexpected blessings. Grant me strength to surrender, trust Your plan, and find peace and joy in Your divine love.
Amen.

...

# Finding Courage in Faith

Lori Miller

...

**Psalm 34:4 (NIV)**
I sought the Lord, and he answered me; he delivered me from all my fears.

...

When I was starting my new business, I faced a challenge that seemed simple on the surface: recording a two-minute live video.

As I prepared to go live, a wave of anxiety hit me like never before. My heart pounded, my hands trembled, and my mind raced.

Logically, I knew that a short video was no big deal, but my body responded with intense fear.

I realized this was more than just nerves—it was a deep-seated fear from my past, triggered by something I couldn't quite put my finger on. The anxiety lingered into the next day, paralyzing me with self-doubt. I knew I had to overcome this, but I couldn't find the strength on my own.

In a moment of desperation, I lifted my hands to the sky and prayed, "God, if this is something I need to do, you need to help me because I can't."

I surrendered my fear, trusting that He would guide me through.

Within fifteen minutes, I felt a profound sense of calm wash over me. It was as if God had reached down to soothe my anxious heart. I received a clear message on how to calm my nervous system, giving me the courage to try again.

Later that day, I went live again, recording another two-minute video. This time, I wasn't just facing my fear—I was embracing it. And for the first time, I smiled.

...

**Heavenly Father,**
I surrender my fears and doubts to You. Grant me strength and peace as I trust Your guidance each step of the way.
Amen.

...

# Soulful Surrender

Rochelle D. Jacobs

...

**Proverbs 16:3 (AMP)**

Commit your works to the Lord; submit and trust them to Him, and your plans will succeed if you respond to His will and guidance.

...

In a world promoting self-sufficiency, surrendering to God can feel counterintuitive. Yet, for me, surrender became a transformative journey—a pathway to experiencing God's favor in every area of my life. I discovered that true fulfillment comes from giving my best to God and being a faithful steward of the resources entrusted to me for His glory.

Determined to honor God with my finances, I examined my budget and spending habits. I realized I was living beyond my means and not prioritizing giving my first fruits to God. Inspired by 2 Corinthians 9:7, "Each one must give as he has decided in his heart, not reluctantly or under compulsion, for God loves a cheerful giver," I began allocating a portion of my income first to God. This practice brought peace and fulfillment, revealing that true joy comes from giving and investing in others. With this mindset, I became a better steward of my talents, answering the call to become an Amazon bestselling author. Through prayer, God blessed me with the gift of writing for His glory. I surrendered my fear of judgment and stepped out in obedience.

I am becoming a woman of faith by surrendering my relationships, talents, and will to God. I evaluated friendships, seeking connections aligned with my values. I prayed for wisdom to let go of toxic relationships and invest in uplifting sisterhoods. Surrendering to God is not about giving up; it's about letting go of our limited understanding to embrace His unlimited possibilities. Through this journey, I've experienced God's favor and deeper intimacy with Him.

...

**Father God,**

May we embrace the favor of surrender, trusting that when we give God our best, He will establish our paths and multiply our efforts.

Amen

# Gears of Surrender

Felicia Pichon

...

### Luke 9:23-24 (NASB)

And He was saying to them all, "If anyone wants to come after Me, he must deny himself, take up his cross daily, and follow Me. For whoever wants to save his life will lose it, but whoever loses his life for My sake, this is the one who will save it.

...

During the pandemic, there wasn't much to do, but I knew I couldn't spend another day cooped up in the house with my husband and kids. We started riding bikes together as a family. My family had bikes with gears, while I only had my cruiser. I'd never cared about gears before—I rode for fun, not speed. But out there with everyone else, I kept getting left behind. That's when I decided it was time for a change.

I'd always wanted a recumbent bike, so I figured if I was getting gears, I'd also get the bike of my dreams. When it arrived, everyone else could ride it with ease—but not me. Struggling like a child without training wheels, I had to rely on my husband to hold the bike steady for me. That's when I realized the problem—it was stuck in the lowest gear, offering no resistance. I couldn't ride without resistance.

It hit me then. That bike was a reflection of my life. I'd always resisted surrender. God would tell me to go left, and I'd go right, thinking I knew better. While riding, I heard Him whisper, "When will you listen to Me, child, and stop trying to steer your own way?"

Sometimes, surrender feels hard, but God knows the path we need to take. What area of your life do you need to surrender to Him fully?

...

### Lord,

I surrender my plans to You. Teach me to trust Your guidance and walk in Your wisdom. Help me release control and lean fully into Your will.

Amen.

...

# Not My Will

### Dr. Nina Addison

...

### Jeremiah 10:23 (AMP)

Humble yourselves [with an attitude of repentance and insignificance] in the presence of the Lord, and He will exalt you [He will lift you up, He will give you purpose].

...

At the end of 2023, God instructed me to make some changes in my business and to embrace new directions. As 2024 began, I followed His guidance and set aside what He asked me to. However, out of fear, I resumed some activities in my business that He had clearly indicated were not meant for this season. This disobedience led to difficulties in various aspects of my business because the grace was not there.

Eventually, I reached a point where I said, "God, I repent, and I surrender it all!"

I then took the necessary steps to let go of my small plans for His greater ones. After making some business announcements, I felt a profound peace in my heart. At that moment of surrender, God did more than I could have imagined. He awarded me an honorary doctorate degree in Christian Leadership and Business, blessed me with the Presidential Lifetime Achievement Award, and I also received a Paige Award for making a difference as a special needs person.

WOW!

The favor of God was, and continues to be, ever-present—all because I surrendered my plans for His!

...

### Abba Father,

May surrender be my posture. May I offer my heart, plans, and dreams to You. In return, may You bless me in ways only You can. In Jesus' Holy name, Amen!

...

# Celebrating The Favor of Surrender

*Surrender is not a sign of weakness but a beautiful act of trust in God's perfect plan. By letting go, you open your heart to His peace and favor, allowing Him to lead you to unimaginable blessings.*

**Now it's your turn to write your story of celebrating The Favor of Surrender.**

Reflect on a time when you surrendered your plans to God and experienced His favor in return. How did this act of letting go change your perspective and outcome? Describe the peace and blessings that emerged from trusting His higher purpose.

_____

_____

_____

_____

_____

_____

_____

_____

_____

_____

_____

_____

_____

_____

_____

_____

_____

_____

# THE FAVOR OF Vision

Embrace God's vision for your life as a guiding light that leads you into His abundant favor and purpose.

# Seeing Beyond the Now

...

### Habakkuk 2:2 (NIV)
Then the LORD replied: 'Write down the revelation and make it plain on tablets so that a herald may run with it.'

...

Vision is not just about peering into the future; it's about tapping into a realm of divine insight where God's purpose for us is revealed. Vision acts as a spiritual compass, anchoring us in clarity and directing our steps. It helps us navigate the complexities of life with unshakeable faith and assurance.

Think of vision as God's whisper to your soul, a reminder that even in chaos, there is a beautiful plan unfolding, one that will lead you to His favor and into the fullness of what He has destined for you.

It is through this divine insight that we are able to align our steps with His purpose, ensuring that every decision and action we take leads us closer to the fulfillment of His promises. Embracing God's vision requires us to look beyond our current circumstances, to see the possibilities that He has crafted just for us.

Reflect on the moments when you've sensed God's vision in your life—those instances when clarity replaced confusion, when you felt an undeniable pull toward a purpose greater than yourself. It's in these revelations that God's favor is most evident, gently steering us toward a future filled with hope and prosperity.

As you journey through this week, take time to seek God's vision for your life. Pray for the clarity to understand His plans and the courage to pursue them wholeheartedly. Remember, God's vision is a promise of His favor, a testament to His unwavering love and desire for your godly success.

...

### God of Vision,
Open my eyes to Your plans for my life. Help me to follow Your path with faith and courage. Guide me with Your wisdom and fill my heart with the assurance of Your favor.

Amen.

...

# First Great Grand

Dr. Joyce S. Mallory

...

### Isaiah 59:21 (ESV)

"My Spirit that is upon you, and my words that I have put in your mouth, shall not depart out of your mouth, or out of the mouth of your offspring, or out of the mouth of your children's offspring," says the Lord, "from this time forth and always."

...

I struggled one warm, humid night. Restless, I kicked off the covers, unable to find sleep.

"Oh, Lord, why am I restless?" I wondered as the clock read 3:35 am.

I began to sing softly, "Holy Spirit, You are welcome to speak..."

Soon, I drifted into sleep.

In my dream, I saw an image, like a sonogram. There was a floating, light-colored form in fluid, with small knobs along its back. I heard a voice, clear and gentle: "You will nurture, guide, and protect what I am sending you."

When my first great-granddaughter arrived, she brought surprise and joy. Her mother graciously gave her my name, a beautiful gesture. This unexpected blessing was a testament to God's love, filling our lives with joy and wonder.

It reminded me that God's plans are full of delightful surprises.

My great-granddaughter, born under the promise of my vision, knows Jesus as her Savior. Now, she stands on the brink of graduation in 2025, a senior ready to embrace her future. She has grown into a remarkable young woman, a living testament to God's faithfulness and the strength of His promises.

Her journey shows that God's vision is true and His promises sure: "May you see your children's children!" (Psalm 128:6 ESV)

...

### Lord,

Thank You for Your divine vision guiding my life. May I trust in Your plans and embrace the blessings You unfold.

Amen.

...

# Life More Abundant

Carol Holesak

...

**John 10:10 (NIV)**
The thief comes only to steal and kill and destroy; I have come that they may have life, and have it to the full.

...

I found myself at the Horizon School of Evangelism in San Diego, California, in 1994, having just turned 44. The three years prior were spent in counseling because of a nervous breakdown. I was a Christian but a new one. As someone who loved connecting with women in the deepest ways, I also found myself mostly upset with them in the deepest ways. But I knew even in my darkest moments of therapy, God was going to use it. I was getting a master's degree in the human condition.

A pastor kept asking me to join the School of Evangelism, and I kept saying no. I told him I hated school and was getting over a nervous breakdown. God had other plans, and off I went. It was a one-year program, and in the second semester, we were asked to pray about a vision of what God would have us do after we graduated. I was praying in the shower, and the Lord impressed upon my heart, "Changing Point for Abundant Life." Jesus said, "I have come that they may have life and have it abundantly." (John 10:10b).

As time went on, God revealed more of the vision. It started with a one-day seminar and grew into a six-week journey of healing. For over thirty years, the Lord has used my pain and my experiences of how only He can make beauty from ashes, to come alongside hundreds of women.

...

**Lord,**
Grant me divine vision and clarity, illuminate my path with Your wisdom, and guide me to see with spiritual insight.
Amen.

...

# Di-Vision Breaks Confidence

### Dr. Theresa Billingsley

...

**James 1:7-8 (AMP)**

For such a person ought not to think or expect that he will receive anything (at all) from the Lord, being a double-minded man, unstable and restless in all his ways (in everything he thinks, feels or decides).

...

The Greek word Di means "double" or "twice." One definition of vision is a mental image of what the future could be like. Without a clear, single focus on what you're striving for, distractions and delays can pull you away from your purpose.

When God plants a vision, dream, or deep desire in your heart, He often makes certain details stand out. This is His invitation to seek Him and ask, "What do you want me to do with this, Lord? Who are You calling me to impact?"

But things can get complicated when we step outside His plan. That's when di-vision happens—your vision and His compete, and everything feels off. I've lived this tension. After my divorce, I threw myself into my career, thinking financial stability and proving myself were the answers. But I kept hitting walls—at work, in parenting, and even in my faith. Nothing felt right.

I remember one night sitting in my living room, exhausted, asking God, "What do You want from me?" The answer wasn't immediate, but as I sought Him, He revealed the vision He had for my life. It wasn't about trying harder; it was about surrendering control. Slowly, He rebuilt my life, leading me to opportunities that aligned with His plan.

When you align your vision with God's, it changes everything. You'll move with purpose, clarity, and peace, knowing you're walking in the destiny He's crafted just for you. Trust Him to guide you through the struggles to something greater.

...

**Lord,**

Align my heart with Your vision. Help me surrender control, trust Your plan, and walk in Your purpose. Amen.

...

# See Yourself

Benecia Ponder

...

**Proverbs 29:18 (KJV)**
Where there is no vision, the people perish.

...

I never thought I had much in common with the Israelites. But then I looked at their forty-year trek to make an eleven-day trip and saw myself. Like them, I've wandered, circling the same mountains, knowing there's more but struggling to take hold of it.

Years ago, God placed a promise on my heart—to use my words to inspire and impact others. It was exhilarating at first, but then fear crept in. I'd tell myself, "It's not the right time," or "I'm not ready yet." And so, I wandered. Round and round I went, spinning my wheels, unable to move closer to God's vision for me.

One day, I came across Proverbs 29:18, where Solomon says, "Without a vision, the people perish." Those words hit me like a boulder. I realized the root of my wandering wasn't God's timing—it was my own lack of belief. The Israelites saw the Promised Land but couldn't see themselves possessing it. And I was doing the same thing.

God's vision wasn't the problem. I needed to see myself stepping into it. I began to picture myself writing, finishing that book, and sharing the message He placed inside me. Slowly, my wandering turned into steps of faith.

The truth is, what keeps us in the wilderness isn't the distance; it's our own doubt. If God has given you a vision, don't just see it—see yourself in it. Step into what He's already promised. Faith doesn't wait for perfect timing; it moves forward, trusting God has equipped you for the journey.

...

**Lord,**
Help me trust Your vision, step boldly in faith, and live fully in the grace of Your salvation.
Amen.

...

# The Gift of Wisdom

Dr. Vanessa D. English

...

## Proverbs 3:13 (NKJV)

Happy is the man who finds wisdom. And the man who gains understanding.

...

Many people assume that knowledge and wisdom are interchangeable. While related, they are not synonymous. One can possess knowledge but lack wisdom.

One Saturday morning, as I headed to church for choir rehearsal, my niece called. She asked if I could visit her house because her mother, my oldest sister, seemed to be in a "depressed state." As a therapist, I was trained to help others with sadness, but as her youngest sister, I simply didn't want to see her in pain. The previous year, we had lost two brothers and her eldest child. Often, I felt like I was barely "holding on." I understood her sadness deeply.

When I parked in her driveway, anxiety made its presence known, reminding me it had come along for the ride. I realized I was so consumed by earthly struggles that I had lost focus on the spiritual truth. God was there, ready to guide me. He reminded me of my task—helping my sister remember Who she belonged to.

"Happy is the one who finds wisdom and gains understanding." I can still picture my sister's smiling face and hear her heartfelt, "Thank you for coming."

...

## Dear God,

Thank You for blessing me with the gift of wisdom, so that you might be glorified in all that you send me to do.

Amen.

...

# Celebrating The Favor of Vision

Vision lights the path to God's favor, offering clarity and direction for your journey. Embrace the dreams and insights He places in your heart, trusting that they are guiding you toward divine purpose and abundant blessings.

Now it's your turn to write your story of celebrating The Favor of Vision.

Reflect on a vision or dream that has guided you toward a significant decision or change. How did this vision influence your actions and strengthen your faith? Consider the ways God's favor has been evident through pursuing this vision and how it has shaped your life's journey.

_____

_____

_____

_____

_____

_____

_____

_____

_____

_____

_____

_____

_____

_____

_____

_____

_____

_____

_____

# THE
# FAVOR
## OF
# *friendship*

Treasure the friendships in your life
that mirror God's unwavering love
and faithfulness, bringing support,
joy, and blessings.

# The Gift of True Companionship

...

Proverbs 18:24 (NIV)
One who has unreliable friends soon comes to ruin, but there is a friend who
sticks closer than a brother.

...

True friendships are divine connections that reflect God's faithful love, offering us support, encouragement, and a sense of belonging. In a world where relationships can often feel superficial or fleeting, genuine friendships stand as a testament to God's favor in our lives.

Friendship is more than shared interests or experiences; it's about hearts that connect on a deeper level, mirroring the love and loyalty that God extends to us. These relationships are like a sanctuary, providing us with comfort and strength when we need it most. They remind us that we are never alone, for God's love is manifested through the caring presence of a true friend.

Reflect on the friendships that have enriched your life—the individuals who have stood by you in times of joy and sorrow, who have celebrated your victories and comforted you in your struggles. These are not mere coincidences; they are expressions of God's grace, handpicked to walk alongside you on your journey.

As you meditate on the gift of friendship this week, take time to nurture these precious bonds. Express gratitude to your friends and seek to be a reflection of God's love in their lives, just as they have been in yours. Remember, in cherishing these connections, we experience God's favor in the most tangible of ways.

...

Loving Father,
Thank You for the gift of friendship. Help me to be a faithful friend,
sharing Your love and favor. Fill my relationships with your presence,
and may they always reflect Your unwavering love.
Amen.

...

# The Hens

Sibyl F. Cole

...

### Proverbs 18:24 (NRSV)

Some friends play at friendship but a true friend sticks closer than one's nearest kin.

...

My friends and I call ourselves "The Hens," and we make it a point to get together every few months to eat, drink (sometimes a bit too much!), and mostly catch up on each other's lives.

Our personalities range from extremely serious to downright nutty, and these differences make each of us unique in our own special way, but what truly connects us is the unbreakable bond of friendship.

We'd gotten together one Saturday afternoon in early spring, and shared memories—both good and bad—some reaching back to childhood, others rooted in the present day. Listening to those who wanted to share was eye-opening. I was surprised to discover aspects of their lives that up until this point, had been hidden, and some of those revelations were painful. From relationship issues, to no longer communicating with certain family members, to various health concerns; the stories were at times heart-wrenching, but also extremely therapeutic.

We've all faced challenges and battled them valiantly, but these ladies supported me during one of the darkest times in my life. My family was there, of course, but my friends' love also helped me get through that terrible chapter.

We gathered in the early afternoon; now, with the sun setting, it was time to say goodbye and return to our daily grinds. We hugged, wished each other well, and looked forward to our next gathering. Lifelong friends are a gift from God, and everyone should have the pleasure of experiencing such a wonderful bond.

...

### Lord,

I'm grateful for the gift of friendship, enriching my life with love, support, and joy.

Amen.

...

# Soulful Sisters

Benecia Ponder

...

**Ecclesiastes 4:9-10 (ESV)**
Two are better than one, because they have a good reward for their toil. For if
they fall, one will lift up his fellow.

...

For years, I wandered through life believing I didn't need close friends, masking a deeper truth: I simply didn't know how to forge those connections.

Making friends never came naturally to me, so I stopped trying.

My daughter leaving for college left a void, a lingering loneliness that grew louder in the silence of an empty home. It was then that the desire for companionship became undeniable. My prayers were simple—asking God to fill my life with friendships that would bring joy and laughter.

And then it happened. A few years ago, I found a group of women who transformed my world. These ladies are nothing short of incredible—witty, spiritually grounded, and overflowing with humor. Our latest adventure took us to Connecticut, where we immersed ourselves in the challenge of an escape room. Hours flew by as we laughed, strategized, and celebrated each small victory. It was a day filled with warmth and joy, a testament to the power of friendships.

These trips have become our tradition, a yearly pilgrimage to rekindle the bonds that have become a vital part of my life. Each meeting is a reminder of the favor I've found in friendship. I'm eternally grateful for the divine intervention that answered my prayers, enriching my life in ways I couldn't have imagined.

Life truly is sweeter, fuller, and more vibrant when shared with friends. As I reflect on this journey, I realize that I was never meant to walk alone.

...

**Lord,**
I am grateful for the divine gift of friendship. Thank You for the joy, support,
and love these bonds bring into my life.
Amen.

...

# I Call You Friend

### Carol Holesak

...

### Ecclesiastes 4:9-10 (NIV)
Two are better than one...For if they fall, one will lift his companion.

...

Friendship provides strength, security, and mutual support, reminding us of our need for community and companionship.

When I think of friendship, I think of my longest friend, Esther—not in height but in time. When I joined the women's ministry at my church, it was the first time I had been around so many women. Esther oversaw this large group, a godly woman filled with wisdom and patience. She needed that patience, especially in those early days of our friendship. Almost 40 years later, she still does!

Esther was the first friend who lovingly suggested that I seek a therapist. Now, that's true friendship.

But an even greater friend I have is Jesus. John 15:15 (NKJV): "No longer do I call you servants, for a servant does not know what his master is doing; but I have called you friends, for all things that I heard from My Father I have made known to you."

This friendship with Jesus invites us into a close, intimate relationship where we are included in God's plans. He is the friend always there for those who call upon His name.

Dear reader, if you're looking for a friend, reach out. I would love to be that for you.

...

Lord,
Thank You for the gift of friendship and the divine companionship found in Jesus.
Amen.

...

# A True Friend, Indeed

Makini Theresa L. Harvey

...

### Proverbs 17:17 (NIV)
A friend loves at all times, and a brother is born for a time of adversity.

...

Queen Esther was a dear friend who truly loved her family and community, the people of Israel. My friend "Esther" is a friend like that—loving, intelligent, wise, compassionate, empathetic, generous, and someone who fights for her family and community. We became best friends through our sons.

As my marriage fell apart, Esther helped me and, more importantly, prayed for me, because I hadn't yet surrendered to Jesus. For the drive to Seattle for the divorce hearing, Esther prayed that I would have a safe 13-hour journey and that the proceedings would go in my favor.

The judge ruled against me, granting full custody of our son to my husband. I was devastated. On the phone, I told Esther the outcome. Suicidal ideation increased; she heard the brokenness in my voice and said, "Makini, don't leave, stay there, I will be there immediately."

Esther caught the next San Francisco-to-Seattle flight, and we drove my car back to California, praying and listening to soul-lifting gospel songs all the way.

...

### Holy Jesus,
Immanuel, thank You for giving me friends who love, live, and serve like You.
May I live, love, and serve like You also;
Hallelujah and Amen.

...

# My Truest Friend

Bonita L. Williams

...

### John 15:15 (NIV)

I no longer call you slaves, because a master doesn't confide in his slaves. Now you are my friends, since I have told you everything the Father told me.

...

Friendships are vital to our existence. The saying "No man is an island" reminds us we were not created to live in isolation. Friends are often placed in our lives to lend a shoulder to cry on, a listening ear, or even a much-needed reprimand. We share cherished thoughts and secrets with them, and they enrich our lives in countless ways.

However, we must ask ourselves—are we prioritizing our friendships correctly? Too often, we turn to our earthly friends for guidance before seeking Jesus. While friends are a valuable blessing, they, too, have their own journeys to travel.

God has given me some incredible friends who have walked through life's ups and downs with me. They are dear to my heart. Yet, as wonderful as they are, they cannot take the place of Jesus. He is the friend who truly understands us, carries our burdens, and provides the perfect guidance.

The lyrics to the hymn What a Friend We Have in Jesus by Joseph M. Scriven remind us of this truth. Jesus is our greatest confidant, the one we can turn to when the world feels heavy. In times of uncertainty, He is the friend we need most.

Cherish your earthly friendships, but don't forget—talking to Jesus is the best conversation you can have. Seek Him first, for His love, wisdom, and guidance are incomparable.

...

### Lord,

Thank You for being my truest friend. Help me seek You first for guidance, comfort, and unwavering love.

Amen.

...

# Celebrating The Favor of Friendship

*Friendship is a precious gift, reflecting God's love and grace in our lives. Through genuine connections, we experience joy, support, and shared strength. Embrace your friendships as expressions of His favor, nurturing and celebrating these bonds with gratitude.*

**Now it's your turn to write your story of celebrating The Favor of Friendship.**

Reflect on a friendship that has significantly impacted your life. How has this relationship enriched your journey and drawn you closer to God's love? Consider the moments you've shared that highlighted His favor and how this friendship has supported your spiritual growth.

_____

_____

_____

_____

_____

_____

_____

_____

_____

_____

_____

_____

_____

_____

_____

_____

_____

# THE FAVOR OF Simplicity

Embrace simplicity. Find true fulfillment. See life's blessings clearly. Experience God's favor. Feel peace and joy in your heart.

# Finding More in Less

...

**1 Timothy 6:6 (NIV)**
But godliness with contentment is great gain.

...

This week, let's step back from the hustle and bustle and dive into the beauty of simplicity. In a world that often tells us more is better, God invites us to find peace and fulfillment in less.

Simplicity is not about deprivation; it's about making room for what truly matters, allowing us to see God's blessings and favor more clearly.

Think about it—how often do we clutter our lives with things and thoughts that steal our joy and cloud our vision? Yet, in the quiet and the simple, we discover a profound richness.

Simplicity teaches us to focus on what God has given us right here, right now, and to appreciate the gifts that can't be bought or measured.

Reflect on moments when simplifying your life brought unexpected joy and peace. Perhaps it was choosing to spend a quiet evening with loved ones or finding delight in nature's beauty. These are the instances where God whispers His love, showing us that He's already provided everything we need.

As you journey through this week, I encourage you to embrace the simplicity God offers. Let go of the unnecessary and make space for His presence to fill your heart.

God's favor isn't always found in abundance, but in a content spirit that recognizes His hand in the small and meaningful.

...

**Lord of Simplicity,**
Guide me to live contentedly in Your favor. Help me to find joy in life's simple blessings and to cherish the moments that reveal Your love.
Amen.

...

# Rich In Spirit

Alethia Saunders

...

### 1 Timothy 6:7-8 (NLT)

After all, we brought nothing with us when we came into the world, and we can't take anything with us when we leave it. So if we have enough food and clothing, let us be content.

...

I thank my God-fearing mother for her ability to turn a dollar into twenty. While I watched people slave to buy the latest cars, technology, and toys with the sole purpose of showing others that they had them, I was content with what I needed. This in no way meant that I didn't buy things I wanted, because I definitely did. However, I learned not to buy things that would complicate my life and expenses just to keep up with the rich and famous.

Finding joy in the simple things was instilled in me from a young age. I also know how to enjoy the finer things in life without relying on them for happiness or fulfillment.

God's riches are greater than any of man's riches. Making the right decisions has allowed me a life where I can give back to others, travel the world, and continue to serve at my highest capacity. I lack nothing and go to sleep each night knowing that I'm full of God's love. For this, I will be forever thankful.

...

**Dear God,**

Thank You for teaching me the beauty of simplicity. Guide my heart to find joy and contentment in Your abundant blessings.

Amen.

...

# Confessions of a Hoarder

Veronica Washington

...

**Proverbs 15:16 (NIV)**
Better a little with the fear of the Lord than great wealth with turmoil.

...

I have a confession to make—I was this close to being a hoarder. Okay, maybe not "TV-show" level, but close enough to feel a little embarrassed now. Back then, I thought I was just sentimental or "prepared for anything." But when I opened my closet one day and half the contents tumbled out, I couldn't ignore it anymore.

There were clothes I hadn't worn in a decade (no, I don't need those bell-bottoms to come back in style), boxes of knick-knacks I didn't even like, and mountains of "just in case" items that were clearly never going to get a justifiable case. My space was overflowing, and oddly, my life felt the same—cluttered, overwhelming, and a little suffocating.

I started cleaning out that closet, expecting to feel lighter when it was all done. What I didn't expect was how tied the clutter in my home was to the clutter in my heart. Stuff and busyness had taken over my life. When had I last really sat with God and just been still?

That day became the start of a bigger shift. I gave away what I didn't need, pared back my commitments, and began finding joy in little things—a walk in the quiet of the morning or sitting on the porch with my Bible. God's favor came flooding into the spaces I created. He wasn't calling me to fill my life with more; He was whispering to me to see the beauty in less.

...

**Lord,**
Thank You for opening my eyes to the freedom that comes with simplicity. Help me clear the clutter—both physical and spiritual—that distracts me from truly walking close to You.
Amen.

...

# The Small Stuff

Melanie Winters

...

**Isaiah 30:15 (NIV)**
This is what the Sovereign Lord, the Holy One of Israel, says: 'In repentance and rest is your salvation, in quietness and trust is your strength.

...

Jane logged in for our Zoom call with a heavy heart. "I just don't feel God's presence anymore," she told me, her eyes glistening with tears. Her calendar was overflowing, her mind was cluttered. She'd been chasing fulfillment through packed schedules and ambitious plans, but all it left her with was exhaustion.

I asked her to start small—really small. "What if, for the next week, you simplify? Start your morning with five minutes of quiet and end the day by writing down three simple things you're grateful for."

At first, she looked doubtful but agreed to try. A week later, Jane came to our session with a notebook in hand. "It's surprising," she said. She had noticed the morning sunlight streaming across her kitchen table. She watched her daughter laugh at something silly. She felt the cool breeze on her walk at lunch.

"I started feeling like God wasn't far away after all—He was in those little moments," she said.

We built on the simplicity, creating space for her to savor life. She began cooking meals from scratch, walking without her phone, and saying 'no' more often. Slowly, she untangled herself from the chaos. Through the unhurried rhythm of an ordinary day, she found God's blessings—right there, in her everyday life. And she found herself, too.

...

**Lord,**
Open my eyes to see Your goodness daily
Amen.
...

213

# Slowing Down Gracefully

Sheryl Simms

...

### John 14:27 (NIV)

Peace I leave with you; my peace I give you. I do not give to you as the world gives.

...

When I was younger, my life was full of noise. I worked long hours, raised three kids, and kept myself busy with church committees, social events, and endless to-do lists. Back then, I thought a full life meant a blessed life. But as the years went on, that busyness left me feeling tired and distant from the God I love.

One evening, after my husband and I retired, we sat on our porch watching the sun dip below the hills. I remember him saying, "Maybe we've overcomplicated things." That idea stuck with me. I started praying about it, asking God to show me what He wanted my life to look like. Little by little, I felt a need to simplify.

First, we downsized our home. We gave away things that no longer served us, finding joy in blessing others. I quit fretting over fancy meals and focused on wholesome suppers shared with family. I spent more time walking in the garden, marveling at God's handiwork in a single flower.

Now, in my 70s, my life feels so much richer in its simplicity. Without all the clutter and busyness, I've learned to listen for God's voice in my day-to-day. His blessings were always there, but when I slowed down, I could finally see them.

...

### Lord,

Thank You for simple blessings. Help me slow down, trust You, and find peace in stillness.

Amen.

...

# No Wi-Fi

Ashley Jenkins

...

**1 Thessalonians 4:11 (NIV)**
Make it your ambition to lead a quiet life: You should mind your own business
and work with your hands.

...

Working from home has its perks, but one thing I underestimated was how noisy my life had become. My days were a constant stream of ringing phones, pinging emails, and blinking computer screens. When I wasn't helping customers troubleshoot their issues, I was juggling class lectures and practice projects. I thought I was managing it well—until one Friday evening when my Wi-Fi went out.

At first, I panicked. No internet meant no work, no class, and apparently, I had no idea of what to do with myself. After running through every fix I could think of and still getting nowhere, I gave up and accepted I'd have to wait for the repair tech. For the first time in months, my home was completely still.

That evening, I sat on my tiny balcony with a warm mug of tea. I watched the sunset without a single notification buzzing in my ear. The quiet felt strange, but then, it hit me how much I'd been missing. God's creation—the clouds, the breeze, and even the neighbor's barking dog—felt like gifts I hadn't unwrapped in ages.

That weekend without Wi-Fi gave me something I didn't realize I needed—a reminder to slow down. God's blessings weren't in everything I was doing but in being present, even in stillness.

...

**Lord,**
Help me embrace simplicity, find peace in stillness, and hear Your voice clearly.
Guide my heart to Your presence.
Amen.

...

# Celebrating The Favor of Simplicity

*Simplicity brings clarity, allowing us to focus on what truly matters and embrace God's blessings with gratitude. In the quiet moments, we find His presence, guiding us toward a life of peace and contentment.*

**Now it's your turn to write your story of celebrating The Favor of Simplicity.**

Reflect on a time when simplifying your life brought unexpected joy and clarity. How did this shift affect your relationship with God and others? Consider the ways His favor was revealed in these moments of simplicity and how they enriched your faith journey.

_____

_____

_____

_____

_____

_____

_____

_____

_____

_____

_____

_____

_____

_____

_____

_____

_____

_____

# THE
# FAVOR
## OF
# *Resilience*

Resilience anchored in faith unlocks limitless favor. Embrace challenges as opportunities, trust in God's strength, and watch His promises manifest in your life.

# Strength in Trials

...

## James 1:12 (NIV)

Blessed is the one who perseveres under trial because, having stood the test, that person will receive the crown of life that the Lord has promised to those who love him.

...

In the journey of faith, resilience becomes our anchor. Life may present trials that shake us, but with God, those very trials mold us into warriors of faith. It's like being refined by fire, emerging stronger and more radiant.

Imagine the favor that emerges when you lean into God's strength, trusting Him completely. It's in those moments of perseverance that you tap into His limitless blessings.

Picture this: you're in the midst of a storm, feeling overwhelmed. Yet, it's in that chaos where God whispers His promises. He sees your struggle and He's ready to crown you with His favor as you hold steadfast. Your resilience is not just about enduring; it's about experiencing God's faithfulness manifesting in your life. Each trial becomes a testimony of His grace and power.

When you embrace resilience, you open the door to God's unfathomable favor. It's about seeing challenges as divine opportunities, knowing that every step taken in faith leads to His promises.

This week, as we explore the Favor of Resilience, let your heart be encouraged, knowing that each trial you face is a stepping stone towards victory.

Stay encouraged, for His favor is upon you, and your resilience is the key to unlocking His promises!

...

## Mighty God,

Grant me resilience in trials. Let Your favor shine through as I persevere in faith. Strengthen my heart and guide me towards Your promises.

Amen.

...

# Redeemed in Resilience

Rochelle D. Jacobs

...

**Isaiah 40:31 (NIV)**

But those who hope in the Lord will renew their strength. They will soar on wings like eagles; they will run and not grow weary; they will walk and not be faint.

...

God's favor of resilience is the strength He gives us to persevere through life's trials. In adversity, His favor empowers us to rise, recover, and move forward with hope. Through His grace, we find resilience to stand firm, trusting He is working for our good even in the hardest times.

Resilience is God's gift of inner strength—His favor that helps us bend without breaking, growing stronger in the storms. When we rely on Him, His favor enables us to overcome obstacles and emerge with greater faith and character.

Beloved, your story of resilience is powerful. You've endured painful seasons yet continued to trust in God's grace. Every step forward reflects deep resilience rooted in faith.

After my childhood trauma, everything stable seemed to crumble. The pain of molestation weighed heavily, obscuring hope. Yet, in those darkest moments, I clung to God's promise: "The Lord is close to the brokenhearted and saves those who are crushed in spirit." (Psalm 34:18 NIV).

In time, God's favor of resilience appeared in unexpected ways—a supportive friend, a moment of peace. As I prayed, God renewed my strength, giving me courage to embrace healing. He transformed my silence into a testimony of resilience.

Today, my story, U.N.L.E.A.S.H.E.D. Destiny, testifies to God's favor of resilience. Resilience isn't just surviving; it's allowing God to rebuild your heart and give you strength that shines brighter than the darkness you've endured.

...

Lord,

Grant us strength and healing, empowering us to rise stronger
in faith, embracing Your enduring love and favor.

Amen.

...

# More Than Able

Benecia Ponder

...

**Joshua 1:9 (NIV)**

Be strong and courageous. Do not be frightened, and do not be dismayed, for the Lord your God is with you wherever you go.

...

For months, I wrestled with my new reality—a pseudo brain tumor diagnosis and the loss of my vision. Anger and depression were my constant companions. How could God allow this to happen to me? I found myself on my bedroom floor, caught in a tempest of tears and rage.

"I want my vision back!" I demanded.

The future seemed bleak, success impossible with a severe visual impairment. In the depths of despair, I cried out to God: "Why? What did I do to deserve this?"

His answer came quietly yet undeniably powerful: "Your life is not over. I still have great plans for you."

At that moment, my wailing ceased. Hope and comfort seeped into my soul. I recognized that my focus on loss was shackling me, preventing me from embracing the future.

I prayed for forgiveness and resolved to trust God completely. I shifted my gaze from limitations to the gifts of His protection and provision. With each step, I discovered new strengths, fueled by a divine resilience.

Today, I am living a life without limits, my heart is filled with gratitude. I have learned that life's challenges are not barriers but opportunities to witness God's favor. With His guidance, I have overcome, not despite my disability, but through it. Embracing resilience, I am free, and I am grateful for every moment of this boundless journey.

...

**Heavenly Father,**

I am grateful for Your unwavering strength and support. Please fill me with resilience and perseverance to face and overcome every challenge. Amen.

...

# Dare to Be Different

Dr. Nina Addison

...

### Romans 5:3-4 (AMP)

3: And not only this, but [with joy] let us exult in our sufferings and rejoice in our hardships, knowing that hardship (distress, pressure, trouble) produces patient endurance; 4: and endurance, proven character (spiritual maturity); and proven character, hope and confident assurance [of eternal salvation].

...

It is not easy to be resilient when it seems as if everyone is against you. You may want to cave in, but you know God has told you to stand out and be strong.

When I decided to fully commit to God, I endured backlash from some family and friends. They were used to me being who I was, and accepting who I was becoming was not in their plans. This led to separations, the loss of friends and family, and much more.

Many would not even talk to me; instead, they often talked about me. This was painful. However, glory be to God that now I am the one they call on for prayer and spiritual guidance. I am the one who gives them hope spiritually and naturally. Rejection did not feel good, but while they rejected me, God accepted me!

I could focus on the fact that they may only reach out when they want something spiritual, but I rejoice greatly. They understand I am not one to gossip or fuss and fight. They come to me for the good, and that is more than well with my soul. Glory Hallelujah to God for others seeing Him in me!

...

### Father,

Help me rejoice in change. Strengthen my heart when others turn away. May I accept Your will, find the resilience to thrive, and rest in Your unwavering acceptance.

Amen!

...

# Broken But Not Defeated

Alethia Saunders

...

### 2 Corinthians 4:8-9 (ESV)

We are pressed on every side by troubles, but we are not crushed. We are perplexed, but not driven to despair. We are hunted down, but never abandoned by God.

...

I was getting a divorce... again... It sucked! This was another failed relationship, and all I could do at certain moments was blame myself for it. I felt myself sinking into depression.

Why was this happening to me?

Why couldn't I just get it right?

I knew what happened the last time things were like this, and I kept reminding myself that God loved me and that this setback didn't mean I wasn't worth love.

I found myself on my knees in tearful prayer. Eventually, I realized that if things were going to get better, then I had to get better. I had to push myself through this season to get out on the other side.

I surrounded myself with people who kept me focused and aware. I woke up every day and found a reason to be thankful. If God was with me, who could be against me? I learned from the mistakes I made, was resilient despite my circumstances, and bounced back even better than before.

...

### Lord,

Thank You for Your unwavering love. Grant me strength to rise from setbacks, learn from my past, and embrace each day with hope and gratitude.

Amen.

...

# 1,513 Days

Jacqueline James

...

**Hebrews 10:36 (ESV)**

For you have need of endurance, so that when you have done the will of God you may receive what is promised.

...

Several years ago, my 95-year-old godmother was tricked out of her home by some of her church members and placed in a nursing home.

She had outlived all her family. I was the only person she could rely on, as she had lived alone since her only sister passed away five years earlier. I prepared her meals, cleaned her house, ran errands, and spent three to four nights a week with her. We attended each other's churches and shared a close, loving bond.

Every year, I hosted Thanksgiving, and Momma Jones was always everyone's favorite guest. She would stay the night before with me, but one year, she wasn't home when I arrived to pick her up. Thanksgiving happened without her, and it took me five terrifying days to locate her. She was in a nursing home placed there by her pastor and two church members.

I hired an attorney, which drained my savings, and spent four long years fighting to free her. Of the 1,513 days she was confined, I visited her almost every day. Getting her released proved to be nearly impossible. Those who had taken over her life, along with the nursing home staff, fought me at every turn. I had to get court orders just to bring her meals, take her to dinner once a week, and even to take her to church.

After every setback, I felt angry and defeated. But Momma Jones, always calm, would gently remind me, "Be still and pray for them." She radiated peace and taught me patience and prayer, even in the face of injustice.

...

**Lord,**

Grant us patience, strength, and unshakable faith, trusting Your salvation and peace amid every trial we endure.

Amen.

...

# Celebrating The Favor of Resilience

*Resilience is the steadfast spirit that rises in adversity, a testament to God's unwavering support. Through trials, His favor strengthens us, turning challenges into opportunities for growth and triumph. Embrace resilience as a pathway to His abundant blessings.*

**Now it's your turn to write your story of celebrating The Favor of Resilience.**

Reflect on a time when resilience carried you through a challenging period. How did this strength shape your character and faith? Describe the ways in which God's favor was evident as you persevered and how this experience has influenced your journey and outlook on life.

_____

_____

_____

_____

_____

_____

_____

_____

_____

_____

_____

_____

_____

_____

_____

_____

# THE
# FAVOR
## OF
# *Reset*

God's daily resets offer fresh starts, filled with His renewing mercies and boundless opportunities.

# Fresh Horizons

...

## Lamentations 3:22-23 (NIV)

"Because of the Lord's great love we are not consumed, for his compassions never fail. They are new every morning; great is your faithfulness.

...

Tap into the soul-stirring reality—each day brings fresh horizons and divine resets crafted just for you.

Life, with all its twists and turns, can sometimes feel overwhelming, as if yesterday's burdens are trying to overshadow the promise of today. But here's the radiant truth: each morning, God's love and mercy renew like the dawn, offering us a chance to rewrite our story.

Imagine waking up to the embrace of God's unfailing compassion, a whisper that today is your canvas, untouched and brimming with His endless possibilities. Each sunrise is an invitation from Him to leave behind what was and step boldly into what can be. His faithfulness is like an anchor, steady and strong, reminding us that every day brings a new wave of possibilities.

The concept of a reset is a profound blessing. It's God extending His hand, pulling you from the shadows of past mistakes, and saying, "Let's try this again, my child."

Each day is a testament to His unwavering love and the potential He sees in you. Reflect on how these resets have shaped your path, how they've been moments where God's favor shined brightest in your life.

This week, choose to embrace the Favor of Reset. Let God's boundless opportunities inspire you to forgive, to dream again, and to walk confidently in His love. Celebrate these resets as tokens of His unending grace, and let them propel you into a future filled with His promises.

...

### Gracious God,

Thank You for the gift of fresh horizons and daily mercies. Help me to embrace each new day with a heart full of gratitude and faith.

Amen.

...

# Break It Off

Karen McKinney Holley

...

### John 15:2 (NIV)

He cuts off every branch in me that bears no fruit, while every branch that does bear fruit he prunes[a] so that it will be even more fruitful.

...

A tooth broke. It was the same tooth where I had my first cavity at age 17. I had not felt any pain. The tooth hadn't been loose, and I hadn't bitten down on anything hard—it just broke off.

When I went to the dentist, I was told it could not be repaired and had to be removed because, if it remained, infection would set in. Once it was removed, there was pain from the procedure for a couple of days. At my checkup, I was told that in four months, I could get an implant.

During those four months, how I chewed my food changed. It was slower, more deliberate, to compensate for the missing molar—and my food tasted better.

We can become so used to negative influences in our lives that we don't even recognize they are eating away at us until they break. An argument, a mean comment, a fractured relationship—they all reveal what's been festering under the surface. When God roots them out, there is pain, discomfort, and a sense that something is missing.

We find ourselves having to "chew" what the world presents differently to compensate for what's gone. Instead of criticizing the choir selection, we listen to the words, and they speak to our soul. We're no longer irritated because the closest parking spaces are filled but thank God for the ability to walk, realizing we're even getting a little exercise.

Ask God to remove what's bad in you before infection sets in and rots you.

...

### Lord,

Thank You for the gift of renewal. Remove what hinders our growth and fill us with Your grace. Help us reset, heal, and draw closer to You.

Amen.

...

# Leaning on Faith

Alethia Saunders

...

**Psalm 32:7 (NIV)**

You are my hiding place; you will protect me from
trouble and surround me with songs of deliverance.

...

Florida was all I knew. It's where this long-term relationship began, and I knew if I stayed in it, my life was in danger. If I really wanted to live, I would have to start over.

The day I packed my car with the few garbage bags of clothes I had been secretly filling while my partner was away at work was one of the hardest days of my life. But I trusted God to cover and protect me as He had up to that point.

I cried. Hard. I cried even harder when I crossed the Florida state line into Georgia. I knew this was the direction I needed to go to get the proper reset in my life. God had created a space for fluidity in my day to get out safely. When I arrived, I moved into the apartment I never thought I would be approved for.

As I stepped into my new home, I thanked God for covering me. No more pain, no more abuse, no more distractions. It was me and Him against the enemy. It couldn't get any better than that.

...

**Dear God,**

Thank You for guiding me out of darkness. Help me embrace this new path with courage and faith, knowing You're always by my side.

Amen

...

# The Reset Button

Bonita L. Williams

...

## Ezekiel 36:26 (NIV)

I will give you a new heart and put a new spirit in you.

...

During one of his sermons, Rev. Cameron Alexander, the former Pastor of Antioch Baptist Church North in Atlanta, said, "Just as every vehicle is equipped with a reverse gear to change direction, our lives hold the power to shift course." His words brought to mind the reset button on many devices. When something isn't working properly, pressing reset restores it to its original settings.

We, too, have a reset button—the Word of God. When life feels off track or unrest overwhelms us, God's Word calls us to reset. It urges us to realign our thoughts, actions, and priorities with His will. But resetting isn't always easy. It requires surrendering control, releasing our own desires, and placing full trust in God's plan. Yet in that surrender, we find restoration, guidance, and the ability to walk the path He has set before us—one filled with hope, renewal, and purpose.

But here's the beauty of it—when we press that reset button, we're not just fixing what's broken. We're stepping into the renewal God has prepared for us. Life flows smoother when we're aligned with Him. Take a moment today and ask, where do I need a reset? Be bold. Surrender. And watch Him restore and guide you to something far greater than you imagined.

...

**Lord,**

Guide me through Your Word. Reset my heart, renew my mind, and align my steps with Your will. I surrender all to You.

Amen.

...

# Turnaround Time

Benecia Ponder

...

**Psalm 25:4-5 (NLT)**

Show me the right path, O Lord; point out the road for me to follow. Lead me by your truth and teach me, for you are the God who saves me. All day long I put my hope in you.

...

We were cruising down I-75 South at a steady 60 miles per hour. My mom was at the wheel, and I was alongside her, staring out at the endless stretch of highway. All of a sudden, she said, "I think we're going in the wrong direction."

I expected her to slow down, maybe take the next exit. But she kept driving. Five minutes passed. Then ten. I stared at the signs whizzing by, each one confirming my growing suspicion. We were heading the wrong way. Every instinct in me screamed, "Get off the highway! Turn back!" But I stayed quiet. After all, she was my mom. Who was I to question her?

This was before GPS, before a calm voice could tell us, "Rerouting." It was just us and the road. Finally, after watching mile after mile disappear, I said, " If we're going the wrong way shouldn't we turn around and get directions?"

Isn't life a lot like that? Sometimes we know in our hearts we're off track. Yet, we press on, afraid of turning around, afraid to admit we need a reset. But here's the beauty of God's grace—it's never too late. You can turn around. You can choose a new direction. His love is the ultimate rerouting.

...

**Lord,**

Guide my steps, redirect my path, and thank You for the grace to start anew in Your love.

Amen.

...

# God Provided That Day

Hazel L. Grant

...

**James 1:17**

...

To look for provision and to ask for it can feel like two different things.

I was standing in the checkout line, asking God to make a way for me to complete a meal we were cooking for the homeless that week. Suddenly, there was an immediate answer—from a stranger a few carts behind me.

He said, "God wants you to stop trying to figure out how you're going to rearrange the food in order to purchase the final bread."

In the next moment, he handed me one hundred dollars. Then, as if on cue, a few more shoppers joined in, asking, "Can we help too?"

That moment wasn't just about provision—it was about perspective. I was so focused on what I didn't have that I almost missed God's goodness in motion. His favor surrounds us, often in ways we don't expect, but we must open our eyes to see it.

Sometimes, favor looks like an unexpected gift, but other times, it's a gentle reminder to trust Him fully. When we release the pressure to figure it all out on our own, we make space for His blessings to flow.

...

**Lord,**

reset my perspective today. Open my eyes to see Your goodness in every moment—big and small—and help me trust Your favor at work.

Amen.

...

# Celebrating The Favor of Reset

*Every new day is an opportunity to reset, leaving behind past burdens and embracing God's fresh mercies. In His grace, we find renewed strength and clarity, allowing us to step forward with hope and purpose.*

**Now it's your turn to write your story of celebrating The Favor of Reset.**

Reflect on a time when you embraced a reset in your life. How did this fresh start impact your mindset and journey with God? Describe the ways His favor was evident through this reset and how it has shaped your path forward.

_____

_____

_____

_____

_____

_____

_____

_____

_____

_____

_____

_____

_____

_____

_____

_____

_____

# THE
# FAVOR
## OF
# *Integrity*

Integrity invites God's lasting favor, opening doors to trust, honor, and divine blessings.

# Walk Upright

...

**Proverbs 10:9 (NIV)**
Whoever walks in integrity walks securely, but whoever takes crooked paths will
be found out.

...

Integrity is the glue that holds our character together, even when life tries to
pull us apart. Integrity isn't just about doing the right thing when someone's
watching; it's about living truthfully, even when no one's around. It's about
choosing the path that reflects God's truth and aligning our actions with His
standards, no matter how tempting shortcuts might seem.

Think about it—living with integrity brings a sense of peace and security
that nothing else can match. It's like having an unshakeable foundation in a
world that's constantly shifting. When we choose integrity, we invite God's
favor to rest upon us. It's not just about avoiding crooked paths; it's about
walking the straight and secure road that God lights up for us.

Have you ever noticed how integrity sparks trust? It opens doors to
relationships built on honesty and respect. And trust me, God sees and
honors every choice we make to stand firm in our values. Integrity isn't
just a moral choice; it's a pathway to His blessings and a reflection of His
character in our lives.

So, this week, embrace integrity with open arms. Let it guide you, knowing
that each choice made in truth is a step toward God's favor. As you walk
uprightly, you not only receive His blessings but also become a blessing
to those around you. Celebrate the strength found in living truthfully, and
watch how God's favor flows through every corner of your life.

...

**Righteous God,**
Tthank You for the gift of integrity. Strengthen my resolve to walk upright,
reflecting Your truth and favor in all I do.
Amen.

...

# Ripple Effect

Miya Mills

...

**Psalm 25:21 (NIV)**

May integrity and uprightness protect me, because my hope, Lord, is in you.

. .

I remember the day I stumbled upon something unsettling at work. There were reports being manipulated, numbers twisted to show false success. I felt uneasy. My conscience screamed that I needed to act, but fear gnawed at me. What if I lost my job? Still, I couldn't ignore the truth. Integrity was something I held dear.

I decided to report the discrepancies; aware of the risks. My heart pounded as I approached the administration offices. I felt like I was stepping into the unknown. Yet, there was a sense of calm, almost like a divine hand guiding me, assuring me I was doing the right thing.

The aftermath was tense. For days, whispers filled the hallways. I stayed focused, trusting in the power of honesty. Slowly, change began to ripple through the building. Policies were revised, and transparency became a priority. A culture of integrity started to take root.

Colleagues who once distanced themselves began to understand and respect my decision. Superiors commended my courage. My standing in the school improved, not because I sought it, but because I stayed true to my values.

In the end, I realized that integrity wasn't just about doing the right thing; it was about inspiring others to do the same. I felt a profound sense of peace, knowing that honesty had not only preserved my integrity, but it also transformed the workplace for the better.

...

**Lord,**

Grant me courage to uphold truth, guide my actions with integrity, and inspire change for the good of all in my workplace.

Amen.

...

# No Shortcuts

Sheryl Simms

...

**Proverbs 4:25-27 (ESV)**

Let your eyes look directly forward, and your gaze be straight before you. Ponder the path of your feet; then all your ways will be sure. Do not swerve to the right or to the left; turn your foot away from evil.

...

"Come on, we need to skip those checks, or we'll never make the deadline!"

The words rang in my ears as I stood at the crossroads of a crucial decision. Leading our community project was no small task, and the pressure was mounting. Everyone was exhausted, driven by the ticking clock. But something inside me knew that the easy way wasn't the right way.

I took a deep breath and addressed the team. "I understand the pressure, but if we compromise now, what does that say about us? We owe it to ourselves and the community to do this right."

The room was silent, but soon heads nodded in agreement. We chose integrity over shortcuts, even if it meant a few long nights. It wasn't easy, but watching the team rally together, driven by a shared commitment to honesty, was inspiring.

In the end, the project was a success. Not just because we completed it, but because we did it with integrity. The support and trust we built were priceless. Our journey proved that sticking to your values might not be the fastest route, but it's always the most rewarding. And that, I realized, was the true victory.

...

**Heavenly Father,**

Grant me strength to lead with integrity, guiding my actions with honesty and inspiring others to uphold truth in all endeavors.

Amen.

...

# When The Doors Close

Alethia Saunders

...

### Proverbs 11:3 (NIV)
The integrity of the upright guides them, but the unfaithful are destroyed by their duplicity.

...

I grew up as a Jehovah's Witness. I was always taught that if I just stuck to the religion, I'd be in line for salvation when "the end" came. I found myself in a deep depression, and at some point, I strayed away from religion. The doors ended up closed on me, and this took me further into depression. Still, I never lost my love for God. I would find myself on my hands and knees praying to Him for guidance and mercy.

I couldn't bring myself to associate with any denomination, but I still felt a strong pull towards God. He was my Father and Protector. My integrity was to Him. I could no longer allow myself to be bound to the rules that men set out. I also knew that years of attending religious gatherings didn't automatically qualify me for salvation. I had to develop and nurture my personal relationship with God.

This was the only way. I had to show integrity to Him regardless of what others around me did or did not do. I also could not allow anyone to make me feel like I wasn't worthy of God's love or that He didn't hear my prayers because I didn't do things their way.

Since I've learned to listen to His Word directly, He has protected me in ways that I could have never imagined. I'm blessed beyond measure and forever grateful!

...

### Dear God,
Thank You for Your unwavering protection and love. Grant me the strength to uphold integrity and deepen my faith in You.
Amen.

...

# The Lost Ring

### L. Marie

...

### Proverbs 20:7 (NKJV)

The righteous man walks in his integrity; his children are blessed after him.

...

Years ago, back when I was still working as a nurse, there was a moment that stuck with me. One of my patients, an elderly woman named Mrs. Sullivan, had a wedding ring she treasured. She told me stories about her late husband and how that ring felt like a piece of him she carried everywhere.

One busy morning, while changing her linens, the ring slipped off her bedside table. I didn't notice until later when I saw it glinting under the dresser. It would've been easy to say nothing, to assume someone else would return it, but something tugged at me. I've always believed if you see something wrong, you make it right.

I picked it up, polished it with a tissue, and slipped it back onto her finger as she slept. When she woke up and noticed it, the relief in her eyes nearly brought tears to mine. "Bless you, dear," she whispered, holding my hand tightly.

The reward wasn't the thanks or recognition—it was knowing I'd honored her love and trust. Sometimes, doing the right thing fills your heart more than any thank-you card could. That day reaffirmed for me that integrity always matters.

...

### Lord,

Thank You for guiding my heart. Help me uphold integrity daily, honoring trust and love in all I do.
Amen

...

# Price of Integrity

Benecia Ponder

...

**Psalm 41:12 (NRSV)**

But you have upheld me because of my integrity, and set me in your presence forever.

...

The opportunity was tempting, no doubt about it. A potential client reached out, eager to hire me for a lucrative project—a five-figure paycheck for work that would have significantly bolstered my bank account. For someone juggling the demands of being a coach, author, and speaker, the offer could have seemed like a dream come true. But as we discussed the project, it became clear that taking on this client would require me to compromise on the values and principles I hold dear.

Their approach clashed with my commitment to authenticity, honesty, and the purpose I strive to serve. It wasn't an easy call to make. Turning down such a high fee brought a mix of emotions—fear of losing out and anxiety about what might come next. But I knew this wasn't just a business decision; it was a choice about who I am at my core.

Walking away wasn't the end of the story. Shortly afterward, doors began to open in ways I hadn't anticipated. New opportunities rolled in, each aligned perfectly with my mission. Clients I could wholeheartedly serve showed up, reaffirming my decision to stand in integrity.

Integrity isn't always the easiest path, but it's always the right one. When we choose to honor our principles, even at a cost, we experience God's favor in ways that far outweigh fleeting rewards.

...

**Lord,**

Thank You for guiding me to honor my values. Help me
trust Your favor and salvation in every choice.

Amen.

...

# Celebrating The Favor of Integrity

*Integrity is the cornerstone of a life blessed by God's favor. By living truthfully and honorably, we invite His guidance and blessings into every aspect of our journey, creating a legacy of trust and character.*

**Now it's your turn to write your story of celebrating The Favor of Integrity.**

Reflect on a moment when choosing integrity made a significant impact on your life. How did this decision shape your path and relationships? Consider how God's favor was revealed through your commitment to truth and how it has influenced your faith and character.

_____

_____

_____

_____

_____

_____

_____

_____

_____

_____

_____

_____

_____

_____

_____

_____

_____

_____

# THE
# FAVOR
## OF
## *Connection*

Deepening your connection with God and others unlocks a powerful flow of divine love, unwavering support, and abundant blessings that transform every aspect of your life.

# Stay Plugged In

...

### John 15:5 (NIV)
I am the vine; you are the branches. If you remain in me and I in you, you will bear much fruit; apart from me you can do nothing.

...

In the flow of our daily commitments, the beauty of connection can easily slip through our fingers. Between juggling work, family, and personal aspirations, it often feels like our to-do lists run the show. We rush through the day, ticking off tasks, sometimes forgetting to pause and truly connect with God. Yet, this connection is the very heart of our life's journey.

Jesus' words in John 15:5 remind us that He is the vine, and we are the branches. This profound imagery illustrates that our vitality and purpose stem from our relationship with Him. When we remain in Christ, we tap into an unending source of strength and grace that nourishes our spirits.

Our connection with God is not just a part of life; it is life itself. Without it, we struggle to find true peace and purpose. With it, we have the support and wisdom we need to navigate life's challenges. It's through this bond that we experience real transformation and favor.

Prioritize this divine connection. Make space in your day for moments of reflection, prayer, and worship. Let His words speak to you, infusing your daily life with purpose and direction.

As we embrace the Favor of Connection this week, remember that you are never alone. God's favor is upon you, and His connection is your lifeline. Stay rooted in Him, and watch how fruitfully your life will unfold.

...

### Heavenly Father,
In the midst of life's busyness, draw me closer to You. Help me to remain rooted in Your love and wisdom, trusting in Your guidance every step of the way. Let Your presence be my strength and Your favor be my foundation. Connect my heart to Yours, so I may flourish in Your grace and walk boldly in Your purpose. Thank You for being my vine, the source of all I need. Amen.

...

# Divine Connections Exist

## Dr. Nina Addison

...

### Matthew 6:6 (NIV)

But when you pray, go into your most private room, close the door and pray to your Father who is in secret, and your Father who sees [what is done] in secret will reward you.

...

When it was time to change my life, everything had to change, including many people I was around. My connections needed to change, and I needed God to change them. His grace, mercy, and favor have given me more than I ever imagined!

When I left a relationship that wasn't for me, I had to give all my furniture away and moved back in with my parents for a while. About six months into this new journey, due to divine connections, God changed my address, church home, and even my car!

My now pastor and first lady, who were my friends at the time, took me into their home for a period so I could have a fresh start. They also supported my journey as an entrepreneur and assisted me with finding a new car, as the one I had had broken down.

Their faith rubbed off on me and still does to this day. I was connected to the right people at the right time, and my life continues to advance for the glory of God. His favor continues to go before me, and He continues to give me divine connections.

...

### Daddy God,

connect me to those who strengthen me spiritually and naturally. May I receive connections openly, be a blessing, and reflect Your love.

Amen!

...

# Writing Class

Sibyl F. Cole

...

**Romans 12:4-5 (NIV)**
No matter what, love others, that's the core of any solid relationship.

...

A few years ago, I signed up for a creative writing course at one of the local universities. I sat in the back because I liked observing people. One of the registration requirements was to be prepared to read a writing sample on the first day.

There was a young lady named Donna sitting two rows in front of me. The instructor asked if she'd be willing to read her piece first, and she agreed. Her story was about how she lost her brother to suicide and the overwhelming guilt she felt at failing to recognize his distress. After she finished, the class was silent, and the instructor thanked her as she went back to her seat. Because time had run out, not all students got to read their work and would have to wait until the following week to share.

After class, I approached Donna. "I'm sorry if I'm intruding, but I just wanted to say I understand," I said, and proceeded to tell her how several years had passed since I'd lost my daughter to an extended illness, but that the grief was still suffocating. There was an instant connection between us, so we agreed to meet for coffee the following week and talk more.

It seemed that writing had been a way for both of us to process our grief. Donna and I eventually lost touch, but I can't help but think that sometimes the most random connections are Heaven-sent and are born from the places where we are most vulnerable.

...

**Lord,**
Thank You for the connections born in our pain. Bless those moments of shared vulnerability, and guide us to comfort and understand one another.
Amen.

...

# Premeditated Provision

Dr. Theresa Billingsley

...

**Philippians 4:19 (NKJV)**
And my God shall supply all your needs according to His riches in glory by Christ Jesus.

...

After exploring entrepreneurial ventures, I found myself needing to return to a regular nine-to-five job. Due to my divorce, my ex-husband had removed me from his benefit package. And, since he had been handling all the major household bills, I knew I had to find a job to cover those expenses once he moved out. I was eager to secure a full-time position to manage both my personal bills and those my ex-husband had previously covered.

I prayed about my situation, and Jesus led me to contact a certain person. Interestingly, this individual and I had been at odds. Nevertheless, I followed the guidance and reached out to them. We addressed our past misunderstandings, and during our conversation, the topic of employment arose. They informed me of someone I could contact for a job opportunity.

I was grateful that Jesus orchestrated this connection, as it resulted in both reconciliation and a new job for me. The person they referred me to submitted my resume, and I was offered the job after successfully passing the pre-employment test.

Glory to King Jesus! This truly is undeniable favor on display.

...

**Heavenly Father,**
Thank You for guiding me to reconciliation and new opportunities. Bless me with strength and wisdom for future endeavors.
Amen.

...

# Amazing Touch

Cynthia Beckles

...

**Matthew 5:16 (NIV)**

In the same way, let your light shine before others, that they may see your good
deeds and glorify your Father in heaven.

...

Volunteering with the Weekend Volunteers was a cherished tradition. One
Saturday, we visited a senior citizens' home to play Bingo. Each time
someone won, happiness erupted. We stayed for hours, laughing and
cheering together, feeling a wonderful sense of community. As we spent time
with the residents, I realized that these small moments of joy held far more
significance than I'd initially understood. It wasn't just about the game—it
was about the connections we built and the difference we made in their lives.

On another visit, we sang for a different group of senior citizens. When
we entered the room, there was silence. The residents sat quietly, their
faces emotionless as we sang gospel songs. There was no response—just
a deep stillness that enveloped the room. But we kept going, hoping to lift
their spirits. When we sang "Amazing Grace," something changed. I saw
silent tears streaming down their faces. Though they didn't speak, their
hearts had heard us.

That experience taught me that the heart never forgets. While we didn't
know their stories, God did. Their tears reminded me that God hears our
prayers, even when unspoken. Acts of kindness don't always require a grand
response. Sometimes, a simple touch or song is enough. As Christ once
asked, "Who touched me?" it's not the number of people we reach, but the
sincerity of our actions that matters. Every small act of kindness creates a
ripple, reminding us that joy, love, and connection are always within reach.

...

**Lord,**

Thank You for the joy of connection and the power of kindness. Guide us to
spread love in every moment.

Amen.

...

# Relationship Over Religion

Bonita L. Williams

...

### John 3:16 (NIV)

For God so loved the world that he gave his one and only Son, that whoever believes in him shall not perish but have eternal life.

...

Religion comes in many forms—Baptist, Catholic, Methodist, and beyond. Yet, at its heart, faith isn't about religion. It's about a personal relationship with God. Too often, people pour themselves into traditions, rituals, and rules while missing this profound truth.

Here's the heart of it—God doesn't seek religious practices. What He desires most is a relationship with us. It's not about attending church, singing in the choir, or performing good deeds. Salvation rests in accepting Jesus Christ as your Savior. His death and resurrection weren't for religion but to restore our relationship with Him.

The powerful story of the two thieves on the cross shows this clearly. Neither man was tied to a particular religion. Yet, one thief recognized Jesus' divinity and asked to be saved. Without rituals or religious works, Jesus assured him a place in paradise. Why? Because salvation comes through faith, not activities.

This challenges us to move beyond checking off religious tasks. Sitting in church or memorizing scripture doesn't secure heaven. Salvation is not inherited or earned through "doing." It's God's gift to those who believe and receive Him. When we choose relationship over religion we experience the love and grace God longs to share.

...

**Lord,**
Draw me closer to You. Help me cherish our relationship and live in Your love, grace, and purpose.
Amen.

...

# Celebrating The Favor of Connection

Connection is a divine gift, weaving our lives together with love, support, and shared purpose. In each relationship, we experience God's favor, enriching our journey and drawing us closer to His heart.

**Now it's your turn to write your story of celebrating The Favor of Connection.**

Reflect on a meaningful connection that has greatly impacted your life. How has this relationship deepened your understanding of God's love and favor? Consider the ways this connection has supported your spiritual growth and how it continues to influence your journey.

_____

_____

_____

_____

_____

_____

_____

_____

_____

_____

_____

_____

_____

_____

_____

_____

_____

_____

_____

# THE
# FAVOR
## OF

## Learning Through Failure

Failures are stepping stones to greater favor, teaching lessons that build character and resilience.

# Rise Again

**Proverbs 24:16 (NIV)**
"For though the righteous fall seven times, they rise again,
but the wicked stumble when calamity strikes.

...

Failure can often feel like a heavy weight, an unwelcome guest that overstays its visit. But let's shift our perspective a bit—what if failure is not a setback, but a setup for something greater?

Proverbs 24:16 reminds us that the righteous may fall multiple times, yet they rise again. This verse is a testament to resilience, a divine promise that God's favor thrives even in our lowest moments.

Has there ever been a time in your life when you stumbled? It might have been a career hurdle, a personal challenge, or a dream deferred. While in it, the pain was real, but think about what came after. Did it lead to unexpected growth? Maybe it opened doors you never considered or taught you lessons that shaped who you are today. Each of these experiences is a stepping stone toward God's favor.

Failures refine us, teaching us humility and perseverance. They are moments where God whispers, "I am not finished with you yet." These trials build our character, preparing us for the blessings to come.

This week, I encourage you to view past failures through the lens of growth. Celebrate the strength you've gained and the journey you've traveled. God's favor is not absent in failure; it's actively working to prepare us for the future He envisions.

Remember, you are not defined by your falls, but by your rises. Embrace each failure as an opportunity to learn and trust that God's favor is guiding you toward greater things.

...

**Merciful Father,**
Teach me to find strength and wisdom in failure. Let Your favor guide my growth.
Amen.

...

# Despair Meets Transformation

Dr. Katherine E. James

...

**Luke 1:37 (NLT)**
For the word of God will never fail.

...

Have you ever made a major investment into a program, system, technology, or experience that you believed to be the answer to your next step, only to discover—after much effort to accompany the investment—that it was, in effect, a monumental failure?

I have.

I retired from my easy, sufficiently paying, cushy job of thirty-six years and entered the foreign land of this radical kind of entrepreneurship. It was an ill-fitting nightmare where I was a desperate misfit. All my life, I fit in. Why would my Abba instruct me to leave guaranteed success to experience colossal failure?

I tried to follow the model set before me. I tried to complete the modules. I tried to fit into a mindset that my soul utterly revolted against. Did I make a mistake by leaving? Did I hear from Abba, or did I make it up? Do I have what it takes to make it in this business? Am I enough for this venture?

This journey of colossal failure began in July 2020, in the heart of the pandemic, and ended in March 2022 when I accepted the truth. Poppa invited me to failure so that I could learn what was only available from being so desperate, afraid, and miserable that surrendering to failure was the only avenue to inner peace.

What if Poppa is inviting you to failure to be gifted with unparalleled growth? Would you be willing to experience colossal failure in exchange for transformation?

...

**Lord,**
Thank You for transforming failure into wisdom. Teach us to find peace in struggles, trust Your plan, and grow through every challenge You lovingly allow. Amen.

...

# From Failure to Favor

Dr. Theresa Billingsley

...

### Luke 7:47 (TPT)

She has been forgiven of all her many sins. This is why she has shown me such extravagant love. But those who assume they have very little to be forgiven, will love me very little.

...

In our everyday lives, failure often touches the roles we hold dear. I vividly recall feeling like a failure in my youth, unable to meet my mother's expectations. Later, as a spouse, I faced the collapse of a marriage, and as a parent, I wondered if I'd ever truly understood my children's needs. As a preacher, there were moments I felt I hadn't conveyed the Word as powerfully as I wished, and as an entrepreneur, financial setbacks shadowed my dreams.

Failure settled on my shoulders like an unwelcome burden, convincing me it was the essence of my identity. It whispered in my ear that I was inadequate, leading me to internalize each misstep. This weight can be crippling, and the fear of repeating past mistakes often paralyzes us, keeping us from trying again. The enemy uses this insidious strategy, turning our thoughts against us, stirring self-doubt, and fostering a relentless cycle of torment.

Yet, in the depths of my despair, a revelation sparked hope. Failure, I realized, is not the end but a powerful teacher. It does not define our worth. When faced with setbacks, instead of retreating into shame, I learned to run to Jesus, embracing His grace and strength. In His presence, I found the courage to transform failure into favor. No longer do I allow past mistakes to bind me; instead, I bring them to my Savior, who turns my trials into triumphs.

...

### Heavenly Father,

Grant me the strength and wisdom to embrace failures as lessons. Guide me to seek Your presence, transforming my setbacks into growth and renewed purpose through faith.

Amen.

...

# Falling Forward

Alethia Saunders

...

**Proverbs 24:16 (NIV)**
For though the righteous fall seven times, they rise again,
but the wicked stumble when calamity strikes.

...

I was getting divorced. The vows that once felt unbreakable—"until death do us part"—now felt like they were shattering before my eyes. The pain was overwhelming. It wasn't just the sorrow of losing my partner, but the deep sense of disappointment in myself and the situation. I couldn't help but ask: How did I end up here?

But through the pain of failure, God began to teach me powerful lessons. I learned the importance of never settling. It's easy to fall into the trap of thinking you have to accept something less than God's best for your life, but He has so much more in store for us. Settling may feel safe in the moment, but it robs us of the fullness that God promises.

God also taught me to take my time. We live in a world that pressures us to rush into relationships, settle for temporary fixes, or move on too quickly. But healing takes time. God wants to heal us from the inside out, and that can't be rushed. Give yourself grace. Healing isn't linear. There will be good days and bad, and in each of those moments, you can choose to lean into God's love and allow Him to rebuild what's broken.

Lastly, I learned to be honest with myself. In the midst of heartache, God was teaching me that it's okay to admit where I was, to own my pain, and to seek healing without pretending it's all okay.

Through this journey, God showed me that failure doesn't have to define us. Healing does.

...

**Lord,**
Thank You for using my failures to teach me and guide me. Help me trust Your plan, find healing in Your love, and grow in grace.
Amen.

253

# ...Good from Bad
Karen McKinney Holley

···

**Genesis 50:20 (NIV)**
You intended to harm me, but God intended it for good to
accomplish what is now being done, the saving of many lives.

···

When I think about Joseph's life, it remains one of my favorite biblical biographies. Everywhere he turned, it seemed like he was getting a raw deal. It's tough when your family members—the people you expect to love you no matter what—betray you. Being punished for a false accusation is heartbreaking. People not keeping their word? That only adds insult to injury.

Yet through it all, Joseph never complained; he simply kept doing his best.

My grandson had a fight at school. The camera showed him attacking another student, so there was no denying what he did. I am not excusing his actions; he absolutely handled the situation the wrong way. However, I'm frustrated that the victim, who had been verbally bullying my grandson for a long time, received no reprimand. This bullying had been reported to the authorities before the fight, but nothing was done.

My grandson was removed from school and sent to alternative learning. Traditionally, this would have meant going to another location with other students who violated the rules. Today, however, it means he has to attend classes virtually. Surprisingly, this has turned out to be better for him. Classes he had been struggling with before, he is now excelling in.

God is so gracious. Even when we mess up, and even when life seems unfair, His faithfulness remains. When we repent, He not only forgives us but uses our experiences—both our failures and hardships—to grow us and align us with His purpose.

···

**Lord,**
Thank You for teaching us through our failures. Help us trust in Your plans and grow from every trial, knowing Your grace turns setbacks into stepping stones.
Amen.

···

# Frozen Moment

Benecia Ponder

...

### Romans 5:3-4 (GNT)

We also boast of our troubles, because we know that trouble produces endurance, endurance brings God's approval, and his approval creates hope.

...

I remember it like it was yesterday. I had applied for a marketing position I was certain was my perfect fit. My qualifications were strong, my resume polished, and the interview started like a dream. There was instant connection, genuine laughter, and the kind of rapport that made me feel at ease. The hiring manager even commented, "I can already tell you're a great fit."

But then came the situational question. "What would you do if this scenario occurred?"

I had an answer. A good one! But when I opened my mouth, the words wouldn't come. My carefully thought-out response suddenly felt tangled, stuck somewhere between my head and my lips. I stammered through a jumbled attempt, feeling confidence slipping through my fingers. I knew, in that moment, my shot had been lost. Sure enough, I didn't get the job.

At first, I was crushed. I kept replaying the moment, wishing I had just spoken up with clarity and confidence. But in the stillness of my reflection, God revealed a powerful truth. That disappointment wasn't the end—it was a lesson. I learned the importance of owning my voice, speaking boldly, and trusting that what I have to say matters.

Today, that lesson carries me in every area of life. Failure isn't final. It's often the doorway to divine growth. That's the favor of failure—it shapes us, strengthens us, and prepares us for what's ahead.

...

Lord,

Thank You for using my failures to guide me. Help me trust Your grace and walk boldly in Your plan for me.

...

# Celebrating The Favor of Learning Through Failure

*In failure, we find life's greatest teachers, guiding us toward growth and transformation. Embrace each setback as a stepping stone, where God's favor turns mistakes into valuable lessons, strengthening your journey and deepening your faith.*

**Now it's your turn to write your story of celebrating The Favor of Learning Through Failure.**

Reflect on a failure that taught you an important lesson and propelled you forward. How did this experience change your perspective and enhance your faith? Describe how God's favor was evident through this learning process and how it continues to shape your journey.

# THE
# FAVOR
## OF

## Sharing Your Story

Through our stories, God's favor
shines, transforming lives, uplifting
faith, and reflecting His glory in
every shared word.

# Testimony of Favor

...

**Revelation 12:11 (NIV)**
They triumphed over him by the blood of the Lamb and by the word of their testimony.

...

Your story is more than a series of events—it is a reflection of God's favor, a living testimony of His faithfulness. Every moment He carried you, every prayer He answered, every valley He walked you through—it all paints a picture of His goodness.

Think about it. When we share our stories, it's like lighting a candle in the darkness. Each testimony radiates hope, a glimmer of light for those walking through their own valleys. It's a reminder that God is still at work, weaving beauty from brokenness, victory from struggle. Your experience becomes a spark, igniting faith in others and pointing them to the God who never fails.

Sharing your story might feel daunting. Maybe you wonder if it's enough, if it even matters. But remember, God doesn't call us to perfection; He calls us to obedience. Your story, no matter how small it seems, holds the power to transform hearts. It's a vessel He uses to pour out His favor—for you and for those who hear it.

This week, consider the story God is writing in your life. Open your heart, speak boldly, and watch how God's grace flows through your testimony, bringing His light into the lives of others.

...

**Lord,**
Thank You for my story. Give me courage to share it with love
and boldness, so Your light may touch and transform lives.
Amen.

...

# Turning Trauma into Testimony

Rochelle D. Jacobs

...

### Mark 5:19 (NIV)

Go home to your own people and tell them how much the
Lord has done for you, and how he has had mercy on you.

...

For so long, I carried a heavy burden. It was like a weight pressing on my chest, making it hard to breathe, hard to speak, hard to be.

Sexual molestation by a friend's brother had left me feeling isolated and afraid. I remember the shame, the confusion, the way the world suddenly felt unfamiliar. For years, I thought silence was my only option—a shield against reliving that night. If I didn't say it out loud, maybe I could pretend it hadn't happened. Maybe the pain would disappear. But it didn't.

I prayed, asking for strength I didn't yet feel and for hope I couldn't yet see. I prayed not just for myself, but for others like me—for the countless people carrying their own heavy burdens in silence.

And then, one day, I found the courage to act. I wrote down my story. Every word felt like releasing a brick from my chest. Writing was both terrifying and freeing. It forced me to confront the pain, but it also gave me a way to rise above it.

That simple act—putting pen to paper—became a turning point. It was no longer just a story of trauma. It became a testimony of resilience. Sharing my story didn't just open the door to my own healing; it invited others to step into the light, too. Healing doesn't happen in isolation. It happens through connection, through faith, and through trusting that God can transform even the darkest pain into something redemptive. My silence is gone now, replaced by a voice that says, "You're not alone. There is hope."

...

**Lord,**

Thank You for turning my pain into purpose. Guide me to
share my story with strength, love, and healing.

Amen.

...

# Is Silence Golden?

Dr. Theresa Billingsley

...

**Exodus 14:14 (KJV)**
The LORD shall fight for you, and ye shall hold your peace.

...

Many people suffer in silence, believing it's the godly way to handle pain. The enemy often traps our minds, emotions, and will in shame—especially from things done to us as children. You stay silent, afraid to speak out, but your actions reveal the hidden hurt. Is that productive? Is it God's way? Is it emotionally healthy? No, it's not. Suffering in silence does not bring healing, wholeness, or reconciliation.

I understand that as a child, fear or threats may have forced you into silence. If that's the case, seeking counseling or confiding in someone you trust can be crucial. Sometimes, it might even mean going to the authorities.

"Hold your peace" doesn't mean staying quiet—it means holding onto the peace God has for you. I remember something that happened to me as a child. It scared me and brought so much shame that I buried it deep. But suppressing it didn't heal me. Years later, it resurfaced, damaging relationships and causing mistrust. For over 20 years, I carried that pain until I finally broke my silence.

When I shared my story in a safe space, it felt like a weight was lifted from my heart. Relationships were restored, and even my body began to heal from the years of stress I had held in.

If you're carrying similar burdens, break the silence. Find a safe place, like therapy or a trusted confidant. God has your back—you don't need to fear. True freedom and healing await.

...

**Lord,**
Grant me courage to break the silence, healing for my soul, and freedom from shame. Help me trust Your love and find peace in Your unfailing support.
Amen.

...

# Messy but Beautiful

Miya Mills

...

## Hebrews 10:24-25 (NIV)

And let us consider how we may spur one another on toward love and good deeds, not giving up meeting together, as some are in the habit of doing, but encouraging one another—and all the more as you see the Day approaching.

...

For years, I thought my story was too messy to share. Who would even care? Wouldn't they just judge me?

One afternoon, I was at lunch with a few close friends. We'd hardly touched our food because the conversation had gotten deep, as it often does when real life gets involved. Jen leaned in and asked, "What's been on your heart lately?"

I froze, my fork hovering mid-air. Everything inside me screamed to change the subject, to keep the walls up. But then, a small voice whispered, "It's time." My heart raced. I swallowed hard and began.

I told them how God met me in my darkest moments, how He stayed even when I thought I was too broken for grace. I shared how tiny steps of faith and raw, unpolished prayers brought light back into my world. My voice trembled, but they didn't interrupt or look away. They listened.

When I finished, my friend Abby reached across the table and grabbed my hand. Tears welled in her eyes. "I thought I was the only one," she said softly. "You don't know what this means to me."

Walking away from that table, something clicked. My messy story wasn't a burden—it was a gift. Sharing it brought hope to my friend, and it left me lighter, too.

....

**Lord,**

Give me courage to share my story, spreading hope and healing. Use my words to bless others and reveal Your light.

Amen.

...

# My Imperfect Loaf

Veronica Washington

...

**Psalm 107:2 (NIV)**
Let the redeemed of the Lord tell their story—those he redeemed from the hand of the foe.

...

I swore I'd never join another church group after The Banana Bread Incident. It involved my lopsided loaf, the first lady's overly honest critique (clearly, she thought she was a judge on some baking show), and me fighting the urge to throw my apron straight into the trash.

But the next Sunday, our pastor said something during his sermon that hit me right in the gut. "Your story—however messy, imperfect, or half-baked—might be exactly what someone else needs to hear."

I couldn't shake it. It was like a nudge that became a shove. Me? Tell my story? My story wasn't a sunny, magazine-cover masterpiece. It was more like a coffee-stained journal with plenty of scratched-out mistakes.

Still, I found myself at the midweek women's gathering, awkwardly agreeing to share. My voice shook, and I laughed more than I'd like to admit, but I told them about the year my life fell apart. I lost my job, doubted God, and felt completely lost. But I also shared the little miracles—how friends showed up, how needs were met in the weirdest ways, and how I eventually found the right job at the right time.

I braced for awkward silence, but instead—I saw nods. People wiped tears. Women came up afterward to tell me my story was their story too. That's when it hit me. Sharing wasn't about being perfect; it was about showing others they're not alone.

...

**Lord,**
Give me the courage to share my story, that it may bring
hope, healing, and connection to those who hear.
Amen.

# Not Alone Anymore

Amanda Blake

...

### John 1:5 (NIV)
The light shines in the darkness, and the darkness has not overcome it.

...

We sat on a worn picnic bench, watching the kids on the swings. The day was beautiful, but my friend didn't seem to notice. Normally, she was the one laughing or cracking jokes, but today she stared at the ground, picking at her nails.

"Hey," I asked, "You okay? You're not yourself."

"Not really. Things at home have been... hard. I feel like I can't keep it all together anymore," she admitted.

Her words hit me. I hesitated but then said, "You're not alone in this. Believe it or not, I've been there too."

Her eyes widened. "You? Really?"

I nodded. "A few years ago, I went through a really dark time. I didn't tell anyone because I was ashamed, but I wish I had. It was then I saw how God can show up when you feel like you've hit rock bottom. I didn't feel it right away, but looking back, I see how He carried me."

Her eyes welled up, and she smiled faintly. "I had no idea. But hearing that... I feel like I can breathe again. Like I'm not alone."

We didn't talk much after that, just watched the kids play. But something shifted. The heaviness hanging over her—and maybe over me too—lifted a little. It wasn't much, but it was enough.

...

### Lord,
Give me the courage to share my story, so Your light shines through.

Amen.

...

# Celebrating The Favor of Sharing Your Story

*When we open our hearts and share our stories, something miraculous happens. The act of sharing is an act of trust, bravery, and vulnerability. It's letting the light of God's work in your life shine for others, and when His light shines through you, it has the power to illuminate someone else's path.*

**Now it's your turn to celebrate The Favor of Sharing Your Story.**

Think about your story—your moments of struggle, redemption, and joy. What chapter of your life shows God's hand most clearly? How has sharing that story brought you closer to Him and to others?

# THE
# FAVOR
# OF
# Abundance

God's favor brings overflowing
abundance, enriching our lives
beyond measure.

# Overflowing Blessings

...

### John 10:10 (NIV)

The thief comes only to steal and kill and destroy; I have
come that they may have life, and have it to the full.

...

Imagine living each day with an awareness of the abundance that surrounds you—a life where every moment is infused with purpose and joy.

This is what Jesus promises us in John 10:10, where He assures us of a life brimming with His blessings. And, these blessings aren't just about tangible gifts; they include the depth of love, the comfort of peace, and the assurance of His presence in every aspect of our lives.

Often, we find ourselves caught up in what we don't have, overlooking the countless blessings we receive daily.

Yet, God's abundance is evident in the beauty of nature, the warmth of a friend's smile, and the peace that calms our worries. By shifting our focus to these blessings, we open ourselves to recognizing the fullness of life that God grants us.

This week, as we celebrate the Favor of Abundance, choose to live with a heart wide open, ready to receive the boundless blessings God has prepared for you. Each day, take a moment to reflect on the gifts that come your way. By focusing on His endless grace, you can experience life in its richest form, knowing you are cherished and provided for beyond measure..

...

### Heavenly Father,

Thank You for the abundance You pour into our lives. Open our eyes to see Your blessings each day. Guide us to live with grateful hearts, always mindful of Your favor. Help us to embrace and celebrate Your gifts, trusting in Your perfect provision. In Jesus' name, Amen.

...

# Blessings Keep Flowing

Adrienne Y. Murphy

...

### Zechariah 8:12 (AMP)

For there the seed will produce peace and prosperity; the vine will yield its fruit, and the ground will produce its increase, and the heavens will give their dew. And I will cause the remnant of this people to inherit and possess all these things.

...

My husband dedicated twenty-four years to the United States Navy. He upheld My husband dedicated twenty-four years to the United States Navy. He upheld his oath with honor and retired with distinction. Together, we built a life of stability and joy, both holding steady jobs that allowed us to support our family and indulge in life's pleasures. Then, the pandemic struck, and I lost my job. Within a year, my husband was diagnosed with cancer, and shortly after, he passed away, leaving me with a limited income.

The Murphys, once celebrated as "relationship goals" by friends and family, now faced an uncertain future. Yet, our journey was not without hope. After losing my job, I chose to leverage my skills and experience to create my own employment. It was a leap of faith, and I was uncertain if it would sustain my lifestyle. However, I soon learned that God's favor can manifest in profound ways.

God favored my husband by bringing him peace. I discovered resources I never anticipated, including new income streams from my business. As a surviving military spouse, I became eligible for various support programs. These unexpected blessings poured in, just when I needed them most, transforming scarcity into abundance.

Through this journey, I've come to understand the presence of abundant favor in my life. God supplies not just our needs, but showers us with abundance from places we never imagined.

...

### Heavenly Father,

Thank You for Your favor of abundance, supplying every need
and blessing us in unexpected ways.

Amen.

# ...More Than Enough

Janice White

...

**Philippians 4:19 (NIV)**
And my God will meet all your needs according to the
riches of his glory in Christ Jesus. Amen

...

I didn't have the rent money. I was two months behind, and I didn't foresee any way to get caught up. I had one month's rent in my bank account, but of course, they wouldn't accept it.

I didn't have any family I could ask for a loan, and I knew all of my associates were struggling. I remember driving around in my car, praying for a miracle. I didn't want to lose my place. I couldn't lose it. I had worked so hard, and it just seemed like the timing was all off. I told God I was tired, but that I wanted to keep pushing because I couldn't give up now.

That's when the phone call came through. One of my previous clients told me she had referred me to her sister, and that she was ready to pay for her service in full.

An hour later, we were on the phone discussing her contract. Within minutes of the discussion, I sent her the contract, she paid in full, and I was scurrying to the store to get a money order. Not only was I able to get caught up on rent, but I was also able to pay ahead a month as well.

This was a miracle indeed! I cried and thanked God as I walked back into my apartment from the leasing office. He provided me with what I needed, plus some!

...

**Lord,**
Thank You for Your timely provision and unending grace. Help me trust You in
every trial, knowing You will always provide more than enough.
Amen.

...

# Abundance Is My Birthright

Dr. Katherine E. James

...

## 2 Corinthians 9:8 (NIV)

And God is able to bless you abundantly, so that in all things at all times, having all that you need, you will abound in every good work.

...

It's been said that a scarcity mindset is a way of thinking characterized by a focus on what you don't have enough of and a belief that you'll never have what you want. What does this have to do with abundance? EVERYTHING. A scarcity mindset was the mountainous divide that stopped me from my birthright of abundant living for years.

Growing up as a Black girl in Detroit during the '60s was rough, particularly because the major media streams didn't offer us much in the way of possibilities for becoming. Their primary messages fostered in me a sense of powerlessness, limitation, being wrong, and feeling unsafe. Abundance was completely unknown to me, except for the love of my family. Thank God for this. Their love was my saving grace that shielded me from also concluding that I was unlovable.

It took decades before I became acquainted with abundant thinking. It wasn't until November 2019 that I heard the phrase, "Abundance is Our Birthright." Like John leapt in Elizabeth's womb when he met Jesus in Mary's womb, my soul leapt in resonation with the truth. My mind didn't know this truth, but my soul was intimately familiar with it. I became my own early adopter. Today, I live in the overflowing blessings of this truth that not only is abundance my birthright, but so is freedom. I now live an abundantly free life to do what I have never done, see what I have never seen, go where I have never gone, and be and have what I never imagined possible.

...

**Lord,**

I thank You for awakening my heart to abundance. Empower me to release fear, trust in Your provision, and walk boldly in the freedom of unlimited blessings. Amen.

...

# Ours For The Asking

Bonita L. Williams

...

### Romans 10:9-10 (NLT)

If you openly declare that Jesus is Lord and believe in your heart that God raised him from the dead, you will be saved. For it is by believing in your heart that you are made right with God, and it is by openly declaring your faith that you are saved.

...

Occasionally, I receive announcements claiming I am the "lucky" recipient of a wonderful offer, seemingly with no strings attached. However, upon closer inspection, there's always a catch: the offer is only free for a limited time, followed by a regular fee. Many have experienced this, as advertising agencies constantly work to convince us something is free or affordable. With so many gimmicks, it's no wonder offers are met with skepticism.

The Bible speaks of the gift of Salvation, yet some dismiss it as just another scheme. Phrases like "Nothing in life is free," "You have to work for what you get," and "I'll just work my way into heaven" reflect common misconceptions. Some plan to come to Christ only when they "get themselves together," rather than accepting the gift of Salvation that Jesus Christ offers.

Believers in Christ have the opportunity to share the truth of God's word: Salvation is indeed free. Christ saved us, and there's nothing we can do to save ourselves. By lifting Jesus up, we allow Him to draw others to Him. Let your actions and deeds demonstrate that there is something truly free for the asking. Help others understand that Salvation is a gift from God, not earned or deserved. It has already been paid for by Christ's sacrifice, available to anyone who seeks it. Share this good news: Salvation is a divine gift, freely offered to us all.

...

### Dear Lord,

I humbly thank You for Your abundant favor and the precious gift of Salvation. May I always cherish and share this free grace with others.
Amen.

...

# Beyond Words

Ebonie T. Pritchett

...

### Hebrews 10:24-25 (NIV)

And let us consider how to stir up one another to love and good works, not neglecting to meet together, as is the habit of some, but encouraging one another, and all the more as you see the Day drawing near.

...

In 8th grade, my world was shaken by my parents' divorce. Their struggles left little room for me. My father, driven by his own unmet dreams, pushed me to excel in school. But his harsh tone often left me feeling like I wasn't enough. Over time, I've come to see that encouragement is as vital as the air we breathe. John Maxwell said it best, "Encouragement is oxygen to the soul."

Life has taught me that constructive feedback, like medicine, helps us grow—when given in the right amount. Too much criticism, like medicine taken in excess, can harm instead of heal. Our world seems flooded with criticism and starved for encouragement.

There's a story in Acts about Paul and Silas, who, after being unjustly imprisoned, visited a believer named Lydia before leaving Philippi. The Bible doesn't give many details, but the message is clear. Paul later wrote in 1 Thessalonians 5:11, "Encourage one another and build each other up." This wasn't just advice—it was a directive to empower each other with words that strengthen weary hearts.

Every person carries unseen battles. Your encouragement might be the light they need. When given sincerely, there's no such thing as too much. Make it a mission—find ways to uplift those around you.

Looking back on my father's efforts, I realize something profound. Even in his flawed way, he never stopped trying to encourage me. And his message lives on.

...

**Lord,**

Thank You for filling my life with abundance—of grace, strength, and love—to overcome challenges and uplift others Amen.

...

# Celebrating The Favor of Abundance

*God's abundance overflows in every aspect of our lives, a testament to His limitless grace and generosity. Open your heart to His blessings, knowing that His favor provides more than you can ask or imagine, enriching your journey with joy and fulfillment.*

**Now it's your turn to write your story of celebrating The Favor of Abundance.**

Reflect on a moment when you felt overwhelmed by God's abundant blessings. How did this experience shape your gratitude and perspective on life? Describe how His favor was evident in these moments of abundance and how it has inspired you to share His blessings with others.

_____

_____

_____

_____

_____

_____

_____

_____

_____

_____

_____

_____

_____

_____

_____

_____

_____

_____

# THE
# FAVOR
## OF
# *Dreaming*

Dream boldly, for God's visions illuminate the path to favor, inspiring courageous action and aligning us with His divine plans.

# Inspired Visions

...

## Joel 2:28 (NIV)

"And afterward, I will pour out my Spirit on all people. Your sons and daughters will prophesy, your old men will dream dreams, your young men will see visions.

...

Have you ever paused to ask yourself what dreams God has sown into your heart?

Joel 2:28 promises that God will pour out His Spirit, gifting us with dreams that are more than mere aspirations—they are divine blueprints for your life's purpose. These dreams are sacred expressions of God's favor, inviting you to explore paths filled with potential and meaning. As you embrace these visions, you're not just moving towards personal growth, but aligning with a greater plan designed by God Himself.

Consider these dreams as God's whispers of encouragement, propelling you towards a future rich in His favor and purpose. Let them inspire you to take bold and courageous steps, trusting that each action brings you closer to living out His divine intentions for your life.

Recognize that the dreams God gives you are not just personal ambitions, but opportunities to collaborate with Him in bringing His plans to fruition.

This week, lean into the Favor of Dreaming. Nurture the dreams God has sown into your heart with prayer, faith, and perseverance, knowing that each step you take is a step towards realizing God's favor in your life. Embrace the journey, and allow your dreams to be a testament to God's loving guidance and provision.

...

### Dear God,

Inspire my heart to dream boldly. Let my dreams reflect Your will and guide me to Your favor. Help me to nurture these dreams with faith and courage, trusting in Your perfect plan for my life.

Amen.

...

# Sacred Collaboration

## Dr. Katherine E. James

...

### 2 Timothy 1:7 (KJV)

For God hath not given us the spirit of fear; but of power, and of love, and of a sound mind.

...

In the latter part of 2021, Poppa invited me to a co-creative experience. My part was to present myself for prayer and meditation daily at our appointed time. His part was to give me a vision of what was to come. It was a palpable experience. My spiritual and natural senses were all employed.

His intention of manifestation was the creation of The Self-Love Queen's Adventure, where women come together for the purposes of:

- Cultivating deep love for all her parts
- Honoring her soul's cry courageously
- Experiencing jubilance with sister interactions
- Building muscles to celebrate her
- Gaining tools to sustain the transformation

This is the product of a co-creative experience between Poppa and me. Poppa's instructions to me were to gather a small group of women, four times a year, travel all over the world to locations where my hand has touched, and create a sisterhood atmosphere filled with Love, Freedom, Jubilation, and Transformation.

In my youth, I yielded dreaming to scarcity. In my latter years, Poppa redeemed and restored. In 2025, we will host our fourth and fifth Self-Love Queen's Adventures.

Beloved, please dare to dream. There is a birthing in you that only you can bring. Invite Poppa to your own co-creative dance. I am in great anticipation of the manifestation of your co-collaboration with the Creator of the Universe.

...

**Lord,**

I thank You for restoring my dreams. Grant me the courage to dream boldly, the faith to trust Your vision, and the joy to see it come alive.

Amen.

# Dreams Come Home

### Stacey Collins

...

### Song of Solomon 3:4 (NIV)
I have found the one whom my soul loves.

...

Like every little girl, I dreamed of becoming a bride, beautiful in my white wedding gown, walking down the aisle to meet my handsome groom. Seeing "HOME" in that unforgettable moment where eyes and two hearts connect as one. I've always been a dreamer. I love a great love story—in books, in movies, in relationships around me—Hallmark are my go-to! As a small girl in church, I'd watch men wrap their arms around their wives, turning to smile at them. In those moments, I knew things were okay. I could see the love and trust in their eyes.

In kindergarten, when the teacher asked, "What do you want to be when you grow up?" this little shy girl with big blue eyes wiggled and squirmed, raising her hand excitedly. "A housewife!" I spoke out with confidence! Then on New Year's Eve in 1991, I met my husband—his sister had been praying for him to meet his wife, and there I was at his home when he returned at 3 a.m. Talk about a dream fulfilled!

Now, 30+ years later, I've been blessed with an incredible husband, home, and family expanding in love. I think back to that tiny girl calling out "housewife." Everything else is a bonus, a blessing. Hold onto your dreams. Don't accept anything less than what God has put within your heart—for your love, for your life, for your destiny.

...

**Lord,**
Thank You for the gift of dreams. Grant me courage and guidance to pursue them, fulfilling the destiny You've placed within my heart.
Amen.

...

# When Dreams Build Bridges

Alethia Saunders

...

**Psalms 37:4 (NIV)**

Take delight in the Lord, and he will give you the desires of your heart.

...

I'm a dreamer. If a fairytale can happen in my world, then I'm ready to make it happen. I've always dreamed I would be in a position to help heal and uplift everyone around me. I wanted to provide a voice to those who were afraid to speak up. Walking in God's purpose for me put me in that exact position. From my desktop, I'm able to communicate with individuals worldwide and aid them in getting better jobs, making more money, and having more resources to provide for their families.

I've also been positioned to help heads of households not just make more money, but also earn what they deserve because of the hard work they put into their careers. Later, I was challenged with the task of writing my first book. I had always been excited about being an author, but to be able to assist someone else in the process and have them include me as a co-author on the book was a dream come true. Since then, I've assisted over thirty individuals in speaking their truth. The topics they were afraid to share, they are now sharing. The secrets they thought they had to hide are now the same ones healing their hearts. I'm so happy to be a part of this journey with them. I'm so happy that my own dreams made way for their dreams of becoming an author to come true. This is my ministry!

...

**Dear God,**

Thank You for the dreams You inspire in me. May I empower
others to realize their aspirations and fulfill Your divine purpose.
Amen.

...

# Beneath the Weeds

Kim Porter

...

### Isaiah 61:11 (ESV)

For as the earth brings forth its sprouts, and as a garden causes what is sown in it to sprout up, so the Lord God will cause righteousness and praise to sprout up before all the nations.

...

One night, years ago, I dreamed I was standing in an old, overgrown garden. It was tangled with thorns and weeds, but beneath the mess, I could see glimpses of beauty—vibrant flowers struggling to break through. I bent down and began gently pulling the weeds away, uncovering patches of life and color that had been hidden for so long. My heart felt so full in that moment, seeing what had been there all along beneath the mess.

When I woke up, I couldn't shake the dream. It felt like God whispering to me, "This is what I've called you to do." At the time, I didn't fully understand, but I knew I had been living in fear—holding back, convincing myself that I wasn't enough. That dream showed me that God's purpose for my life wasn't buried or lost. It had just been waiting for me to uncover it.

I've carried that vision in my heart. I see the women I meet like that garden—beautiful, chosen, and filled with God's design, even if pain or life's struggles have tried to cover it up. My purpose is to help clear away the doubts and lies, so they can walk boldly in the purpose He's already planted in them. It starts with one question: What beauty is waiting for you to uncover?

...

**Lord,**
Uncover the beauty within us, restore what's been
hidden, and guide us to boldly walk in Your purpose.
Amen.

...

# Never Too Late

Veronica Washington

...

**Psalm 92:14 (ESV)**

They still bear fruit in old age; they are ever full of sap and green.

...

If you'd told me last year I'd be tutoring kids on a computer screen, I would've laughed until I cried and called you crazy. At 72, I assumed my dreaming days were past me. I figured I'd stick to my puzzles, watch my church's livestream, and leave the big plans to the young folk. But God has a funny way of stretching us when we least expect it.

It all started when Sister Melba from church mentioned during a prayer call that her grandson was struggling in math. I joked, "Well, I used to be a teacher—maybe I could help if he don't mind the 'old school' way." Next thing I know, she's talking about setting up a Zoom meeting. Zoom? I thought she was talking about a new workout class! Lord, have mercy.

I asked my granddaughter to teach me the ropes. It took me some time, and Lord knows I had my moments, but before long, I was in business. Now every Tuesday and Thursday, my kitchen transforms into my virtual classroom. One student has turned into eight. When one of them passes a test, I almost jump up and shout, "Thank you, Lord!" (though I save my knees and just clap instead).

The funny thing is, while I'm teaching math, God has been teaching me something, too. He's been showing me that dreams don't have an expiration date. I thought I'd just be coasting by now, but here I am discovering this whole new chapter where I'm still useful, still growing, and still dreaming. God told me, "Veronica, as long as there's breath in your body, there's work to do."

What a joy to be reminded that we're never too old to dream, and never too old to say, "Yes, Lord, use me."

...

**Lord,**

Thank You for dreams that never fade and for using me, at any age, to fulfill Your purpose.

Amen.

...

# Celebrating The Favor of Dreaming

*Dreaming is the canvas where God paints His visions for our future. Embrace your dreams with faith and courage, knowing they are pathways to His favor, inspiring growth, purpose, and the realization of His divine plans.*

**Now it's your turn to write your story of celebrating The Favor of Dreaming.**

Reflect on a dream or aspiration that has fueled your passion and purpose. How has pursuing this dream revealed God's favor in your life? Consider the ways these dreams have guided your decisions and how they've shaped your faith and journey.

_____

_____

_____

_____

_____

_____

_____

_____

_____

_____

_____

_____

_____

_____

_____

_____

_____

_____

# THE
# FAVOR
# OF
# *Transformation*

Transformation in Christ brings new life and divine favor.

# New Creation

...

## 2 Corinthians 5:17 (NIV)

Therefore, if anyone is in Christ, the new creation has
come: The old has gone, the new is here!

...

Transformation is at the heart of our walk with Christ. When we step into a relationship with Him, we are invited into a process of renewal and change that touches every aspect of our lives. This transformation is not just a change of habits but a profound shift in our identity.

In Christ, the old self, weighed down by past mistakes and regrets, is replaced by a new creation, full of promise and potential.

God expresses His favor through transformation by equipping us with the grace to let go and the strength to embrace the new. This divine favor means we are no longer defined by our failures but are instead marked by His love and power. As we grow in faith, we begin to reflect the character of Christ, showing kindness, compassion, and forgiveness to others.

Your journey may have moments of struggle as you shed old patterns and adopt new ones. Remember, transformation is a process, and God is patient and faithful in His work within you. Embrace each step, knowing that with every change, you are becoming more aligned with God's purpose and plan for your life.

Celebrate the Favor of Transformation this week. Allow yourself to feel the excitement of becoming a new creation. God's favor is upon you, guiding each step you take. Trust in His timing and rejoice in the progress you make.

...

## Heavenly Father,

I thank You for the gift of transformation through Christ. Help me to embrace the new creation You are making me to be. Fill me with Your love and power, and guide me as I walk this path of change. May Your divine favor lead me into a life that reflects Your glory.

Amen.

...

# Dancing to a Different Beat

Alethia Saunders

...

**Romans 12:2 (NLT)**

Don't copy the behavior and customs of this world, but let God transform you
into a new person by changing the way you think. Then you will learn to know
God's will for you, which is good and pleasing and perfect.

...

I used to be a stripper. I always say that I did it because I needed to make
more money, and that's true. However, in many ways, I also think I did it
because I was missing something. I was drawn to beautiful women who
were desired, and I felt as though I needed that same acceptance. Night
after night, I would get drunk and high to handle being touched or lusted
over. What I thought was building my confidence was actually lowering it.

So, I set a date, and I quit. I still remember the party they threw for me on
my last day as a dancer.

I also remember the words, "You'll be back."

But I never went back.

I walked away, focused on my career, and let Jesus take the wheel. I gained
confidence in who I was designed to be by God, and not in the things that
society emphasized!

Now I dance to a different beat. I wouldn't want it any other way.

...

**Dear God,**

Thank You for guiding me through transformation. Grant me strength to embrace my true self and continue on this new path with confidence and grace.

Amen.

...

# Transformed by the Master

Vanessa Fortenberry

...

**Colossians 3:10 (NLT)**

Put on your new nature, and be renewed as you learn
to know your Creator and become like him.

...

The name Vanessa, derived from Greek origins, means butterfly. Interestingly, Jonathan Swift first introduced the name in his 1713 poem, Cadenus and Vanessa. Later, entomologist Johan Christian Fabricius named a butterfly genus "Vanessa." Regardless of the name's debated origins, I feel deeply connected to the butterfly—a symbol of transformation.

The butterfly's life, evolving through metamorphosis, parallels our spiritual transformation in Christ. While we change physically over time, God invites us to undergo a deeper, spiritual renewal. This transformation is not about superficial adjustments but a complete reshaping of the heart and soul.

Looking back, I see God's handiwork in my life. Years ago, I held grudges and cut off people who wronged me. Over time, through God's mercy, my heart softened. I reconnected with people I had distanced myself from and grew more mindful of my actions and attitudes. God's grace transformed me, teaching me to extend that grace to others.

True transformation begins with renewing our minds, detaching from worldly desires, and discerning God's will. While we have responsibilities—praying, studying scripture, repenting, and sharing our faith—it is the Holy Spirit that drives the change.

The Master of Transformation calls us to grow spiritually, love generously, and build His kingdom. By aligning ourselves with God's will, we can emerge, like butterflies, renewed and transformed for His glory..

...

**Lord,**

Thank You for transforming my heart. Help me extend grace, love deeply, and walk
faithfully in Your will.

Amen.

...

# Spiritual Exercise

Bonita L. Williams

...

**Galatians 5:25 (NIV)**

Since we are living by the Spirit, let us follow the Spirit's leading in every part of our lives.

...

A friend of mine faithfully goes to the gym every morning at 6:30. Her commitment to this routine has transformed her—she looks decades younger and radiates energy, a result of her healthy choices over the years.

This made me reflect on what happens when we stay spiritually fit. When we rise early to meet with our spiritual trainer, the Holy Spirit, we equip ourselves for the challenges of the day. Just as a physical trainer pushes their clients to grow and stretch, the Holy Spirit guides and transforms us, taking us where God wants us to be.

Like physical training, spiritual growth requires discipline, time, and commitment. It's not always easy, but the results are undeniable. Transformation comes through consistent effort, dedication, and allowing the Holy Spirit to shape us.

When we commit to this process, we're not only strengthened for the day ahead, but we also become more like Christ—our ultimate goal. The effort may be hard, but the reward is eternal. Trust your trainer and keep showing up for the session. Transformation, both inside and out, is within reach when we allow the Holy Spirit to work in us.

...

**Lord,**

Shape my heart through Your Spirit. Grant me faith to grow, strength to persevere, and a transformed life that reflects Your glory. Amen.

...

# A Mended Heart

Dr. Nina Addison

...

**Jeremiah 17:14 (NIV)**

Heal me, O Lord, and I will be healed; Save me and I will be saved, For You are my praise.

...

I have my share of giving my heart to the wrong person. I ended up in situations that caused my heart to be broken. I even spent 14 hours in a jail cell because I was trying to please a man. I ended up in bad relationships because I was broken and needed to be healed. I lost myself in many situations I thought was love but it was lust.

In September of 2010, I decided to allow God to heal my brokenness. By November, I fasted and told God I would not date until I was healed and whole. I became celibate and I went through my process of healing.

Sin is designed to feel good in the moment, and healing could be a journey. The enemy never willingly gives up his grip. You must fight for your healing, and I did just that! I did not know my journey would take nearly a decade, but in 2020, I began to date a man that would become my husband. We dated, got engaged, and married all in 2020 during the pandemic.

When I allowed God to heal me and teach me what love was, I was then ready for the right type of love. That healing brought about His favor of marriage.

...

**Dear God,**

Please heal my broken heart. Mend the pieces and shower me with Your unfailing love. Help me submerge myself in Your peace. In Jesus' Name, may it forever be so.

Amen!

...

# God Did It

Veronica Washington

...

### Joel 2:25 (KJV)

And I will restore to you the years that the locust hath eaten, the cankerworm, and the caterpillar, and the palmerworm, my great army which I sent among you.

...

My grandson was in trouble. He had gotten mixed up with the wrong crowd, and it hurt my heart to see a boy with so much promise heading down the wrong road. His mama had done all she could, but he wasn't listening to a word she said.

One night, I sat in my chair, staring out the window, tears welling up. "Lord, I can't fix this. But I know You can."

The next morning, something told me to speak to Marlon, no yelling, no begging—just speak. I invited him over, cooked his favorite fried chicken and greens, and showed him some love. Once we were done eating, I said, "Baby, you are worth more than this life you're living right now. God didn't bring you into this world for all this foolishness."

Marlon sat quiet. Tears rolled down his cheeks. "Grandma," he said, "I want to change, but I don't know how."

We prayed together that day. Soon after, Marlon started going to church. He found mentors, got a job, and turned his life around.

...

Lord,
Thank You for Your saving grace. Guide us with patience and
love, restoring hearts and leading lives to You.
Amen.

...

# Celebrating The Favor of Transformation

*Transformation is a testament to God's renewing power, turning our old selves into new, vibrant creations. Embrace the changes He brings, knowing each transformation leads you closer to His purpose and fills your life with His abundant favor.*

**Now it's your turn to write your story of celebrating The Favor of Transformation.**

Reflect on a significant transformation in your life that brought you closer to God. How did this change impact your faith and perspective? Describe the ways His favor was evident throughout this transformation and how it has shaped your journey and identity in Him.

_____

_____

_____

_____

_____

_____

_____

_____

_____

_____

_____

_____

_____

_____

_____

_____

_____

# THE
# FAVOR
## OF
# *Worship*

Worship is the key that unlocks a profound connection with God, allowing His favor to flow abundantly into our lives.

# Joyful Presence

...

**Psalm 100:2 (NIV)**
Worship the Lord with gladness; come before him with joyful songs.

...

Worship is a beautiful expression of our love and reverence for God. It is in the act of worship that we open our hearts to receive His profound favor.

When we come before the Lord with gladness, singing joyful songs, we create a space where His presence can dwell, filling us with joy and peace beyond understanding.

In worship, we move beyond the noise of daily life and step into a sacred communion with the Divine. This encounter is not about formality or perfection; it's about authenticity and a genuine desire to connect with God.

Through worship, God expresses His love by meeting us where we are, transforming our burdens into blessings, and our worries into worship.

As you journey through life, there will be moments when you feel distant or disconnected from God. These are the times when worship becomes even more essential. It serves as a bridge to His presence, reminding you that you are never alone. Embrace worship as a daily practice, not just reserved for Sundays but as a way of life that keeps your heart aligned with His will.

Let your worship be filled with gratitude and expectation, knowing that God delights in your praises. Celebrate the opportunity to draw near to Him, and discover the favor that comes through this intimate connection.

As you worship this week, feel the joy and peace that His presence brings, and let it transform every aspect of your life.

...

**Gracious God,**
I come before You with a joyful heart, ready to worship and adore You. May my songs of praise draw me closer to Your presence and open my heart to Your favor. Fill my life with Your joy and peace as I honor You with my worship.
Amen.

...

# Heaven's Symphony

## Stacey Collins

...

### Revelation 4:11 (NIV)

You are worthy, our Lord and God, to receive glory and honor and power, for
you created all things, and by your will they were created and have their being.

...

Wow! Listening to "Agnus Dei" on Resurrection morning, I imagine angels
and multitudes worshiping in heaven! All singing in unison... in harmony...
I see loved ones gone ahead... standing before His throne... kneeling...
dancing with exuberant joy... singing out... shouting out... I see the
beautiful sea of glass... colors I don't even recognize... all voices joining:
"You are HOLY, HOLY are You, Lord God Almighty. Worthy is the Lamb!
Worthy is the Lamb!"

Since I was a small girl, I would place my fingers on the piano keys and
play melodies—before any lessons. I knew even then there was something
sacred in sound for me! I would open my voice, and a powerful resonance
would pour out of my tiny body and cover the room. I've seen people set
free, chains broken, relationships restored, bodies and minds healed, ones
coming out of comas, and those who are suicidal choosing life—all through
releasing the sound of God's heart in warfare and worship.

When I have no words, I have music! The sound I carry and release is His
heart. Love... healing... forgiveness... hope... resurrection... restoration...
peace... identity and purpose. Only IN and through Him. Strategies of heaven
flow when I'm IN Him. The sound of obedience and trust are KEY! I say
"YES" when He prompts—and they are there! It never ceases to profoundly
impact me, knowing it was God who placed me there for that moment!

...

**Lord,**
We worship You! You are HOLY, HOLY are You, Lord God
Almighty. Worthy is the Lamb! Worthy is the Lamb.
Amen.

...

# The Blessing of Worship

Dr. Nina Addison

...

**1 Chronicles 16:34 (NIV)**

O give thanks to the Lord, for He is good; For His lovingkindness endures forever.

...

Worship is something you can grow to love doing and do easily once you get into the habit of it. I enjoy worshiping when I need to boost my mood or emotions. There are times when God calls me into a random moment of worship because He knows what He is about to do.

One day, God called me into worship. I began to thank and praise Him like never before, expecting nothing in return. When He says, "Worship me," I do it because He is God and He is deserving.

On this particular day, I was having coffee, and I went into worship as instructed. I gave Him what He deserved. Immediately after my time in worship, I was offered an opportunity to speak to youth and get paid to do it. I love speaking life to youth, so I was excited.

See, God is our Father, our parent. Parents like giving gifts to grateful children. Give God worship and watch the doors that sling open for you!

...

**Dear Daddy God,**

May You receive the worship from Your child. May the worship be pure and from the heart. We honor You simply because of who You are. In Jesus' name, we thank You for every opportunity to give You what You deserve. Amen!

...

# Worship Over Worry

Bonita L. Williams

...

### Romans 14:8 (NIV)

If we live, it's to honor the Lord. And if we die, it's to honor the Lord. So whether we live or die, we belong to the Lord.

...

During my hospital stays, I reflected deeply on my faith. Before surgery, I thanked God for the medical professionals managing my care and acknowledged Him as the true healer. When a blood clot was discovered, leading to my readmission, I wrote a heartfelt letter to God. This situation elevated my faith to a new level. There was a real risk of the clot dislodging and reaching my lungs, and I was reminded of the seriousness of my condition. Seeking peace, I realized that no matter the outcome, I was a winner. This understanding echoed Paul's message in Romans 14:8 about trusting God completely.

My faith looks to God unwaveringly. I am certain that regardless of what I face, He will deliver me according to His plan. If God chose to end my journey here, it meant eternal life with Him. If He decided there was more for me to do, that was also gain. I learned I had a choice: to worry or worship God. I chose worship, trusting in His wisdom. I refused to let fear and despair take hold of my thoughts.

Trials on our journey often lead to fear, doubt, and frustration. Allowing these feelings to dominate can cause us to lose hope. We may talk about faith, but it becomes real only when tested. Where we turn in need reveals our trust. My faith is steadfast in God, knowing He will guide me in alignment with His divine plan for my life.

...

### Lord,

Strengthen my faith, guiding me to trust Your plan. In every trial, let me choose worship over worry, embracing Your peace and wisdom.

Amen.

...

# Great is Thy Faithfulness

L. Marie

...

**Psalm 23:3 (KJV)**
He restoreth my soul: he leadeth me in the paths of righteousness for his name's sake.

...

The church was humming with life that morning, and honestly, I almost stayed home. Grief weighed heavy on me after James passed, and worship felt like a routine I could barely follow. But that day, I pushed myself out the door and into the sanctuary, unsure of what I needed but desperate for relief.

Then the music started—"Great Is Thy Faithfulness." It wasn't a new song to me, but something about it hit differently that day.

When everyone sang, "Morning by morning, new mercies I see," I felt my chest tighten.

Then the choir moved to their next selection. Tears streamed down my face as they sang, "It Is Well With My Soul." I felt God's presence so clearly, wrapping me in His peace.

It wasn't that my sorrow disappeared, but I left that service changed. Worship became my anchor after that day, guiding me through the darkest valleys into the light. Even now, when my grief threatens to overtake me instead of wallowing in the pain. I turned to worship and soak in God's goodness.

...

**Lord,**
Thank You for Your unending faithfulness. Renew my spirit each day and guide me in Your grace and love. Amen.

...

# God Is My Healer

Makini Theresa L. Harvey

...

**Psalms 150:1-2 (NIV)**

Praise the Lord. Praise God in his sanctuary; praise him in his mighty heavens.
Praise him for his acts of power; praise him for his surpassing greatness.

...

Internal turmoil can take a toll on the body. Working 60-80 hour weeks, eating poorly, and living under constant stress landed me in the hospital. On November 30, 2008, I suffered a massive stroke and required a craniotomy and craniectomy.

The morning after surgery, Deacon and Deaconess visited and began singing "Awesome God." Though unconscious, they say I began mouthing the words and even sang along.

The next thing I fully remember is December 6th. I woke up to the gentle touch of water on my cheek—my youngest son was lying beside me, crying.

Weeks later, I walked into my follow-up appointment. The doctor said, "Ms. Harvey, you are a walking miracle." I replied, "Thank you, Doctor, but I am Jesus Christ's walking miracle."

When someone asked if I was mad at God, I said, "Why be mad at God for my own irresponsibility?" Here are my life lessons:

- Trust God and lay your burdens at The Cross.
- Care for your body and mind.
- Seek joy, even in suffering.

Praise God through it all!

...

**Lord,**

I praise You for Your miracles, for turning pain into purpose, and for Your unending grace and faithful love.
Hallelujah and Amen.

...

# Celebrating The Favor of Worship

*Worship is our heartfelt response to God's greatness, a powerful connection that draws us into His presence. Through worship, we are renewed and enveloped in His love and favor, transforming our hearts and aligning us with His divine will.*

**Now it's your turn to write your story of celebrating The Favor of Worship.**

Reflect on a worship experience that profoundly touched your heart and spirit. How did this encounter deepen your relationship with God and enhance your faith? Describe the ways in which His favor was revealed through this act of worship and how it continues to inspire your spiritual journey.

# THE FAVOR OF Redemption

Redemption through Christ's sacrifice is God's ultimate favor, offering forgiveness, renewal, and a fresh start in life.

# Forgiven and Restored

...

**Ephesians 1:7 (NIV)**
In him we have redemption through his blood, the forgiveness of sins, in accordance with the riches of God's grace.

...

Redemption is like getting a do-over, a fresh start, and it's all thanks to God's incredible love for us. Through Jesus' sacrifice, we're offered this beautiful gift where the mistakes and burdens of our past don't define us anymore.

Ephesians 1:7 reminds us that through Christ's blood, we have forgiveness and redemption. It's not something we have to earn or strive for; it's freely given because God loves us that much.

Imagine that—God's favor is so vast and rich that He chooses to see us through the lens of grace rather than our flaws.

In your own life, redemption means you're not stuck in the past. Those slip-ups and regrets? They don't have to hold you back. Instead, you're invited to step into the joy and freedom that come from being forgiven.

Sure, the journey isn't always smooth, but it's a path worth taking because it deepens your connection with God and helps you discover His purpose for you.

So, celebrate this incredible favor of redemption. Let go of the guilt and embrace the peace that comes with knowing you're loved and forgiven. Allow God's grace to transform your heart, renewing your spirit every single day.

...

**Dear God,**
Thank You for the gift of redemption through Jesus. Help me embrace this new life and leave the past behind. Fill me with Your peace and guide me as I walk in the freedom of Your forgiveness.
Amen.

...

# A Mother's Redemption

Mary Riley

...

**2 Corinthians 12:9 (NIV)**
But he said to me, 'My grace is sufficient for you, for my power is made perfect in weakness.' Therefore I will boast all the more gladly about my weaknesses, so that Christ's power may rest on me.

...

Slumped against the headboard of my bed, I stared at the ceiling, feeling the familiar weight of exhaustion. My mind raced with thoughts of overdue bills, demanding work emails, and the empty void left by my recent divorce. My two kids, playing in their rooms down the hall, were my only source of solace, but even their precious laughter couldn't drown out the overwhelming responsibility I felt as a single mother.

One Sunday, a friend invited us to her church. The church was small and my girls and I were welcomed with open arms. As the pastor spoke about grace, his words resonated deeply within me. He spoke of brokenness— something I was all too familiar with. Then, he told us about Christ's redemption. For the first time, I felt less alone in my struggles.

Over the weeks that followed, I noticed a change within myself. As I changed, the things around me seemed to change too. I wish I could say that all my bills were instantly paid or that my job suddenly became less demanding, but that's not what happened. Instead dealing with my day-to-day life was less stressful and I began to enjoy it a little more.

I learned that redemption is a journey that transforms not just my circumstances, but the very core of who I am. I now cherish the chance to share my story, hoping to offer encouragement to others navigating their own storms.

...

**Heavenly Father,**
Thank You for Your unwavering grace and strength. Guide us through our trials, renewing our spirits and filling us with hope and peace.
Amen.

...

# Do You Trust Jesus?

Dr. Theresa Billingsley

...

**Isaiah 12:2 (NIV)**

Behold, God is my salvation; I will trust, and will not be afraid; for the Lord God is my strength and my song, and he has become my salvation.

...

"What have I done?"

The question echoed in my mind as I sat alone, feeling the weight of my choice.

I was just a teenager, still in school, without a job. When I found out I was pregnant, panic set in.

How would I tell my mother?

Society kept saying, "It's your body, your choice," but I knew the life inside me was its own.

Out of fear, I made a decision I couldn't take back. I ended the life growing within me, thinking it was for the best. I promised God I'd never do it again, praying for forgiveness. But the regret hung over me.

Years later, I found myself in the same situation. Fear knocked again, but this time, I reached out to God. I chose to trust Him, choosing life instead of giving in to fear. That decision was a turning point. My son became my greatest joy, a living testament to God's grace.

Looking back, I realize fear had clouded my vision. I had believed in the enemy's lies. By trusting God, I found the courage to see the preciousness of life. My sons are more than just my children; they are divine gifts that bring joy and purpose to my life. Embracing them has filled my world with a richness and fulfillment I never imagined. Through my faith, I discovered a love and strength that transformed me completely.

...

**Lord,**

Thank You for guiding me through fear, granting strength, and leading me to redemption. I trust in Your plan for my life. Amen.

...

# In Spite of Stupid

Kim Porter

...

**Psalm 51:10 (NIV)**

Create in me a pure heart, O God, and renew a steadfast spirit within me.

...

In my teenage years and early twenties, life was one big, wild party. I lived for those nights that seamlessly turned into mornings, where boundaries didn't exist, and nothing was off limits. The thrill of each moment was intoxicating, and I chased every reckless decision with open arms, believing I was untouchable.

Then, just a few months after my 22nd birthday, the music abruptly stopped. I discovered I was pregnant. The realization hit me like a tidal wave: I had no idea who the father could be. The carefree lifestyle I'd indulged in had finally caught up to me, and I found myself standing at a crossroads.

The news was a sobering wake-up call. I was engulfed by fear and uncertainty, and thoughts of ending the pregnancy clouded my mind. Yet, something deep within me resisted. I chose to keep my baby. Despite all the foolish choices that had marked my path, this was one decision I knew was right.

God is so big and so good. He is more than amazing, capable of transforming our mistakes into blessings beyond our imagination. My greatest gift, my child, emerged from what I once deemed my most foolish decisions. It's astounding how God can work through our messes to create something truly beautiful.

To anyone who feels trapped by their past, remember this: Even your stupidest choices can't keep you from God's goodness. God can offer you favor despite and even through your shortcomings.

...

**Lord,**

Guide us through our mistakes, turning them into blessings, and help us embrace Your grace and love.

Amen.

...

# Taking Ownership

Benecia Ponder

...

**Zechariah 10:6 (NIV)**

I will strengthen Judah and save the tribes of Joseph. I will restore them because
I have compassion on them. They will be as though I had not rejected them, for I
am the Lord their God and I will answer them.

...

Redemption often finds its way into our lives in the quiet moments of humility. I remember one time, early in my career as a Certified Personal and Executive Coach, when I missed an important client deadline. I had overcommitted, believing I could handle everything on my plate. I was the coach who preached balance, yet here I was, drowning in my own chaos. When I realized my mistake, the guilt felt overwhelming. I had failed to deliver on my word, something that struck deeply at the core of my values.

Instead of dodging responsibility, I reached out to the client with sincerity. I admitted my mistake, apologized, and offered a solution to make things right. To my surprise, they responded with grace. Not only were they willing to give me another chance, but they also shared how my honesty strengthened their trust in me.

That moment taught me that redemption isn't about perfection—it's about ownership. When we're willing to face our mistakes, God uses them as tools to refine us. The situation reminded me of His redemptive power, turning failures into stepping stones. And through that client's kindness, I saw a glimpse of God's unmerited favor.

We all stumble. But when we choose to rise, acknowledge our missteps, and learn from them, we open the door to unexpected blessings. Take heart—redemption awaits every honest step forward.

...

**Lord,**

Thank You for transforming my failures into grace. Guide me to grow, seek
redemption, and trust Your eternal salvation.

Amen.

...

# Beyond the Wound

Ebonie T. Pritchett

...

**Matthew 6:14 (NIV)**
For if you forgive other people when they sin against you, your heavenly Father
will also forgive you

...

In 2016, I thought I had found true love. We greatly cared about each other until communication broke down and things became ugly. The relationship turned violent. I was stabbed and forced to drive myself to the hospital. It was a case of "love is blind." I carried that pain and anger until, seven years later, I chose to heal, let go, and open my heart again.

I told myself, "Ebonie, if you let God help you forgive that person, your old life can end." I reminded myself how God used imperfect people throughout the Bible—people who did terrible things. David and Moses were killers. Mary Magdalene and Rahab were sex workers. Society would never give them a second chance, yet Jesus said, "Father, forgive them."

This is the beautiful truth about our Lord—He desires forgiveness over punishment. He wants us to come to Him. Wrongdoers may carry guilt and feel their life is over, but God can transform their story. Sometimes He places us in positions to demonstrate forgiveness to others. Rather than punishment, He may be molding them into living testimonies of His life-changing grace.

As Ezekiel 33:11 tells us: "As surely as I live, says the Sovereign Lord, I do not enjoy the death of the wicked. I would rather they turn away from their sins and live." Our job is to turn away from darkness and choose a new path.

...

**Lord,**
Thank You for redeeming my brokenness, replacing pain with peace, and granting me the strength to forgive and begin anew.
Amen.

...

# Celebrating The Favor of Redemption

*Redemption is God's promise of new beginnings, a powerful transformation from past to purpose. Embrace the freedom and hope that His redemption brings, knowing it is a profound reflection of His love and favor in your life.*

**Now it's your turn to write your story of celebrating The Favor of Redemption.**

Reflect on a time when you felt the impact of God's redeeming grace in your life. How did this experience change your perspective and path? Describe how His favor was evident through this redemption, and how it has shaped your faith and identity in Him.

_____

_____

_____

_____

_____

_____

_____

_____

_____

_____

_____

_____

_____

_____

_____

_____

_____

_____

_____

# THE FAVOR OF *Balance*

Discovering balance is essential to align with God's favor, bringing profound peace and a deep sense of fulfillment.

# Harmony in Every Season

## Ecclesiastes 3:1 (NIV)

There is a time for everything, and a season for every activity under the heavens.

...

Achieving balance in our lives can sometimes seem like an impossible dream. The constant juggling act between work, family, and personal time often feels like walking a tightrope, barely managing to keep everything from falling apart. We've all been there, feeling stretched thin and overwhelmed. Yet, in the midst of it all, Ecclesiastes 3:1 offers a comforting truth: there is a rhythm to life, a divine order that assures us there's a suitable time for everything. Trusting in this divine timing allows us to let go of the pressure to control it all ourselves.

Balance is not about making everything equal but about aligning with God's purpose and timing. It's about knowing when to push forward and when to pause, when to speak and when to listen. Living in harmony with this rhythm brings peace and fulfillment, allowing us to fully experience the depth of God's favor.

In your personal journey, consider what areas of your life might need rebalancing. Are you overextending in some areas while neglecting others? Remember, God's favor shines brightest when we live in harmony with His plan. Embrace the peace that comes with knowing there's a season for everything, and trust that God's timing is always perfect.

Celebrate the Favor of Balance this week by taking a step back to evaluate and adjust. Let God's wisdom guide your choices, and watch how your life transforms, filled with His grace and favor.

...

## Heavenly Father,

Thank You for the gift of balance in my life. Help me to embrace Your timing and purpose, living in harmony with Your plan. Guide me as I seek to balance my priorities, finding peace and fulfillment in Your perfect favor.

Amen.

...

# Balanced By Grace

Alethia Saunders

...

### Philippians 4:11 (ESV)
Not that I am speaking of being in need, for I have learned in whatever situation I am to be content.

...

I've never needed a lot of things. However, at one point in my life, I needed to be in the mix. I found it hard to be alone and wanted to be liked by people, so I'd go to work and spend most evenings in the club, drinking and dancing. Instead of creating the happiness I sought, it produced more anxiety. I'd end up with hangovers or feeling high the next day at work, regretting the previous night's events.

After a while, I decided it was time to create a shift. I had to determine what I was really feeling, face those emotions, and move differently. I learned the importance of self-care, which is produced by self-love. The only way I could truly understand self-love was by getting to know God's love.

Knowing that I was made in God's love taught me to be more balanced. I learned how to enjoy my own company and the company of others. This is a lesson I'll always appreciate.

...

**Lord,**
Thank You for Your love. Help me find balance and embrace self-love in my journey.
Amen.

...

# Seasons of Balance

Janice White

...

### Ecclesiastes 3:1 (NIV)

There is a time for everything, and a season for every activity under the heavens.

...

It felt like I was juggling too many balls in the air—work, family, church commitments, and personal goals. Every moment of my day was packed, yet I still felt like I wasn't doing enough.

The weight of my responsibilities left me drained and irritable. One day, while rushing to finish a project, I noticed my daughter sitting quietly on the couch, holding a book she'd asked me to read to her earlier. I realized I'd told her, "Maybe later," too many times that week. My heart sank. I put the project aside, sat down, and read with her. In that moment, I felt God whisper, You can't pour from an empty cup.

That evening, I prayed for guidance and clarity. I started setting boundaries—learning to say no to things that weren't aligned with my priorities and yes to the moments that truly mattered.

Slowly, I found peace in letting go of the need to do it all. Balance isn't about perfection; it's about recognizing that every season of life requires us to focus on what's most important. When we seek God's wisdom, He shows us how to prioritize and embrace His timing for everything.

...

### Lord,

Guide me to seek Your wisdom and align my life with Your timing. Help me find balance, cherishing the moments that truly matter.

Amen.

...

# Journey to Wholeness

Beverley Anderson

...

### 1 Corinthians 6:19 (NIV)

Do you not know that your bodies are temples of the Holy Spirit, who is in you, whom you have received from God? You are not your own.

...

In the bustle of daily life, self-care can feel like a luxury and may even seem selfish, but it's a biblical mandate for fulfilling God's purpose. Have you ever felt overwhelmed, neglecting your well-being amid endless tasks? I've been there, and it taught me the importance of caring for my body as a temple of the Holy Spirit. This insight inspired me to develop B.A.L.A.N.C.E., a self-care method rooted in Bible-based principles that have transformed lives.

Why Biblical self-care?

Biblical self-care prioritizes time for God, self, and others. It's not just about routines, but aligning our lives with God's plan. These practices are acts of stewardship and worship that renew us holistically. With balanced time, nutrition, exercise, and spiritual disciplines, we honor God and equip ourselves to serve with joy and grace.

Today, reflect on your habits and consider their alignment with biblical principles. Embrace the wholeness God desires for you, finding peace through stillness, prayer, and reflection. Establish clear and healthy boundaries to prioritize self-care, ensuring that you make time for what truly matters and that your needs are met.

God promises to enrich your life and enable you to be generous in every way. As you nurture the fruits of the Spirit, let them shine through your efforts. Your journey to wholeness will fill your cup to overflowing and uplift those around you.

...

### Lord,

Guide me in caring for my body as your temple. Help me embrace true self-care and live a life of balance and wholeness.

Amen.

...

# One Hat at a Time

Bonita L. Williams

...

**Psalm 25:4 (TLB)**
Show me the path where I should go, O Lord; point out the right road for me to walk.

...

A word of advice I like to give students entering college is to balance studying with enjoying life. There's a saying: "All work and no play makes life dull," and I believe there's truth to that. God's Word tells us that Jesus came so we could have life and have it more abundantly. God desires for us to have joy on this journey. Unfortunately, there was a time when I didn't fully understand what that meant.

Years ago, as I reflected on my life and all the roles I played—daughter, sister, wife, mother, friend—I realized my life was out of balance. It felt like a constant juggling act. While all these roles are important, there must be order to the chaos that can creep in. I remember feeling overwhelmed by the endless list of things I thought I had to do. It wasn't until I came to understand that balance is essential for well-being that I was able to turn to God for help.

Now, when I seek God's guidance and ask Him to prioritize my workload, He graciously points me in the right direction. He helps me turn my "to-do" list into a "to-be" list. He gives me the discernment I need to focus on the key areas of life. We simply cannot be everything to everyone all the time. Allowing the Holy Spirit to direct our paths keeps us aligned with God's plans for us and helps us find the peace and balance we need to live abundantly.

...

**Lord,**
Grant me Your wisdom and peace to seek balance, aligning my steps with Your purpose and abundant grace.
Amen.

...

# Finding Balance

Sheryl Simms

...

**Proverbs 11:1 (ESV)**
A false balance is an abomination to the Lord, but a just weight is his delight.

...

I used to think balance was about splitting my time evenly between everything—family, friends, my own needs—like a perfectly stacked tower of blocks. But then came the day it all came crashing down.

It all started two weeks before my youngest daughter's school recital. My mom called, needing help organizing her attic. My best friend asked if I could watch her kids for a weekend. And I decided it was the perfect time to start a major home project—repainting the living room. I kept saying yes, believing I could handle it all. After all, if I scheduled everything just right, it would all fit, wouldn't it?

Spoiler alert—it didn't. The paint cans sat unopened for days. I missed a planning call for the recital that my daughter had begged me to attend. And the attic was still a clutter-filled mess when my mom gave me a disappointed sigh over the phone.

That evening, I sank into the couch, exhausted and overwhelmed. That's when it hit me— I couldn't do everything. I had to learn when to say "yes" and when to say "no." I found out that balance is recognizing that life isn't built like a tower of blocks, but more like a seesaw, constantly shifting and adjusting.

The next day, I started fresh. I apologized to my daughter and promised I'd be fully there for her recital. The living room could wait. I said no to a few requests, something that once felt impossible, but now felt freeing.

...

**Lord,**
guide my steps, grant me balance in life, and help me rest in the perfect grace of Your salvation.
Amen.

# Celebrating The Favor of Balance

*Balance is the art of aligning our lives with God's perfect rhythm, finding harmony in His presence. By embracing balance, we invite His peace and favor into every aspect of our journey, experiencing fulfillment and joy in His divine order.*

**Now it's your turn to write your story of celebrating The Favor of Balance.**

Reflect on a time when achieving balance brought peace and clarity to your life. How did this shift help you align with God's purpose and favor? Consider the ways balance has enriched your spiritual journey and how it continues to influence your decisions and well-being.

_____

_____

_____

_____

_____

_____

_____

_____

_____

_____

_____

_____

_____

_____

_____

_____

_____

# THE FAVOR OF *Growth*

Growth in God brings lasting favor. As we deepen our faith, we bear fruit and reflect His glory.

# Fruitful Faith

...

**Colossians 1:10 (NIV)**
so that you may live a life worthy of the Lord and please him in every way: bearing fruit in every good work, growing in the knowledge of God.

...

Growth isn't just about change; it's about aligning with God's purpose for our lives. Spiritual growth is like a garden—faith is the seed planted in rich soil, and with devotion and God's care, it flourishes into a bountiful harvest.

Colossians 1:10 reminds us to live a life that pleases the Lord, bearing fruit in every good work. This isn't merely about doing more; it's about growing in the knowledge of God, allowing His wisdom to transform us. When we deepen our faith, we bear fruit—acts of kindness, patience, and love—that reflect His glory. This is the evidence of His favor, a sign that we're walking in His light.

Personal growth often challenges us. It pushes us beyond comfort, but like a tree facing storms, these struggles strengthen our roots and deepen our trust in God. Each step, no matter how small, draws us closer to Him and aligns us with His will.

This week, reflect on how God has guided your growth. Celebrate progress, no matter how incremental, and welcome the changes He brings into your life. Remember, growth is a lifelong process, one filled with storms and seasons, but always abundant with God's favor. Each step forward is part of His divine plan for you.

...

**Heavenly Father,**
Thank You for guiding my growth and nurturing my faith. Help me to embrace each season of change, trusting in Your perfect plan. Grant me the wisdom to see Your hand in every step of my journey. In Jesus' name,
Amen.

...

# Becoming Through Being

Dr. Katherine E. James

...

**Proverbs 3:5-6 (KJV)**

Trust in the Lord with all thine heart; and lean not unto thine own understanding. In all thy ways acknowledge him, and he shall direct thy paths.

...

Here I was, retired from an educational career of 36 years, in the process of retiring from a professional teaching career of almost 20 years. And yet, my new venture into a foreign world had me questioning what I was able to bring to the table.

Fear invited me to doubt myself, and I did.

I was transitioning into life coaching. To say that I was beyond qualified is an understatement: five degrees, including a master's in Pastoral Counseling and a PhD in Educational Psychology, along with being a seasoned licensed therapist.

And yet, because I was trying to fit in instead of BEing in this foreign world, fear had its heyday with me.

I didn't know that Poppa had set the whole thing up. He knew that eventually, I would press my way back to my soul place of knowing and BEing, and that the two years of wilderness sojourning would produce unparalleled growth that would reposition me in Him. I am grateful for it all. My knowing of Him was deeply enriched and ever-growing because of the experience. For this place of knowing, I would do it all over again.

If Poppa invites you to the wilderness, please go. The growth that awaits is more than worth the discomfort of development.

...

Lord,

Thank You for the gift of growth. Grant me courage to change, faith to trust, and wisdom to thrive.

Amen.

...

# From Insecurity to Blessings

Alethia Saunders

...

**Psalms 1:3 (NIV)**

That person is like a tree planted by streams of water, which yields its fruit in season and whose leaf does not wither— whatever they do prospers.

...

I watched myself blossom, and it was nothing short of miraculous. I remember a time when I was trapped in low self-esteem, feeling insecure, and completely unsure of my path. I struggled daily, trying to survive off the validation of others, relying on external sources to tell me who I was and what I could be. I felt as if I was barely making it, living moment to moment, hoping that somehow things would fall into place.

But then, God began to move in my life. I realized that before I could truly grow, I had to plant the right seeds within myself. I had to stop waiting for others to validate me and start finding my value in God's love and purpose for me.

It wasn't easy, but as I surrendered to God's will, something incredible happened. I started to move full speed ahead, directly toward my blessings. I learned that I wasn't defined by the opinions of others, but by who God says I am. His love became the foundation upon which I built my life. I watched as my confidence grew and as I started walking confidently in the direction He had called me to go.

It wasn't just me that saw the change. The people around me began to blossom too. As I planted the right seeds of faith, strength, and purpose, they too felt the encouragement and strength to grow. With God's guidance, I became a living testimony of His ability to transform, heal, and guide us toward our true blessings. When we let Him plant the right seeds in our hearts, the growth is inevitable. It is in His love that we truly begin to thrive.

...

**Lord,**

Thank You for transforming me through Your love. Help me plant seeds of faith, trust Your timing, and grow boldly into the purpose You've designed.

Amen.

...

# Goals: Mine or God's?

Karen McKinney Holley

...

**Psalm 119:105 (CEV)**
Your word is a lamp to my feet and a light to my path.

...

When my cousin became pregnant out of wedlock at 17 years old, my mother came to my bedroom to have "the talk" with me. I was supposed to be doing my homework, but I was reading a book I wanted to finish.

Thinking I had been caught, I expected to be scolded. Instead, my mother asked, "What are your goals in life?"

Since the age of four, I'd wanted to be a teacher, so the answer came easily. "How are you going to become a teacher?" she asked.

I had expected an additional statement like, "You're not even doing your homework." Instead, I stammered out something about going to college and getting a degree.

My mother's reply was, "You have to set goals, stay focused, and work to accomplish them, or you will end up like your cousin." End of talk.

I still find lists of goals tucked inside old notebooks. One of those goals, for many years, was to read the Bible in a year. I have read the Bible several times over, but one day, the Holy Spirit clearly asked, "What are you getting out of racing through the scriptures? The Bible wasn't written in a year."

Since that day, I have let the Holy Spirit guide my reading—sometimes reading only one verse and meditating on it all day.

My relationship with Christ has become closer than I could have imagined. I can't quote chapter and verse, but daily, God's Word lives in my heart and guides my footsteps.

...

**Lord,**
Thank You for guiding our steps and teaching us to grow. Help us set purposeful goals and draw closer to You, letting Your Word shape our lives.
Amen.

...

317

# Lessons in the Valley

Felicia Pichon

...

### Philippians 4:12-13 (NIV)

I know what it is to be in need, and I know what it is to have plenty. I have learned the secret of being content in any and every situation, whether well-fed or hungry, whether living in plenty or in want. I can do all this through him who gives me strength.

...

God often uses our mistakes to teach us and shape us into better stewards. I learned this the hard way when my family faced a financial crisis. I had lost my job, bills were mounting, and we were waiting on a settlement my husband had received. When the money finally came, it saved us just in time, but I spent it all within three months on things we didn't truly need.

That money was meant to pull us out of debt, but instead, we ended up right back where we started—struggling, stressed, and with nothing to show for it. It took an entire year to climb out of the financial hole I'd carelessly placed us in. I was overwhelmed with guilt and disappointment in myself.

Yet, even in my lowest moments, God met me right where I was. He used that season to humble me, reshape my priorities, and teach me about grace. I extended to myself the same grace that God freely gives. Through Him, I learned to focus on what truly matters and to trust His guidance as we weathered the storm.

What about you? What areas in your life is God using to challenge, grow, and transform you? Are you leaning into His grace and trusting the process of growth?

...

**Lord,**

Thank You for growing me through trials. Shape my heart, refine my ways, and guide me to walk in Your wisdom, always trusting Your purpose for my life.

Amen.

...

# Faith Over Feelings

Bonita L. Williams

...

### Jeremiah 17:7-8 (NIV)

But blessed is the one who trusts in the Lord, whose confidence is in him. They will be like a tree planted by the water that sends out its roots by the stream. It does not fear when heat comes; its leaves are always green. It has no worries in a year of drought and never fails to bear fruit.

...

Growth is a process of learning, refining, and becoming better, and often, it requires acknowledging the limitations of our feelings. I've come to realize that my emotions can be unreliable, leading me down paths of fear and doubt. Feelings are fleeting and subject to change, which means they cannot always serve as a foundation for wise decisions or a healthy outlook on life. Instead of letting fear dictate my actions, I need to respond with faith, trusting in the divine plan already set for me.

Even when I can't see how circumstances will work out, I'm reminded that God knows the plans He has for me—plans to give me hope and a future. Fear doesn't have to be my response; praise can replace it. The battle isn't mine to fight alone because the victory has already been won through Christ. His work on the cross ensures I can trust in His provision.

To grow, I must daily renew my mind by spending time in God's Word. When I look away from Him and focus too much on my worries, I lose perspective. My growth depends on surrendering my feelings and allowing God to lead. True strength and peace come not from circumstances or emotions but from the unchanging truth of His guidance and love.

...

### Lord,

Guide my steps, strengthen my faith, renew my spirit daily, and lead me into Your eternal grace and salvation. Amen.

...

# Celebrating The Favor of Growth

*Growth is the journey of blossoming into the potential God has sown within us. Each step forward is a testament to His favor, transforming trials into triumphs and nurturing us with wisdom and strength. Embrace growth as a divine blessing, fueling your path with purpose and joy.*

**Now it's your turn to write your story of celebrating The Favor of Growth.**

Reflect on a period of growth that reshaped your life and strengthened your faith. How did this transformation impact your perspectives and relationships? Describe the ways God's favor was evident throughout this process and how it continues to guide your journey.

_____

_____

_____

_____

_____

_____

_____

_____

_____

_____

_____

_____

_____

_____

_____

_____

# THE FAVOR OF *Revelation*

Revelation from God leads to clarity and favor. His insights guide our paths, revealing His plans and purpose.

# Insights

### Amos 3:7 (NIV)
Surely the Sovereign LORD does nothing without
revealing his plan to his servants the prophets.

...

Navigating life without guidance can feel like walking through a dense fog, leaving us unsure of the path ahead. Yet, as Amos 3:7 tells us, God reveals His plans to those who serve Him, ensuring we're never left in the dark about His purpose for our lives.

Revelation is more than just hearing from God; it's an invitation to join His grand plans. It clears the fog, showing us the road ahead and filling us with the confidence to move forward. It's not just about what the future holds but about understanding the present, making choices rooted in divine wisdom.

Think about those moments in your life when clarity emerged unexpectedly. These are expressions of God's favor through revelation. Each insight is a step closer to realizing His purpose for you. Embrace these moments, recognizing them as pathways to favor and deeper connection with God.

As you ponder the Favor of Revelation, keep your heart open to God's insights. Seek His revelations through prayer and reflection, and celebrate the new clarity they bring. Understand that these divine revelations are gifts, guiding you to live a life that aligns with His will and reflects His glory.

...

### Gracious Lord,
Thank You for the clarity Your revelations bring. Help me to seek and embrace Your wisdom, guiding my steps with Your divine insights. Let me walk in Your favor, understanding Your purpose for my life. May my journey honor You, as I live in the light of Your revelations. In Jesus' name,
Amen.

...

# Trash or Treasure

Sibyl F. Cole

...

## Acts 11:15-18 (MSG)

So I started in, talking. Before I'd spoken half a dozen sentences, the Holy Spirit fell on them just as he did on us the first time. I remembered Jesus' words: 'John baptized with water; you will be baptized with the Holy Spirit.' So I ask you: If God gave the same exact gift to them as to us when we believed in the Master Jesus Christ, how could I object to God?" Hearing it all laid out like that, they quieted down. And then, as it sank in, they started praising God. "It's really happened! God has broken through to the other nations, opened them up to Life!"

...

I was sitting on my bed, surrounded by boxes filled with memories. Looking at them, I wondered how I'd gotten to this point. This wasn't how I'd envisioned my life, but I knew I had to make a change. I was leaving my husband, and today was the day; it was a matter of survival. The years of physical, emotional, and verbal abuse had finally taken their toll. Whoever made up the phrase "sticks and stones may break my bones, but words will never hurt me" lied, big time. Being called "fat, dumb, and stupid" daily becomes ingrained in your psyche, and you start to believe it.

Needing a break from packing, I stood up, stretched, and happened to catch a glimpse of myself in the mirror. The person staring back was momentarily beaten down and broken, but also resilient. My life was about to change in a major way, and so was my mindset. One of my soon-to-be ex-husband's favorite quotes was, "one man's trash is another man's treasure."

In his eyes, I was trash, but the revelation was that I was someone else's treasure—my own. My life was the only one God had given me, and if I didn't love myself, no one else would.

I stepped out my door for the last time, boxes packed and loaded in my car. As I drove away, I exhaled, feeling a sense of freedom and looking forward to embarking on this new chapter of life.

...

### Dear God,

Thank You for the revelation of self-worth and strength. Guide me as I embrace this new chapter in freedom and love.

Amen.

...

# Uniquely Gifted

### Alethia Saunders

...

### Psalms 139:14 (NIV)

I praise you because I am fearfully and wonderfully
made; your works are wonderful, I know that full well.

...

I believe that we are all born with special gifts. We read about them all the time in the Bible—those who had the ability to see and interpret visions, perform miracles, and speak in tongues.

As a child, I didn't always understand or appreciate these gifts. It wasn't until I realized that I had my own that my eyes were opened. Thanks to those who were spiritually inclined around me, even in my adult years, I was exposed to people who chose to freely live and walk in their purpose and utilize those gifts. I am forever grateful that they chose to share them with me, thus providing me with enlightenment and understanding. Not only were they able to help me understand myself better with their gifts, but they also provided me with insight into my own spiritual gifts. I no longer had to feel crazy or out of place because I understood that what I was experiencing was merely a manifestation of what God had provided within me to walk in His purpose fully.

We are all wonderfully and uniquely made. Sometimes we spend so much time comparing ourselves to others and feeling left out that we don't celebrate our differences and recognize how amazing we are. I'm grateful for what God has given me.

...

### Dear God,

Thank You for revealing the gifts within me and guiding me toward my purpose.
May Your wisdom continue to enlighten my path, and may I always honor these
divine revelations.
Amen.

...

# A Real Relationship

Dr. Nina Addison

...

## John 15:15 (AMP)

I do not call you servants any longer, for the servant does not know what his master is doing; but I have called you [My] friends, because I have revealed to you everything that I have heard from My Father.

...

A relationship is defined as being connected to another person. God wants us to be connected to Him. He wants us to know Him, and He already knows everything about us. This is so comforting to know.

Growing up, I went to church, but I was not invited to have a relationship with God. I was almost 30 years old before I really understood that God wanted a relationship with me. This changed my life. We love good relationships, and a relationship with God is the best relationship we can have.

When I think of a relationship, I want people who really care for me, show interest in me, and get to know the real me. Well, God covers all those areas. He wants us to get to know Him in that way. YES, He wants a relationship with us.

This was revelation knowledge to me. I did not realize how many people today do not know that God wants a relationship with us. He wants to be intimate with us, and He won't take advantage of us nor misuse or abuse us. It is the best relationship ever. Get to know Him. Start with His word and prayer.

...

## Our Father in Heaven,

Thank You for being our friend. Thank You for desiring a relationship with us. God, teach us how to grow in relationship with You. Thank You for calling us friend. In Jesus' name, we are grateful.

Amen!

...

# God's Will

Karen McKinney Holley

...

### Matthew 28:18-20 (NIV)

Then Jesus came to them and said, "All authority in heaven and on earth has been given to me. Therefore go and make disciples of all nations, baptizing them in the name of the Father and of the Son and of the Holy Spirit, and teaching them to obey everything I have commanded you. And surely I am with you always, to the very end of the age."

...

I kept asking God what His will was for my life. I had both taken and administered spiritual gifts and personality trait tests. I was actively involved in the church and the community. I had read pamphlets and books about discerning God's purpose. However, every time I attended a service or program and heard someone say, "God told me to [fill-in-the-blank]," I found myself wondering why God hadn't given me a specific assignment. I started praying again.

One afternoon, while walking and praying, I heard the Holy Spirit as clearly as if He were walking right next to me. "You aren't doing what I commanded all believers to do; why would I give you something else?"

My mind immediately went to the Ten Commandments. I looked them up and repented for the ones I had broken. I waited—a few days, a few months. I was disappointed because I still didn't receive a specific assignment.

By nature, I am shy. When the Holy Spirit prompted me to share Christ with one of my students who was going through a great deal of distress in her life, I resisted. I was flat-out scared. "What if she gets mad?" "What if she reports me?"

The urging was so strong that I finally asked her, "Do you believe in Jesus Christ?" She told me she used to attend church. I shared with her about the saving grace of Jesus Christ.

Driving home, I heard two words, "My will."

...

### Lord,

Thank You for Your revelations. Help us obey Your commands and trust Your guidance, knowing You align our hearts with Your perfect will.

Amen.

...

# God Says I Am

Bonita L. Williams

...

**Ephesians 1:17 (NIV)**

I keep asking that the God of our Lord Jesus Christ, the glorious Father, may give you the Spirit of wisdom and revelation, so that you may know him better.

...

One of my greatest joys in life is sharing the lessons God is teaching me with others. One of those opportunities arose when I worked with a group of individuals recovering from various addictions. During a ceremony recognizing their achievements, I was tasked with presenting certificates to those who had completed one of the sessions I taught.

As I sat, waiting for my moment to present, I asked God how He wanted me to introduce myself. To my surprise and great joy, He replied, "Tell them you are an assurance agent." My heart filled with delight at this new revelation. An assurance agent—wow. That title resonated deeply with me.

I love telling people about the goodness of God—His love, His grace, and His mercy. I realized long ago how vital it is to assure people of their salvation, to help them understand that eternal life isn't something we earn. Entry into heaven isn't about what we do; it's about what Jesus accomplished on the cross. Hearing God call me an "assurance agent" felt like a perfect fit. What an incredible title and privilege to be given by Him.

I am so grateful that God chooses to use me to share His amazing story. Now, it looks like it's time to print some new business cards.

Bonita Williams, Assurance Agent

...

**Lord,**

Thank You for letting me share Your salvation. Through Your Holy Spirit, help others receive and understand this precious gift.

Amen.

...

# Celebrating The Favor of Revelation

*Revelation illuminates the path of truth, unveiling God's wisdom and purpose for our lives. Embrace these divine insights with an open heart, knowing that each revelation is a gift of His favor, guiding you toward greater understanding and spiritual growth.*

**Now it's your turn to write your story of celebrating The Favor of Revelation.**

Reflect on a moment when a revelation from God brought clarity and direction to your life. How did this insight change your perspective and decisions? Describe how His favor was evident through this revelation and how it has influenced your faith journey and understanding of His plans.

_____

_____

_____

_____

_____

_____

_____

_____

_____

_____

_____

_____

_____

_____

_____

_____

_____

_____

_____

# THE FAVOR OF Change

Embrace change, for God's favor is constant. His unchanging nature assures us of His presence through life's transitions.

# Presence

...

**Malachi 3:6 (NIV)**
I the LORD do not change. So you, the descendants of Jacob, are not destroyed.

...

Let's be real—change is one of those things that can shake us up and leave us wondering what's next. But here's the thing: change is where growth happens. It pushes us out of the comfortable and into the extraordinary. And while change can feel like a storm, we have an anchor in God's unchanging nature.

Malachi 3:6 is a promise that no matter how wild the ride gets, God is our constant.

Imagine riding through life's changes with the confidence of knowing that your Creator is unshakeable. God's favor is like that unwavering friend who stands by you when everything else is in flux. It's His stable love that gives you the courage to embrace each new season, knowing He's got you.

Picture those times in your life when change seemed overwhelming. Remember how you found peace in the assurance that God was right there with you? That's His favor at work, weaving strength and resilience into your journey.

So, as you think about the Favor of Change, challenge yourself to invite God into your transitions. Celebrate the changes as opportunities for new beginnings that are all part of His plan for you. Step into each moment with the boldness of knowing His love and favor are constant.

...

**Lord,**
I thank You for being my rock when everything around me is shifting. Help me to lean into change with faith, trusting Your eternal presence. Guide me through life's transitions with Your unwavering love, and let me find my strength in You.
In Jesus' name, Amen.

...

# The Risk Revolution

Dr. Katherine E. James

...

**Ephesians 4:23-24 (NLT)**

Instead, let the Spirit renew your thoughts and attitudes. Put on your new nature, created to be like God—truly righteous and holy.

...

Poppa God said, "Kathy, I'm gonna need you to start breaking rules and taking risks." Yes, this was the impression I received from my heavenly Father.

I didn't need more explanation because I knew the kind of safe life I had curated for myself. I was the color-within-the-lines kind of girl. Scarcity had me confined to a predictable life. Ignorantly, with pride, I often adamantly declared that I don't take risks.

Today, I shudder at the idea of living a life without risks. Back then, in my safe haven of a life, I had no idea that not taking risks confined me to a life of limited growth.

Poppa was inviting His daughter to be transformed, to make the change of a lifetime. I accepted the invitation. Glory to God for the inner structural change that I have experienced over the last four years of my life.

The blessings of BEing my most authentic self.

The blessings of truly living out my dreams daily (the significance: until 2020, scarcity robbed me of my willingness to dream).

The blessings of doing what makes my heart sing and helping others to do the same.

My greatest lesson of change is my offer to you: Discover who you are, be who you are, and serve others from your truth.

...

**Lord,**

Thank You for guiding my transformation. Grant me the courage to change, faith to trust, and strength to grow.

Amen.

...

# Embracing The New

Janice White

...

### Isaiah 43:19 (NIV)

See, I am doing a new thing! Now it springs up; do you not perceive it? I am
making a way in the wilderness and streams in the wasteland.

...

Change has never been easy for me. I love routine and predictability. So, when
I was laid off from a job I'd had for years, my world felt like it had been flipped
upside down.

At first, I resisted, desperately clinging to what was familiar. But the doors I
tried to reopen stayed firmly shut.

One night, I cried out to God, "Why is this happening?"

Almost immediately, I felt Him press on my heart: This is not the end—it's a
redirection.

From that moment, I shifted my perspective and began seeking opportunities
I'd never considered. Within months, I found a role that aligned perfectly with
my passions, something I never would have pursued if I hadn't been pushed
out of my comfort zone.

Change can feel like loss, but it's often God's way of positioning us for something greater. When we trust Him, He turns what feels like a wilderness into a
path filled with new possibilities.

...

### Lord,

Guide my steps through change. Help me trust Your plan, opening my heart to
new opportunities. Turn uncertainty into faith and transform this season into
something greater. Amen.

...

# Be The Change

Alethia Saunders

...

**Romans 12:2 (NIV)**

Do not conform to the pattern of this world, but be transformed by the renewing of your mind. Then you will be able to test and approve what God's will is—his good, pleasing and perfect will.

...

Life is a journey of constant adjustment. Seasons shift, people come and go, and circumstances change. To navigate this world, we must learn to adapt to what's happening around us. But as believers, we are called to go beyond mere survival. We are called to listen for God's voice and obey when He asks us to shift—not just outwardly, but inwardly.

I've had to make adjustments many times in my life, often just to survive. Whether it was financial struggles, emotional trials, or unexpected life events, adapting was necessary to keep moving forward. But some changes went deeper—changes that didn't come from external circumstances but from God speaking directly to me. These were the moments when God asked me to let go of things that were holding me back and step into the person He was calling me to be.

One such moment came when God told me it was time to revamp my friend group. Some relationships, though familiar, were no longer serving the purpose God had for my life. The hardest part wasn't just walking away—it was realizing that I had to change too. If I wanted to attract better people into my life, I had to actively be better. If I wanted a life that reflected God's love, purpose, and peace, I had to embody those qualities myself.

Change isn't easy. It requires sacrifice, humility, and trust in God's plan. But the beauty of transformation is that it's not something we do alone. God walks with us every step of the way, providing wisdom, strength, and grace to become who He's called us to be.

...

**Lord,**

Thank You for guiding my steps. Help me humbly release what holds me back, trust Your plan, and become the person You've called me to be.

Amen.

...

# I Get To

Bonita L. Williams

...

### Proverbs 16:3 (NIV)
Commit your actions to the Lord, and your plans will succeed.

...

"I have to clean the house." "I have to go to the grocery store." "I have to pay the bills." "I have to, I have to, I have to."

This was a frequent saying of mine for quite a long time. The "have to do's" of life were taking a toll on my existence. The weariness of having to complete a long list of tasks each day can be nerve-wracking.

Through the guidance of the Holy Spirit, I came to understand that I have been blessed with the opportunity to do many things. My attitude needed changing. Instead of dreading all the tasks before me, I now see them as blessings.

I get to clean a house that God blessed me with. I have a roof over my head and a floor under my feet. I am blessed to wake up each morning. I am blessed to go to the grocery store. I am blessed to interact with my family, friends, and others. I am blessed to be able to drive in traffic. I am blessed to do the laundry. I am blessed, blessed, blessed. I thank God that I am blessed to do the things He allows me to do.

By viewing our obligations through a lens of gratitude, we witness the favor of change and its power to renew our spirits.

Change your perspective, and watch your burdens become blessings. Embrace gratitude and witness miracles every day.

...

### Lord,
Help us embrace change, transforming burdens into blessings. May gratitude guide us, revealing Your grace in every moment.
Amen.

...

# I Need Exact Change

Dr. Theresa Billingsley

...

**Proverbs 18:21 (AMPC)**

Death and life are in the power of the tongue, and they who
indulge in it shall eat the fruit of it [for death or life].

...

You have the right to remain silent, and whatever you say can and will be used against you—this phrase carries more truth than we might realize. Our words hold incredible power. They are vessels, transporting outcomes from one realm to another. If we desire change, we must apply the principles from God's Word.

Think of creation itself. God saw darkness and said, "Let there be light," and light appeared. He didn't describe the darkness or complain about it—He spoke what He desired into existence. We are made in His image, with that same creative power. Yet too often, we speak negativity. We focus on what's wrong, agreeing with what we see, and unintentionally create even more of it. Then, we turn around and blame God.

I remember a time when my finances were an absolute mess. I'd wake up saying things like, "I'll never get ahead," or "I'm always broke." Nothing changed—until I caught myself. I realized I was framing my reality with my words. Instead of speaking loss, I began declaring, "God is my provider," and "My needs are met." It didn't happen overnight, but as I continued to speak life over my situation, opportunities and provision started to flow.

Hebrews 11:3 reminds us that the worlds were framed by God's Word. Words may be invisible, but their impact is undeniable. From now on, let's speak only what we desire to see—God's truth, life, and promises over every circumstance. Our words create. Choose wisely, and watch the change unfold.

...

**Lord,**

Guide my words to reflect Your truth. Help me speak life, hope, and promise,
creating a reality aligned with Your will and abundant grace.

Amen.

...

# Celebrating The Favor of Change

*Change is a constant invitation to grow and experience God's unchanging love and favor. Embrace each change with faith, knowing it brings new opportunities and blessings, aligning you with His divine purpose and transforming your journey.*

**Now it's your turn to write your story of celebrating The Favor of Change.**

Reflect on a change in your life that brought unexpected blessings or insights. How did embracing this change influence your faith and perspective? Describe the ways in which God's favor was evident through this transition and how it has shaped your path and understanding of His will.

_____

_____

_____

_____

_____

_____

_____

_____

_____

_____

_____

_____

_____

_____

_____

_____

_____

_____

_____

_____

_____

_____

# THE FAVOR OF *Anointing*

Embrace God's anointing—the divine empowerment that equips you for your unique calling, leading to breakthroughs and clarity.

# Divine Empowerment

...

## 1 John 2:27 (NIV)

As for you, the anointing you received from him remains in you, and you do not need anyone to teach you. But as his anointing teaches you about all things and as that anointing is real, not counterfeit—just as it has taught you, remain in him.

...

Anointing is like God giving you a nudge, saying, "I've got something amazing planned just for you." Picture it as having a divine toolkit at your disposal, filled with everything you need to walk confidently in your calling. It's God's way of saying you're not just another face in the crowd; you're chosen for something extraordinary. It's His stamp of approval, showing you are set apart for something significant.

The best part is, God's anointing isn't just a one-time gift. It's ongoing, teaching and guiding you every day. It doesn't rely on human wisdom but taps into a deeper, spiritual truth that lights up your path. When you embrace this anointing, it helps clear the fog in times of confusion and gives you strength when you feel weak. It's like having a quiet inner voice that assures you, "You've got this because I'm with you."

And, in those moments when you're standing at the edge of something new, feeling that knot of uncertainty in your stomach, the anointing kicks in, whis-pering to your spirit, "You're ready. You're chosen for this moment."

Now, this empowerment isn't just about you; it's about transforming the world around you, illuminating those shadowy corners with your light, and bringing God's Kingdom alive right where you are.

As you ponder the Favor of Anointing, let your heart burst wide open to the limitless possibilities that God's anointing brings into your life. This is your moment to celebrate this divine empowerment, knowing deep down it's the key to unlocking breakthroughs and gaining true understanding. Embrace this gift and let it direct your path, fully confident that with God's favor, there's nothing that can stand in your way.

...

Dear God,

Thank You for Your anointing that sets me apart. Help me embrace this power and walk confidently in Your favor.

Amen.

...

# My Anointed Difference

Dr. Nina Addison

...

## Luke 4:18 (AMP)

The Spirit of the Lord is upon Me (the Messiah), Because He has anointed Me to preach the good news to the poor. He has sent Me to announce release (pardon, forgiveness) to the captives, And recovery of sight to the blind, To set free those who are oppressed (downtrodden, bruised, crushed by tragedy),

...

I was born a physically disabled Black girl on the South Side of Chicago. Society might say I had several strikes against me. However, God had His hand on me because He formed me in my mother's womb. He created me, just like He created you.

Even having a physical difference is an anointing from God.

How?

I use my physical difference to teach the Word and show others that God does not make mistakes. I am also a youth pastor and speaker, helping people love themselves. People are drawn to me because of my disability, allowing me to speak life to them.

I am typing this and can barely move my left hand due to my special need. That in itself is an anointing.

The anointing on your life may not look like you expected, but there is an anointing on your life. I am sure of it. It may be the very thing the enemy wants you to overlook. I used to want to hide my hands, but now I show them proudly.

...

**God,**

Please reveal the anointing You have on Your child's life. Show them what You desire to use for Your glory and their story. May they walk in the anointing You have placed on their life. In Jesus' name,

Amen!

...

# God Qualified

Benecia Ponder

...

**Acts 4:13 (NIV)**

When they saw the courage of Peter and John and realized that they were unschooled, ordinary men, they were astonished and they took note that these men had been with Jesus.

...

As a book coach, I often tell the remarkable story of one of my clients, Jessica, a Christian author whose journey is a testament to the favor of God's anointing.

Jessica writes devotional books that empower and encourage women of faith. A few years ago, Jessica spoke at a large women's conference in Dallas, Texas. After her presentation, one of the other speakers at the conference approached her. The woman was a well-known ministry leader at a prominent mega-church. She was someone Jessica greatly admired and respected. The ministry leader gave Jessica a big hug and expressed how much she loved Jessica's presentation. She marveled at how eloquently Jessica spoke, and she commended her on her grasp of biblical truths.

"What seminary did you attend?" the ministry leader asked.

"I didn't go to seminary," Jessica replied. "I dropped out of high school in the tenth grade. I went back to get my GED, but I never made it to college."

The ministry leader was even more impressed with Jessica. "To God be the glory!" she said.

Jessica's story is a story of divine favor, where God's anointing shines through. Her story reinforces that it's not your education or training that God wants to use. If you have it, that's good. But God's ability to do great things through you is not limited by your qualifications. No matter how extensive (or limited) your education or experience, your obedience to God's call far outweighs anything else.
Her journey reminds us all that when we step into our purpose with faith, God's favor can open doors we never imagined.

...

**Lord,**

Thank You for qualifying me. Thank You for using me just as I am. I pray that others will see how You are working through me and glorify You. In Jesus' Name,
Amen.

...

# Assignments

Bonita L. Williams

...

### Ephesians 2:10 (NLT)

For we are God's masterpiece. He has created us anew in Christ Jesus,
so we can do the good things he planned for us long ago.

...

Students often receive assignments from their instructors, varying in length and complexity. Regardless of duration, each comes with a set of instructions detailing how to complete it. Similarly, as Christians, our Master Teacher, Jesus, has entrusted us with assignments and provided directions (the Bible) to guide us.

Each of us has specific tasks. Some are clear, while others require further explanation. Some can be completed quickly, while others may take years, even a lifetime, to fulfill. Reverend Carmon Alexander of Atlanta, GA, preached about a prophet tasked with delivering a challenging message to a king. Despite previous troubles with his peers, the prophet remained faithful, trusting God with the outcome.

This faithfulness is what we must embrace. We should diligently pursue the assignments God gives us, striving to follow His directions wholeheartedly. Remember, we are not alone in this journey. The Holy Spirit is ever ready to assist us whenever we need help. Trust Him to guide your steps as you align with God's plan for your life.

Whatever the assignment may be, let us commit to carrying it out with all our might, knowing that we are supported and guided by the divine.

...

### Heavenly Father,

Guide my steps as I fulfill Your assignments. Grant me strength and wisdom,
and let Your Holy Spirit be my constant aid.

Amen.

...

# Aligning with God's Purpose

Beverley Anderson

...

### Ephesians 2:10 (NIV)

For we are God's handiwork, created in Christ Jesus to do good works, which
God prepared in advance for us to do.

...

Amidst life's demands, it's easy to lose sight of our true calling, leaving us unfulfilled and directionless. There was a season when I was running on empty. Despite my achievements, something was missing—I felt adrift, disconnected from my purpose. Have you felt this way?

A life-altering event, a brush with death, awakened me to the reality that I was out of alignment with God's plan. The busyness of life and the secular marketplace had overshadowed my divine calling. God has a unique purpose for each of us. Imagine how enriched your life could be by realigning with His vision.

After my wake-up call, I intentionally reconnected with my purpose through prayer and listening to the Holy Spirit. I learned to trust in God's provision and timing. As you reflect on your purpose, remember that God's plans are abundant and filled with hope. His promises are like a harvest yielding 30-, 60-, or even 100-fold!

Align your actions with His purpose, and embrace a future that reflects His glory. Living with purpose transforms every moment into an opportunity to glorify Him. Start your day with a "power hour" of communion with God. Let this practice guide your decisions and actions, creating a deeper understanding of His plans. By aligning your daily life with His divine purpose, you open the door to a life rich with meaning and fulfillment.

...

**Lord,**

Guide my steps and align my heart with Your will.
Help me to trust in Your timing and provision.
Amen.

...

# Anointed to Inspire

Benecia Ponder

...

## Matthew 5:16 (ESV)

In the same way, let your light shine before others, so that they may see your good works and give glory to your Father who is in heaven.

...

Each morning, I find myself reflecting on the words, "Your kingdom come, Your will be done." These words remind me of my purpose as a book and business coach. I have been anointed not just to pursue my own dreams, but to help others share their stories and impact lives. This calling isn't about personal gain; it's about expanding the Kingdom, one book and one business at a time.

When I first started, my prayers were small and focused on immediate needs. But then, I realized that God wants us to pray bold prayers. He wants us to ask for big things that align with His purpose. So, I began to pray for the courage and wisdom to guide others in their journey, to help them find their voice and amplify their message.

As I work with each client, my heart is full of gratitude. I see how their stories have the power to change lives, to uplift and to inspire. Each success is a testament to the incredible plans God has for us when we align our motives with His will. It's not just about building successful businesses; it's about building His Kingdom.

Every day, I am reminded that when we put God first, He does amazing things through us. My prayer is to always honor Him with my work, to live with the right motives, and to help others do the same. Together, we can make a lasting difference, leaving the world a better place.

...

**Lord,**

Anoint me to serve others, build Your kingdom, and
fulfill my purpose with love and humility.
Amen.

...

# Celebrating The Favor of Anointing

*Anointing is God's special empowerment, setting you apart for His purpose and glory. Embrace this divine gift, knowing His favor equips you with everything needed to fulfill your calling and witness His power through your life.*

**Now it's your turn to write your story of celebrating The Favor of Anointing.**

Reflect on a time when you felt God's anointing guiding and empowering you for a specific purpose. How did this anointing influence your actions and confidence? Describe the ways in which His favor was evident during this experience and how it has shaped your journey and faith.

_____

_____

_____

_____

_____

_____

_____

_____

_____

_____

_____

_____

_____

_____

_____

_____

_____

_____

_____

_____

# THE FAVOR OF *Identity*

Embracing who you truly are in Christ opens the door to purpose, strength, and divine blessings in every aspect of your life.

# True Self

### Galatians 2:20 (NIV)

I have been crucified with Christ and I no longer live, but Christ lives in me. The life I now live in the body, I live by faith in the Son of God, who loved me and gave himself for me.

...

Understanding who you are in Christ is a transformative journey. It's more than just a label. It's about realizing the incredible life you're called to live. When you fully embrace your identity in Him, you unlock doors to purpose, belonging, and direction that you never imagined possible. You live each day with the confidence that you are loved, chosen, and equipped to fulfill a divine purpose. This is not a mere motivational thought; it's the reality of God's favor manifesting in your life.

In a world that constantly tries to define and confine you, knowing your true identity in Christ becomes your anchor. It allows you to navigate life's challenges with a sense of belonging and clarity, knowing exactly where you're meant to be. Embracing this identity means stepping into a life of favor, where God's blessings and guidance become evident in your everyday experiences.

Think about the possibilities that lie ahead when you see yourself through the eyes of your Creator. Let this understanding fuel your journey, propelling you toward your calling with renewed vigor and faith.

As you celebrate the Favor of Identity this week, remember that you are not alone. Your path is lit by the truth of who you are in Christ—an empowered, favored child of God.

...

### Heavenly Father,

Thank You for the identity I have in Christ. Help me embrace who I am in You, unlocking the fullness of Your favor in my life. Guide my steps as I walk in purpose and belonging.

Amen.

...

# Through The Creator's Eyes

Benecia Ponder

...

### Jeremiah 1:5 (NIV)

Before I formed you in the womb I knew you, before you were born I set you apart; I appointed you as a prophet to the nations.

...

"What are you doing, Mommy?"

My daughter's curious voice pulled me from my thoughts. "That goes on your head. It's a hat."

I glanced at the paper she handed me. One side was blank, the other a lively tangle of colors—yellow, blue, orange, and red.

A hat? To me, it seemed like a picture destined for the fridge gallery of toddler art. But my daughter, wise beyond her years, had a different vision.

I hesitated, not wanting to crush her budding creativity. "Are you sure, Pumpkin?" I asked, turning the paper again.

Her eyes sparkled with a mix of patience and determination. "Silly, Mommy," she said, climbing onto a chair. She folded the paper, placing it gently on my head. Then she dashed away, returning with a mirror.

"See, Mommy? I told you. It's a hat."

At that moment, her vision was clear. She saw what I couldn't. Her certainty was unwavering; she knew exactly what she had created from the start. It wasn't about my perception. She was the creator, and only she could define its purpose.

This simple act held a profound lesson. Just as my daughter saw the hat in that paper, we must trust the identity crafted by our own Creator. It's not about what others see; it's about knowing, deep within, who we truly are. Only when we view ourselves through the eyes of our Creator, do we uncover our true identity.

...

### Creator of all,

Guide me in seeing myself through Your eyes. Illuminate my path to true identity, unfolding purpose and strength within me.

Amen.

...

# Journey Back to Me

Dr. Katherine E. James

...

### Galatians 2:20 (NIV)

I have been crucified with Christ and I no longer live, but Christ lives in me. The life I now live in the body, I live by faith in the Son of God, who loved me and gave himself for me.

...

If Poppa will use a donkey to get Balaam's attention, will He not use India Arie?

India Arie's "Just Do You" is an invitation to authenticity. This song acted as an anchor when I was desperate, lost, and trying to find my way back to my true self.

I was in a foreign world of radical entrepreneurship; it just wasn't a good fit for me. Simultaneously, it was for the lessons Poppa intended. Now, I am grateful for the entire experience and the people involved.

I wasn't being my authentic self because I was trying—desperately—to fit where I wasn't supposed to. I was confused, scared, and desperate to figure it all out, flailing, and scarcity was running rampant. Fear invited me to be liked. Fear invited me to shrink. Fear invited me to compete. Fear invited me to not show up as my authentic self. I accepted all the invitations because fear, not faith, was running this show.

It took almost two years to regain my sense of self. I was preparing to do it the prescribed way again. By now, however, I was so exasperated with not BEing me that I simply—out of pure frustration—said, "I just have to do me." At that very moment, the words to India Arie's song, "Just Do You," bellowed from my soul.

I came to myself and remembered Katherine as Poppa intended and realized that Poppa intended this journey to redefine my identity and renew my freedom to BE in Him.

Is fear blocking your faith and ability to know who you are in Him?

...

### Lord,

Thank You for creating me with purpose. Help me shed fear, trust Your plan, and fully embrace the identity You've given me.

Amen.

...

# Truth Shatters Lies

Stacey Collins

...

### 1 Peter 2:9 (NIV)

But you are a chosen people, a royal priesthood, a holy nation, God's special possession, that you may declare the praises of him who called you out of darkness into his wonderful light.

...

"Are you POOR?" A question so randomly thrown out to me when I was a 9-year-old girl on my way to school one day. I can still hear its echo.

"Are you poor?… Are you poor?… Are you poor?"

A ball so quickly tossed up in the air in front of me. Do I catch it? Or do I run away? I look up and see this imaginary ball—pausing in the air—then dropping right into my heart. For a moment, my breath catches, and I unknowingly receive this verdict as my own. I still hear it like it was yesterday. "Are you poor?"

I remember the stares... whispers... accusing eyes boring into mine... trying to find the weaknesses... put a "label"... place an "identity"... I absorbed every bitter word and soaked up the lies. One day, sharing with my friend about feeling disregarded and dishonored, I said, "I don't deserve to be treated like this!" She made me repeat it, but I didn't believe it. I was allowing others to hurt me because of my own insecurities.

I saw myself as a baby who fell off the assembly line just before receiving the stamp that said VALID. I'd been running after everyone else's approval my whole life. Then God's truth broke through, shattering every lie—Repeat after me... I am BLESSED—not poor. I am WORTHY—not unworthy. I am a TREASURE—not trash. I am VALID—not invalid. I am LOVED.

...

**Lord,**

Thank You for defining our worth. Help us to see ourselves through Your eyes—blessed, treasured, and deeply loved.

Amen.

...

349

# God is my Husband

Makini Theresa L. Harvey

...

### Isaiah 54:5 (NIV)

For your Maker is your husband, The Lord of hosts is His name; And your Redeemer is the Holy One of Israel; He is called the God of the whole earth.

...

Toward the end of my second marriage, I discarded my identity. I saw myself as his wife, my children's mother, and a businesswoman, and not good in any role, forgetting the woman I once knew I could be.

Still grieving and having a pity party over the second divorce, I acknowledged that I had a lot of "me-fixing" to do. During my Bible study time, Isaiah 54:1-8 jumped out at me. After reading it several times, I fell to the floor and cried like a baby. Then I heard the Holy Spirit say, "I told you I got you."

I stopped preparing for, or waiting for, the right man and I truly live in peace beyond understanding. I am striving to live like, and for, Jesus Christ. I know who I am, I know whose I am.

...

### Dear God Almighty,

I thank You that I am Yours and You are mine. Give me the wisdom and commitment to live my life for Your glory, honor, and praise, in the Name of Jesus Christ; Hallelujah and Amen.

...

# The Courage to Shine

Benecia Ponder

...

### Joshua 1:9 (CSB)

Haven't I commanded you: be strong and courageous? Do not be afraid or discouraged, for the Lord your God is with you wherever you go.

...

I used to feel as if I were merely a spectator in my own life, watching from the sidelines as fear kept me shackled. The fear of what others might think or say was a relentless shadow that held me captive. I stayed quiet, hidden, never daring to step into the light.

Then, one day, I encountered a truth that shattered my chains: Joyce Meyer's words echoed in my heart, "We need a backbone, not a wishbone." It was time to claim my identity in Christ, to find that spiritual backbone. Galatians 2:20 became my anthem: "I have been crucified with Christ, and I no longer live, but Christ lives in me." These words resonated deeply, marking a turning point in my life.

I realized that my identity wasn't defined by past mistakes or the opinions of others. In Christ, I was given a new identity, a fresh start. I was no longer just a spectator but a co-heir with Christ, deeply loved and valued by God. This revelation infused me with a boldness I had never known.

Today, I dance through life, each step filled with the joy of knowing I am His. My fear has transformed into courage, grounded in the unshakeable fortress of Christ's love. I face challenges with a renewed spirit, knowing I am not alone. My life, once shadowed by hesitation, now shines with the radiance of a heart fully alive in Him.

...

### Heavenly Father,

Grant me courage to embrace my identity in Christ, overcoming fear and living boldly in Your love and purpose.

Amen.

...

# Celebrating The Favor of Identity

*Embrace your true identity in Christ, where His love and purpose define who you are. In understanding your worth through His eyes, you unlock the fullness of His favor, walking confidently in the path He has set before you.*

**Now it's your turn to write your story of celebrating The Favor of Identity.**

Reflect on a moment when you discovered a deeper sense of your identity in Christ. How did this understanding transform your perspective and actions? Describe how God's favor became evident as you embraced your true self and how it continues to guide your journey.

# THE FAVOR OF *Hope*

Hope in God never disappoints. It sustains us through trials and renews our spirit, revealing His boundless favor.

# Enduring Assurance

...

## Romans 15:13 (NIV)

May the God of hope fill you with all joy and peace as you trust in him, so that you may overflow with hope by the power of the Holy Spirit.

...

Hope is a powerful force that anchors us in the midst of life's storms. In Romans 15:13, we find a profound reminder that our hope in God is not just a wishful thought but a divine assurance that fills us with joy and peace.

This hope is alive and active, sustaining us through trials and renewing our spirit when the journey seems tough.

When we place our hope in God, we tap into a source that never runs dry. His boundless favor becomes evident as we navigate challenges with a heart full of hope. This hope is not rooted in our circumstances but in His promises, which are steadfast and true. It is this unwavering hope that illuminates our path, even in the darkest moments, reminding us that we are never alone.

As you reflect on the Favor of Hope this week, consider the ways it has lifted you up and carried you forward. Embrace the assurance that with God's hope, you have the strength to endure and the spirit to rise above any obstacle. Let this hope overflow from you, touching those around you and spreading the joy and peace that only God can provide. Celebrate this gift of hope, knowing it's a testament to His endless favor in your life.

...

Heavenly Father,

Thank You for the hope that never disappoints. Fill my heart with Your joy and peace as I trust in You. Help me to overflow with hope, revealing Your boundless favor in my life and to those around me.

Amen.

...

# A Whisper of Hope

Lori Miller

...

**Psalm 30:5 (NIV)**

For his anger lasts only a moment, but his favor lasts a lifetime; weeping may stay for the night, but rejoicing comes in the morning.

...

As a teenager, I lived in a difficult home environment that felt impossible to escape. The atmosphere was tense and stressful. With all my siblings grown and gone, I was the last one left at home.

I felt alone, trapped, and uncertain.

I couldn't imagine a future because of the heaviness that surrounded me.

One day, feeling overwhelmed by my circumstances, I went for a walk down the country road. My heart was heavy. My soul felt weary, silently crying out, "I don't know how much longer I can do this."

I stopped to pet a cow grazing by the fence. It was a sweet moment—focusing on the cow's gentle presence. I felt a rare calm settle over me as I appreciated the beauty in front of me.

In that stillness, I heard a voice speak to me, "It won't be much longer now."

I didn't know where the voice came from, but it filled me with an unexpected sense of peace. I walked back home, feeling as if a burden had been lifted. I didn't dwell on what I had heard or question when or how things would change. I simply felt a quiet assurance that somehow, things would get better.

Two months later, a series of unexpected events unfolded, and I was able to leave that difficult environment behind.

My life changed for the better, moving me toward a brighter, more hopeful future holding onto the promise that God had whispered to my heart.

...

Heavenly Father,
Thank You for Your enduring favor and the promise of hope. Guide us through darkness to the joy of a new dawn.
Amen.

...

# Divine Timing

Ebonie T. Pritchett

...

**Romans 12:12 (NIV)**
Rejoice in hope, be patient in tribulation, be constant in prayer.

...

From May to September 2024, I went through one of the roughest seasons of my life. Lost and overwhelmed, I found myself at a crossroads—unsure where to turn or who to call. Then it hit me: Jesus was the answer I'd been seeking all along.

During this difficult period, financial hardships seemed to multiply daily. Debt mounted as I scrambled between various gigs, doing whatever it took to keep food on the table and bills paid. Through it all, God's word became my anchor. I immersed myself in my faith, faithfully attending Sunday services and Bible studies on Wednesdays and Thursdays. Deep down, I sensed this wasn't just another trial or spiritual warfare—this was a time of growth in the wilderness.

Then, on September 3, 2024, everything changed. I received an unexpected call about a recent, forgotten job opportunity. Even as the Director mentioned his company's name, I couldn't recall applying. On September 12, I received an email inviting me to train as a Crisis Counselor, working with homeless individuals facing mental health challenges. By the 17th, I was starting my new role.

My dedication didn't go unnoticed. Within just six weeks, numerous colleagues recommended me for a supervisor position. Today, I've been promoted to Program Administrator—a testament to God's faithfulness in guiding me through that challenging season and into a position where I can truly make a difference in others' lives.

...

**Lord,**
Thank You for Your unwavering favor, guiding us through life's storms
into purpose, provision, and the path You've prepared.
Amen.

...

# Finding True Love

Adrienne Y. Murphy

...

**Proverbs 8:35 (AMP)**
For whoever finds me (Wisdom) finds life and obtains favor and grace from the Lord.

...

The first time I got married, I was young and full of dreams. Little did I know how unprepared we were for the lifelong commitment we were making. Six years later, that dream crumbled, leaving me a single mother with two young children and a heart full of questions. Could I ever find true love again? Was there hope for someone like me?

Enter Carlie Murphy, a man with a presence so compelling it was hard to ignore. He worked security at the office where I was an independent contractor. One day, as I fumbled through a list looking for my name, he approached with a simple, "May I?" With a confident flip of the page, he found my name and pointed to it, asking, "Is this you?" A small moment, yet it sparked a connection that would change my life.

Carlie offered to walk me to my car, and in that short journey, a friendship began to blossom. Both navigating the aftermath of our divorces, with small children and hesitant hearts, we found solace in each other's company. Conversations flowed effortlessly, and as time went on, those talks turned into something deeper.

Despite the hesitations and the complexities of blending families, hope whispered that love was possible. A little over a year later, trusting in that hope, we took a leap of faith and got married. Together, we built a life filled with laughter, cherished memories, and unwavering support, a testament to the power of love and resilience.

For 24 beautiful years, we loved and cared for each other until his passing. Though our marriage ended, the love we shared lives on, a beacon of hope for all who have faced similar journeys. Our story is one of faith and transformation, proof that God can mend broken hearts and forge new paths to true love.

...

**Heavenly Father,**
Fill our souls with steadfast hope, trusting in Your
infinite blessings and unwavering love.
Amen.

...

# Hope Through Tears

Stacey Collins

...

### Romans 15:13 (NIV)

May the God of hope fill you with all joy and peace as you trust in him, so that you may overflow with hope by the power of the Holy Spirit.

...

"Grieving doesn't make you a victim, but when you grieve alone, you can become a victim."

A year after my beautiful sister passed away, a few of my sisters and I got together to paint and remember her life. I sat down on the floor, picked up a blank white canvas, and chose the color orange. I painted the whole background, then sketched the letters "HOPE" in black. The word looked awkward... crooked... off-center... misplaced... alone... just as I felt in my life... in such great loss.

I suddenly stopped painting, tears filling my eyes, and I cried out, "This is hopeless!"

I felt a prompting, "Pick up the yellow paint."

So I picked up the paintbrush and dipped it into the paint. I began to drop dots of yellow onto the orange canvas... drip... drip... then again on the black letters of hope. As each drop fell, a teardrop would come... and another... I could barely see through the tears. In that moment, I felt a shift in my heart—hopelessness turning to hope. The black letters were now a bright yellow sunshine... HOPE!!!

Hope isn't perfect or polished—it's messy and real, like my painting. But like those yellow dots of light, it breaks through our darkest moments... one drop at a time. I took my picture home and hung it on my wall for another year. Each time I looked at it, more healing and courage would come, and I would remember... HOPE. It's not a perfect painting, but it shares my story... a story of hope... "Hope against hope."

...

Lord,

Thank You for the gift of hope. In my darkest moments, help me embrace its light and find strength. May hope transform my heart, one drop at a time.

Amen.

...

# When Hope Returns

### Alethia Saunders

...

### Job 22:21 (NIV)

Submit to God and be at peace with him; in this way prosperity will come to you.

...

I was lying on my bathroom floor, completely lost in time. Hours, maybe days, had passed, but at that moment, I didn't care. I felt nothing—numbness had replaced the storm of emotions I could no longer bear. The pain that consumed me had been dulled by liquor, my chosen escape. I was exhausted—physically, emotionally, and spiritually. I had tried everything I thought would help me heal, yet nothing worked. I was stuck, sinking deeper into despair.

Deep down, though, I knew there was one thing I hadn't tried. My anger—at family, at friends, and even at life—had built a wall between God and me. I hadn't been praying, even though I knew He was the only one who could truly help me. In that moment of desperation, I swallowed my pride. I prayed, called out, and pleaded for Him to hear me.

I begged Him to give me the strength to get off that bathroom floor and find a reason to keep going. And He did. He reminded me of the work I'd done, the gifts He'd given me, and the lives I'd touched. He showed me that there was still more to do—that my purpose wasn't finished.

God lifted me from that cold, hard floor and guided me to my bed. I cried and prayed, prayed and cried, until sleep finally came. The next morning, I woke up feeling different—renewed. I wasn't completely healed, but surrendering to Him had set me on a path toward recovery. That was the turning point, the moment I realized that with Him, I could face anything.

...

### Lord,

When all feels lost, renew my heart with Your hope.
Restore my purpose and guide me in Your grace.
Amen.

...

# Celebrating The Favor of Hope

*Hope in God is a beacon of light, guiding us through life's uncertainties with the promise of His unfailing love. Embrace hope as a powerful force that renews your spirit and draws you closer to His boundless favor and grace.*

**Now it's your turn to write your story of celebrating The Favor of Hope.**

Reflect on a time when hope sustained you during a challenging period. How did this hope influence your outlook and actions? Describe how God's favor was evident through this experience and how hope continues to inspire and guide your faith journey.

# THE
# FAVOR
## OF

# *Mindfulness*

Mindfulness of God's presence opens the heart to favor. By focusing on His goodness, we align our thoughts with His truth, bringing clarity and peace.

# Present Awareness

## Philippians 4:8 (NIV)

Finally, brothers and sisters, whatever is true, whatever is noble, whatever is right, whatever is pure, whatever is lovely, whatever is admirable—if anything is excellent or praiseworthy—think about such things.

...

Mindfulness is not just a distant concept but a daily, intimate journey with God. It's about choosing to focus on His goodness rather than letting worry dictate your day. This choice is a powerful alignment with His truth that sets your spirit free. By being mindful of God's presence, you create space for His favor to manifest in your life in ways you might never have imagined.

Philippians 4:8 isn't just a suggestion; it's your roadmap. It's an invitation to fill your mind with thoughts that lift you up—thoughts that are true, noble, right, pure, lovely, and admirable. When we allow these things to guide our thoughts, we create an environment where peace and clarity can thrive. This isn't about ignoring the realities of life, but rather about embracing a mindset that aligns with God's truth, opening our hearts to His favor.

I challenge you to be intentional about what occupies your mind. When chaos starts to creep in, take a moment to pause. It's in that pause that you can redirect your thoughts towards what's good and praiseworthy. Acknowledge your worries but don't let them take the lead. Choose to dwell on the positive, on the promises God has laid out for you. This practice of mindfulness can transform your perspective, granting you the clarity to navigate powerfully through life. Celebrate the Favor of Mindfulness this. Use it to clear the fog that sometimes clouds your vision and see the path God has laid out for you with fresh eyes. Trust that with clarity and peace, you're unstoppable. God's favor is not just a gift; it's a way of life that fuels your journey. As you cultivate mindfulness, you'll find that you're not just getting through life, but you're thriving, armed with the assurance that God's truth is the foundation beneath your feet. Embrace it, live it, and watch how it transforms not just your mind but your entire life.

...

### God,

Thank You for the clarity and peace that comes from focusing on Your goodness. Help me to be mindful of my thoughts and align them with Your truth. Empower me to embrace each day with Your favor.

Amen.

...

# Everyday Sacred Moments

Sheryl Simms

...

**Psalm 46:10 (NIV)**
Be still, and know that I am God.

...

Life sometimes feels like a whirlwind, doesn't it? Between the endless to-do lists and constant notifications, it's easy to overlook the simple, yet profound moments that remind us of something greater. I remember one evening when this realization struck me. I was in my kitchen, washing dishes after dinner, a mundane task I usually rush through while thinking about the next thing on my agenda.

As the warm water ran over my hands and the scent of lemon soap filled the air, I paused. A soft light from the setting sun filtered through the window, casting a golden hue on everything around me. At that moment, the clatter of the day faded away, and I was enveloped in a gentle stillness. It was then that I felt it— an awareness of God's comforting presence, like a quiet whisper in the chaos.

I looked out the window and saw a neighbor walking their dog, a child's laughter echoing from down the street. It reminded me of the interconnectedness of our lives and the unseen threads that bind us all. It was a simple scene, yet it felt profound. I realized how often I rush through life, missing these everyday miracles.

That evening taught me to cherish the ordinary, to find the divine in the details, and to be fully present. It was a gentle nudge to open my heart to the beauty and grace woven into the fabric of daily life.

...

**Lord,**
Open my heart to Your presence in each moment. May I embrace the beauty of the ordinary and cherish Your divine grace daily.
Amen.

...

# Stay In The Moment

Ishaq Edwards

...

### Matthew 6:33 (NIV)

Therefore do not worry about tomorrow, for tomorrow will worry
about itself. Each day has enough trouble of its own.

...

One day, my Grandma and I were driving to Target. I was so excited because I wanted to buy this cool toy I had been saving up for. I had my wallet with me, and I kept asking Grandma, "Do you think they'll have it? What if it's too expensive? What if they're out of stock?"

Grandma said, "Stop worrying so much. We'll see when we get there."

But I couldn't stop! What if something went wrong? What if I couldn't get the toy I wanted?

Finally, Grandma said, "You can't change what hasn't even happened yet. Just enjoy the ride, and we'll figure it out when we're there."

That made me stop and think. I looked out the window and saw the trees and sunlight. I noticed how peaceful it was.

Then, an idea popped into my head. I told Grandma, "You know what? People should just live in the moment! Like, 'Let the past be the past, let the present be the present, and let the future be the future. If you worry about tomorrow, you won't worry about today. If you get stuck on last month, it will bother you forever!'"

Grandma grinned and said, "That's pretty smart for an eight-year-old."

When we got to Target, the toy was there, and it was the perfect price. I was so happy! But I was more thankful that I had learned to stop worrying and trust God.

...

### Dear God,

Thank You for loving me and taking care of tomorrow. Help
me to trust You, not worry, and enjoy today.
Amen.

...

# Silent Hearts Hear God

Bonita L. Williams

...

**I Thessalonians 4:11 (NIV)**
Make it your goal to live a quiet life, minding your own business and working
with your hands, just as we instructed you before.

...

Over the years, I've embraced the gift of gab—speaking my mind, sharing my opinions, eager to be heard. While there is nothing wrong with verbalizing, I've learned the importance of knowing when to be silent.

Recently, I saw a post that highlighted an interesting fact—the words silent and listen contain the same letters. That simple connection stayed with me. Silence has never been my strongest trait, but it reminded me of a prayer I once prayed, asking God for a discerning spirit.

At times, I've wanted to speak, and yet I hear that still, small voice urging me to remain quiet. Why? Because silence is powerful. It creates space to listen—truly listen—to the promptings of the Holy Spirit.

God has granted us the freedom to say whatever we want, but as His children, our words should reflect our relationship with Him. Learning to pause, to listen, and to obey that nudge to stay silent isn't a sign of weakness; it's a reflection of a heart seeking to please God.

Through His Word, I'm learning to trust the moments of stillness. Silence isn't just the absence of words; it's the presence of wisdom. And in those quiet moments, I find His guidance more clearly.

May we all seek to honor God by cultivating the favor of silence and listening to His voice.

...

**Lord,**
Teach me to treasure silence, to listen closely to Your
voice, and to follow the wisdom You reveal.
Amen.

...

# Hearing God's Voice

Cody Persell

...

## 1 Thessalonians 5:19-22 (GNT)

Do not restrain the Holy Spirit; do not despise inspired messages. Put all things to the test: keep what is good and avoid every kind of evil.

...

Did you know you can hear God's voice? The Bible tells us that the gift of prophecy—hearing God's guidance for yourself and others—is available to all believers. Acts 2:17 declares, "In the last days... your sons and daughters will prophesy." This promise is alive today and meant for everyone.

Prophecy isn't just about knowing the future; it's about hearing God's heart for you and those around you. Paul encourages us in 1 Corinthians 14:1 to "eagerly desire gifts of the Spirit, especially prophecy." Why? Because prophecy strengthens, comforts, and brings hope. It's a reminder that God is near, that He sees you, and that He knows what you need.

To hear God's voice, we must cultivate mindfulness. Just as Jesus withdrew to pray, we can create quiet spaces to focus on Him. Mindfulness opens our hearts and minds, helping us tune in to His whispers, even in a noisy world. John 10:27 reminds us, "My sheep listen to my voice." When we take time to be still, we can experience His presence and discern His words more clearly.

God longs to speak to and through you. No matter your age or background, you can hear His voice. Be mindful, be open, and trust that He's ready to guide and encourage you.

...

**Lord,**

Thank You that You still speak today. Help me to quiet my heart and hear Your voice. Give me the courage to share Your words with others. Amen.

...

# Listening for God's Whisper

### Rochelle D. Jacobs

...

**Psalm 46:10 (ESV)**
Be still and know that I am God.

...

In our fast-paced world, finding stillness is challenging. Life pulls us in countless directions—deadlines, responsibilities, the endless hum of notifications. Yet, it's in the quiet that we hear God's voice most clearly. God's favor is found in silence, where we receive His wisdom, guidance, and love.

There have been times when I felt distant from God. My days were filled with noise—meetings, family obligations, and constant chatter. In these moments I crave stillness. No music, no phone. Just the rhythm of my breath. In the silence, I hear a whisper in my heart, a reassurance that I'm not alone, that God is steering me through life's storm.

Stillness requires us to lay down our worries and distractions, allowing God to speak to our hearts. It's a sacred space where peace and clarity take root. Silence lets us reflect on our challenges, fears, or decisions, not with the rush of anxiety but with the calm of His presence. Instead of filling the void with noise, we pause, pray, and listen. And in these quiet moments, God reveals His plans, reassures our weary souls, and pours out His favor.

Silence is not an absence but a presence—an invitation to listen to God's whisper and embrace His guiding love.

When we seek this stillness, transforming our hearts becomes possible. His word brings peace, understanding, and a deeper connection to Him, reminding us that His voice is clearest in the quiet.

...

**Heavenly Father,**
Grant us healing and strength in silence. Guide us with Your
wisdom, and fill our hearts with peace and understanding.
Amen.

...

# Celebrating The Favor of Mindfulness

*Mindfulness invites us to be present in God's presence, opening our hearts to His daily blessings and guidance. By focusing on His goodness, we align our thoughts with His truth, experiencing peace, clarity, and divine favor in every moment.*

**Now it's your turn to write your story of celebrating The Favor of Mindfulness.**

Reflect on a moment when practicing mindfulness deepened your connection with God. How did this awareness transform your perspective and actions? Describe how His favor was evident through this practice and how mindfulness continues to enrich your spiritual journey and daily life.

# THE FAVOR OF

## Confidence

Stand firm in confidence and embrace God's abundant favor.. When we lean into His promises, we're given a boldness and assurance that empowers us to tackle life head-on, knowing we're backed by the Creator Himself.

# Unshakeable Trust

...

## Hebrews 10:35 (NIV)
So do not throw away your confidence; it will be richly rewarded.

...

Confidence in God's promises empowers us to handle whatever life throws our way. It's the unshakeable trust that keeps us moving forward, even when the journey feels uncertain.

Hebrews 10:35 reminds us not to discard this confidence, for it holds great reward.

When you're standing on the edge of a daunting challenge, your natural instinct might be to retreat or doubt. But when you anchor yourself in faith, you find a new kind of strength. This is not about arrogance but about a deep, abiding assurance that God is true to His word. This confidence gives us courage, a courage that stands unwavering in the face of trials, knowing that God's promises are the bedrock on which we stand.

When you hold on to this kind of faith, you begin to see challenges not as insurmountable walls but as stepping stones to witness God's favor. Every obstacle met with confidence becomes a story of His faithfulness, a testament to your strength in Him. Embrace the confidence that God has placed within you. Reflect on His promises, let them embolden your spirit, and recognize that your confidence is a divine gift that enriches your journey.

Celebrate the unwavering trust you can have in God. Let your faith be the cornerstone of your life, knowing that God is working in every situation, revealing His favor in ways you might not have imagined.

As you lean into the Favor of Confidence this week, know that God has equipped you not just to survive. You're built to thrive, armed with the assurance that God's truth is the foundation beneath your feet.

...

### Lord,
Thank You for the confidence we find in Your promises. Help us to stand firm in faith and trust in Your unfailing love. May we face each challenge with courage, assured of Your abundant favor in our lives. Empower us to walk boldly, knowing that with You, we are richly rewarded.
Amen.

...

# From Fear to Faith

Alethia Saunders

...

**Hebrews 13:6 (ESV)**

So we say with confidence, "The Lord is my helper; I
will not be afraid. What can mere mortals do to me?"

...

I've always been afraid to stand out. Even though I grew up as an only child, I didn't like having all eyes on me. Still, when I left my job and started working for myself, I could hear God's voice telling me it was time to use my writing skills to help others see their true value. After being complimented on my skills in helping people get jobs, I told God that if this was my path, I would follow it. However, I knew I couldn't just pray about it—I had to do something.

So, I took a leap of faith and started promoting my services. When asked, I would confidently tell people, "I can help you get the job." And then I did. This was a great faith booster for me, and the more I moved with confidence, the more doors opened not only for myself but also for others.

Always move with confidence when walking in your purpose!

...

**Lord,**

Thank You for guiding me beyond fear. Grant me
courage to embrace my purpose with confidence.

Amen.

...

# Not a Copy

Benecia Ponder

...

### Romans 12:2 (NIV)

Do not conform to the pattern of this world, but be transformed by the renewing of your mind. Then you will be able to test and approve what God's will is—his good, pleasing and perfect will.

...

When I started writing and sharing the messages God placed in my heart to share, I often looked to other influential leaders. Some of them were Christian, and others were not, but I loved how they all were able to express themselves and create the kinds of results I wanted. I immersed myself in what they were doing. I patterned my style of communication after theirs.

Slowly, I began to distrust my own ideas and instincts. Instead of trusting the inspiration and visions God gave me, I would ask, "What is X doing?" "How would You do this?"

My purpose was paralyzed as I second-guessed everything about my message and how I shared it with others. It wasn't until a wise friend called me out. She told me, "God didn't call you to look like everyone else. Do it the way God told you to do it."

Over time, imitation and comparison can chip away at our confidence. In an effort to "get it right," we compromise our unique calling and become carbon copies of someone else's vision of success.

Embracing our unique calling requires courage and faith, a reminder that God's purpose is not a one-size-fits-all blueprint. Trust in the path He has paved uniquely for you, and let His favor guide your every step. Be bold, be authentic, and let the world see the true reflection of God's purpose in your life.

...

### Dear God,

Thank You for the unique gifts You have given me. Forgive me for limiting my calling and trying to make it look like someone else's. My desire is to do the work You've called me to do, in the way You've called me to do it.

Amen.

...

# Trust Without Answers

Felicia Pichon

...

### Isaiah 55:8-9 (NIV)

For my thoughts are not your thoughts, neither are your ways my ways," declares the Lord. "As the heavens are higher than the earth, so are my ways higher than your ways and my thoughts than your thoughts.

...

My cousin went to Punta Cana for a girls' trip with her friends. When I say "cousin," some may not grasp the depth of our relationship. She wasn't just family by blood—she was my first two daughters' sister and playmate, my youngest daughters' older sister who kept them in line, and to me, she was like a fifth daughter.

While scrolling through Facebook, I saw she'd injured her knee on vacation. Immediately, I felt something wasn't right. God was stirring my spirit, warning me. When she returned, I checked in and expressed my concern about her knee. She reassured me everything was fine, that her doctor had cleared her. The next day, I found her lifeless in her home.

The grief and despair I felt cannot be put into words. Her death turned my world upside down. Even years later, waves of grief still come, but so do the lessons God has taught me through it all. These lessons have shaped my life. I wouldn't trade what I've learned, yet I still wrestle with God, asking, "Was there no other way for me to learn this?"

When have you had to trust God without knowing all the answers? Blindly, painfully, assured only that His ways are higher than ours. Even in uncertainty, will you rest in the confidence that His plan is always better?

...

### Lord,

I trust You fully, even when I don't understand. Strengthen my faith, guide my steps, and help me rest in the confidence of Your perfect plan.

Amen.

...

# Out of the Valley

Bonita L. Williams

...

### Psalms 23:4 (NIV)

Even though I walk through the darkest valley, I will fear no evil,
for you are with me; your rod and your staff, they comfort me.

...

Recently, I found myself in an uncomfortable place. I knew something was wrong, but I couldn't pinpoint what it was. After a period in the valley, I know God has brought me through. My desire in sharing this is to help someone with what I've learned from God. Part of this experience, I believe, was meant to teach and strengthen both me and others.

My time in the valley left me spiritually drained. I prayed and read God's Word but still felt stuck. No effort of mine seemed to work. God eventually used a sermon to show me the path out. He reminded me of a truth I had stopped living out—"With God, all things are possible."

While I knew this, I had failed to daily proclaim it in my life. Instead of praying with victory, I prayed out of need, focusing on my struggles rather than God's power.

I went from feeling on top of the world to sinking deeper until God lifted me up. To those of you in the valley now, I assure you, God will bring you out. To those on the mountain, stay focused and ask God to keep you on the straight and narrow.

I thank God for His love, mercy, and patience as I continue this journey. I encourage you to daily proclaim the power of God and trust Him fully—He is faithful to guide us through every challenge.

...

**Lord,**

Guide my steps, strengthen my faith, and help me trust Your
power to overcome, grow, and walk in salvation.
Amen.

...

# Never Hopeless

Dr. Vanessa D. English

...

## Psalms 121:1-2 (NKJV)

I will lift up my eyes to the hills, From whence comes my help? My help comes from the Lord, Who made heaven and earth.

...

Jewish tradition holds that Psalms 121-134 were sung by pilgrims traveling to Jerusalem. They made this journey to the temple for one of their annual worship festivals. These Psalms affirm their trust in God to guide and protect them on life's journey.

After giving birth to my third child and only daughter, I developed a fever from an abscess on my incision. As the night went on, my fever rose. When it reached 104 degrees, the nurses placed a "cooling sheet" on my bed.

My mama never left my side. She volunteered to stay through the night, declining the cot the nurses offered, saying she would sit in the chair. During the night, I would open my eyes and see her mouth moving. I knew she was praying for God to protect me from whatever was causing my fever.

My mama was never discouraged because she knew what God could do. She prayed all night, trusting in a God who never sleeps.

No matter the circumstances, I am encouraged. I lift my eyes to the hills, and God is always there to help me.

...

**Heavenly Father,**

Because You are my everlasting security, I am never hopeless.

Amen.

...

# Celebrating The Favor of Confidence

*Confidence in God's promises empowers us to face challenges with boldness and certainty. Trusting in His unwavering support, we find the courage to step forward, knowing His favor paves the way for triumph and growth in every endeavor.*

**Now it's your turn to write your story of celebrating The Favor of Confidence.**

Reflect on a time when confidence in God guided you through a difficult situation. How did this trust influence your decisions and outcomes? Describe how His favor was evident through your confidence and how it continues to inspire your faith and actions.

_____

_____

_____

_____

_____

_____

_____

_____

_____

_____

_____

_____

_____

_____

_____

_____

_____

_____

# THE
# FAVOR
## OF
# Direction

Trust in God's guidance to direct you to His favor. His loving counsel illuminates our path.

# Guided Steps

...

**Psalm 32:8**

I will instruct you and teach you in the way you should go; I will counsel you with my loving eye on you.

...

Life often feels like navigating through a maze. There are turns that look promising, paths that seem unclear, and times we feel lost. Yet, in the midst of uncertainty, God offers the gift of direction. His promise to guide us and teach us is not just comforting; it's transformational.

When we embrace His guidance, He doesn't just point out the way; He walks with us, ensuring that each step we take is secure and purpose-driven.

Think of God's direction as a compass, revealing the right path even when we're surrounded by confusion. He sees the full picture, the destination we're heading towards, and the obstacles we might encounter. Trusting in His guidance means allowing Him to take the lead, to steer us away from pitfalls and towards His abundant favor.

You might be facing decisions that feel overwhelming or situations that seem to have no clear solution. In these moments, lean into God's promise in Psalm 32:8. Let His wisdom calm your fears and His counsel guide your choices. Remember, you are not alone on this journey. His loving eye is upon you, ensuring that every step you take aligns with His divine purpose.

Celebrate the Favor of Direction in your life. Embrace the assurance that comes from knowing that God's hand is directing your path. Take bold steps, knowing that with Him, you are always on the right track.

...

**Dear Lord,**

Thank You for being our guide and counselor. Help us trust in Your direction, knowing that Your loving eye watches over us. Teach us to follow Your path with confidence and wisdom. May we seek Your guidance in every decision and celebrate the favor of Your direction.
Amen.

...

# At Your Age

Dr. Joyce S. Mallory

...

### James 1:5 (NIV)

If any of you lacks wisdom, you should ask God, who gives generously to all without finding fault, and it will be given to you.

...

After a brief 10-minute screening, the neurologist informed me that I have minimal cognitive decline; he said this was common for people my age. My immediate reaction was disbelief; I refused to accept this fate of losing my memory and mental clarity. Instead, I prayed, "Lord, please help me not to forget so that I can write for you!"

I prayed for wisdom, not fame or money. I was determined to explore every possible option to maintain my cognitive health and inspire others who read my writing.

The concept of living a good life occupies my thoughts constantly. I usually wake up with a praise song in my heart or a person's name to pray for. Many times, I am urged to pray in various circumstances. Since retiring in 2019 following a layoff from my part-time teaching position, I have immersed myself in reading and writing. I also teach in a summer adult Vacation Bible School and enroll in various classes my church offers. Despite the prevalence of social media and technology, I still derive immense joy from holding a physical book, appreciating the traditional method over reading on a screen. Embracing this phase of life, I continue to seek growth and connection through my passions for crafting, learning, teaching, and writing.

...

### Dear Lord,

Thank you for your continuous guidance as I share and write your Word. May clarity and favor reside with the reader of my written messages.

Amen.

...

379

# From Resistance to Blessing

Alethia Saunders

...

**Psalms 32:8 (NIV)**
I will instruct you and teach you in the way you should
go; I will counsel you with my loving eye on you.

...

I've always been known for my stubbornness—a trait my mother frequently reminded me of. I had a knack for listening, smiling, nodding in agreement, and then doing exactly what I had intended in the first place. When I began working for myself, that streak of defiance stayed with me. I was determined to preserve my identity and operate my business my way, no matter the advice I received.

One day, a God-fearing professional pulled me aside and gently admonished me, pointing out how certain aspects of my appearance might hinder my image and, ultimately, my business growth. At first, I brushed it off. I fought their advice tooth and nail, believing I knew what was best for me. But they didn't give up. They sat me down, walked me through the numbers, and presented tangible proof of the consequences of my choices. For the first time, I truly listened.

After much reflection, I decided to follow their direction. I made the changes they suggested, humbled myself, and aligned my actions with wisdom and God's guidance. That decision transformed everything. In just three months, my business tripled in size. My income followed suit, and my confidence soared.

This wasn't just about improving my business—it was about learning to trust the process, heed sound advice, and boldly walk in God's path for me. That moment of surrender taught me that sometimes the greatest strength lies in letting go of pride and embracing the lessons others are sent to teach us.

...

**Lord,**
Thank You for guiding my steps. Grant me humility to accept wisdom, courage
to follow Your direction, and faith to trust Your plan. Amen.

...

# The Right Way

Dr. Nina Addison

...

**Psalms 25:4 (NIV)**

Let me know Your ways, O Lord; Teach me Your paths.

...

Can you imagine being on a road and realizing you are going the long way or the wrong way?

I felt like that before God opened my eyes to His truth. I grew up not knowing that God still speaks or that He could perform miracles. I thought that was just in the Bible, not applicable today.

In 2010, when God changed my life, He did it in a way that proved to me He not only hears but also speaks. This changed the direction of my life.

Whereas I was making choices that made me feel good, I decided to follow God for real and go in the direction that pleases Him. These changes brought about so much favor. I have been able to be one of His lights He uses on the earth. Following the direction He has led me in has brought about so much peace. It has opened many doors and closed those that needed to close for my good. I promise you that if you go in the direction that pleases God and that He leads you in, you will NOT be disappointed.

...

**Father God,**

May You lead and direct Your child in the way they should go, so that
it pleases You and gives them peace that surpasses all understanding.
May it be so, in the name above all names, Jesus,
Amen!

...

# HOW

Bonita L. Williams

...

### Philippians 4:19 (NLT)

And this same God who takes care of me will supply all your needs from his glorious riches, which have been given to us in Christ Jesus.

...

During a morning prayer, I made an incredible discovery involving the letters H-O-W, which form the word "how." I realized that I have spent a significant part of my life worrying about the "how's."

How will I pass this test? How will I lose weight? How will this bill get paid?

I noticed I wasn't alone in this struggle; many people I have met have faced the same issue. The "how's" of life were weighing them down too.

How am I going to make ends meet? How will I meet Mr. Right? How will I get that promotion? How will I navigate these teenage years? How can I become a better person?

These "how's" can sometimes lead us to despair.

While I was pondering a "how" situation, the Lord spoke to me and said, "Turn the letters around." I discovered that by rearranging the letters H-O-W, they form the word "who."

Isn't our God amazing? That's what He does—He turns things around. Instead of wasting time focusing on the "how's," I need to shift my attention to the "who."

Who is my strong tower? Who is my bridge over troubled waters? Who turns my midnight into day? Who wipes away all my tears? Who is my all in all?
Luke 12:31 reminds us that instead of worrying about how we will eat, what we will wear, or how we will be better parents or spouses, we should seek God first. Focusing on the "how's" only brings worry and unrest. The "Who" in our lives, the center of our joy, brings "peace that surpasses all understanding" (Philippians 4:7).

...

### Lord,

Help me shift my focus from worries to Your presence. Guide me to trust in You, finding peace and strength in Your unwavering support and love.

Amen.

...

# Called to Thrive

Felicia Pichon

...

**Psalm 32:8 (NIV)**

I will instruct you and teach you in the way you should
go; I will counsel you with my loving eye on you.

...

It was in the stillness and quiet that I heard, as clear as day, "Check your breasts." WHAT???

I had not had a mammogram in over seven years, and I didn't do routine breast exams. But I obeyed that whisper and acted that very day. I found something and mentioned it to a friend so she could hold me accountable. Less than a month later, I was diagnosed with breast cancer.

I knew God had a greater purpose for me, but I had no idea what it was. I understood that this was a calling on my life. God was calling me to something greater by allowing this to happen, and I was ready to listen. God kept leading me down different paths, but I would always circle back to my comfort zone. However, this diagnosis shed new light on everything.

I had breast cancer!!! Yet, I also knew God would deliver me and that there would be a testimony in this test.

I started a nonprofit that focuses on the health and wellness of women of color. Sisters Thrive advocates for BIWOC (Black Indigenous Women of Color) for better health outcomes based on health equity. We amplify our voices to ensure we are heard above the noise and to change the trajectory of health outcomes. Because health is wealth, we're committed to ensuring we thrive, not just survive.

What is the Lord calling you to do that is greater than you?

...

**Lord,**

Thank You for guiding me to this purpose. I trust Your plan and seek Your wisdom
to continue serving others. Help me walk boldly in Your favor and direction.

Amen.

...

# Celebrating The Favor of Direction

*God's direction lights the path to His promises, guiding us with clarity and purpose. As you follow His lead, trust that His favor is paving the way for you to walk confidently into the future He has prepared.*

**Now it's your turn to write your story of celebrating The Favor of Direction.**

Reflect on a time when you felt God's guidance directing your path. How did this direction influence your decisions and lead to unexpected blessings? Describe how His favor was evident through this guidance and how it continues to shape your journey and faith.

_____

_____

_____

_____

_____

_____

_____

_____

_____

_____

_____

_____

_____

_____

_____

_____

_____

_____

# THE
# FAVOR
## OF
# *Breakthrough*

Breakthroughs come when God's favor is upon you. In His timing, He breaks barriers and opens doors.

# Divine Openings

...

**1 Chronicles 14:11**

So David and his men went up to Baal Perazim, and there he defeated them. He said, 'As waters break out, God has broken out against my enemies by my hand.' So that place was called Baal Perazim.

...

Life can sometimes feel like you're stuck in a holding pattern, circling the same mountain over and over again. We all know what it's like to feel boxed in by circumstances, whether it's waiting for a new job opportunity, healing in a relationship, or a personal breakthrough in your spiritual walk. But here's the truth: God's favor has a way of showing up right when you need it most, like a flood that washes away every obstacle in its path.

David's experience at Baal Perazim is a testament to that. When God shows up, He doesn't tiptoe around your problems—He breaks through with power and purpose. That same force is available for you today. His favor is the catalyst that transforms insurmountable walls into open doors.

Think about a time you felt like you were at the end of your rope. Maybe you were under financial stress, dealing with a deep loss, or questioning your path. Then suddenly, something shifted. A door opened, a phone call came, or a peace settled in your spirit. That's what a breakthrough feels like, and it's not by accident. It's God aligning things in His perfect timing.

Breakthroughs often come when we least expect them, in ways we could never have orchestrated ourselves. That's why it's important to stay expectant and open to His leading. Look for the small victories and celebrate them, because they're indicators of the larger work God is doing in your life.

This week, lean into the breakthroughs you need. Keep your heart full of gratitude for what God has already done, and stay hopeful for what's ahead. Let the anticipation of His favor fuel your faith, knowing that when God moves, He moves in extraordinary ways.

...

**Heavenly Father,**

Thank You for the favor of breakthrough. Teach us to trust Your timing and remain steadfast in our faith. Break down the barriers that hold us back and open doors to new possibilities. Let Your power and mercy be evident in every area of our lives.

Amen.

...

# Broke Down to Breakthrough

Rochelle D. Jacobs

...

**Jeremiah 30:17 (NIV)**
But I will restore you to health and heal your wounds.

...

Amid uncertainty and fear during the COVID-19 pandemic, I faced a journey battling the virus that was both a physical and spiritual struggle. As my health deteriorated, anxiety and doubt overwhelmed me, and I questioned if I would ever be well again.

In my darkest moments, I turned to God's word for comfort. Jeremiah 30:17 became a lifeline, sparking hope in my heart. I prayed fervently for healing, strength, and a breakthrough. The days were challenging; relentless headaches and fever left me wishing for relief. Each breath was laborious, yet I found solace in the 23rd Psalm (KJV), learning to lean into God's presence and trust His goodness. Repeating, "The Lord is my shepherd, I shall not want," reminded me of God's promise of restoration.

As weeks passed, I noticed small signs of improvement. The fever broke, and I could take longer walks around the house. Each step forward felt like a victory, signaling not just physical healing but a spiritual breakthrough. God was restoring my body and spirit, showing me there was a message in this mess.

"Breakthrough begins with a heart of faith, believing that God's favor can turn our trials into testimonies of His healing power."

I fully recovered from COVID-19, but the experience left an indelible mark on my faith. I emerged with a renewed sense of purpose, sharing my story in the ladies' Bible class about the importance of faith during adversity. I encouraged others to trust in God's favor for healing and breakthrough.

God's favor is not just about immediate healing but also about the transformation in our hearts. May we hold onto hope in His promises, knowing His grace is sufficient in our times of need.

...

**Heavenly Father,**
Thank You for Your healing and favor. Grant us strength and faith to overcome trials, transforming our struggles into testimonies.
Amen.

...

# Breaking Free

Alethia Saunders

...

### Psalms 118:17 (NIV)

I will not die but live, and will proclaim what the Lord has done.

...

For two years, I was trapped. It started with a surgery and a prescription. What seemed like a necessary solution to my pain turned into a cycle that held me captive. I didn't recognize it at first, but I was functioning as a shadow of myself. The pills numbed the pain, but they also numbed my spirit. I moved through life like a zombie, unnoticed by those around me, and, most importantly, unnoticed by myself.

But God had a different plan. He saw me even when I couldn't see myself. One day, as I sat in the stillness of my own life, I realized I didn't want to stay stuck anymore. The pills had controlled me long enough, and I knew I needed to make a change. I took this burden to God in prayer, asking for the strength and clarity to break free. In that moment, a shift occurred.

I heard a sermon that would forever change my life. It spoke directly to my heart, reminding me that God's favor was not just for the moments when things were easy, but also for the times when we take a stand for our healing. I knew then that I was no longer a prisoner to my circumstances. I began to wean myself off the pills, one day at a time, relying on God's strength to carry me through.

That was my breakthrough. The favor of God came over me as I made the conscious decision to trust Him fully, to let go of what was holding me back, and to embrace the freedom He had for me.

...

### Lord,

Thank You for Your favor and strength. Help me break free from all that binds me, trust Your plan, and walk boldly into the freedom You've prepared for me.

Amen.

...

# Break Through Those Walls

Dr. Theresa Billingsley

...

**Joshua 6:5 (NKJV)**

It shall come to pass, when they make a long blast with the ram's horn, and when you hear the sound of the trumpet, that all the people shall shout with a great shout; then the wall of the city will fall down flat.

...

Walls serve a purpose. They protect, set boundaries, and create space for privacy. But here's the thing—walls don't just keep people out; they can lock you in. I know because I built them around my heart after being hurt so many times.

I thought I was safe behind those walls. No one could hurt me anymore. But over time, I realized I was trapped. I couldn't connect with anyone. I couldn't even fully love the people who stood patiently on the other side, waiting for a crack in my defenses. I was guarded, bitter, and lonely.

I remember one moment vividly. A close friend gently pointed out that I had stopped sharing anything real with them. "You're here, but you're not," they said. It stung, but they were right. That night, I sat with God, tears running down my face, and asked, "What now? How do I tear these walls down?"

God didn't give me an easy out. He worked on my heart layer by layer. He showed me that while it was okay to set healthy boundaries, locking everyone out wasn't the answer. Through forgiveness and trust in Him, I started letting people in again. It wasn't easy, but something beautiful happened—I felt free.

Now, I see those walls for what they were—a defense mechanism that kept me from being my authentic self, from sharing God's love with others. Whatever walls you've built, trust Him to break through them. There's love and freedom waiting on the other side.

...

**Lord,**

Soften my heart and tear down these walls. Help me
trust, forgive, and love freely as You lead me.

Amen.

...

# Brokenness Produces Breakthroughs

Vanessa Fortenberry

...

**Psalm 34:18 (NIV)**

The Lord is close to the brokenhearted and saves those who are crushed in spirit."

...

Have you ever refused help, determined to solve things on your own? I have. Too often, we reject God's help, clinging to self-reliance. This resistance only leads to frustration and failure.

A few years ago, I faced a crisis that left me broken and lifeless. Depression consumed me, and I went through the motions of life without joy. Though I attended church and sang in the choir, my passion was gone. I isolated myself, sharing my struggles with no one, not even God. My efforts to handle it alone only deepened my despair.

One Sunday, overwhelmed, I walked to the altar, fell to my knees, and cried out to Jesus. I repented, surrendered my pride, and opened my heart to God's will. I also sought help from a Christian therapist, whom God used to guide me through the pain. With time, I was restored and even accomplished a lifelong dream of publishing my first children's book. This season of brokenness was the catalyst for immense spiritual growth.

Like King David, whose broken spirit and guilt drove him to repentance, I found hope in God's mercy (Psalm 51). David learned that we cannot hide from God, and neither can we. God knows our hearts and longs to bring us healing and restoration.

Take your brokenness to God. Lay your worries and struggles before Him, ask for healing, and align yourself with His will. He is the God of breakthroughs— ready to transform brokenness into wholeness and purpose.

...

**Lord,**

I surrender my brokenness to You. Heal my heart, renew my spirit, and guide me toward breakthroughs that reflect Your glory. Transform my pain into purpose, Father. Amen.

...

# God Provides

Veronica Washington

...

**Isaiah 65:24 (NIV)**

Before they call I will answer; while they are still speaking I will hear.

...

My car suddenly broke down on my way home from school. It wasn't just an inconvenience—it was the end of a long month, and my budget was stretched thin. I remember sitting in that car, rain tapping on the windshield, wondering how I was going to afford the repairs.

Instead of spiraling into worry, I took a deep breath and prayed right there in the driver's seat. "Lord, I don't know how, but I trust You will provide."

The following day, a parent of one of my students stopped by my classroom with an unexpected gift. She handed me an envelope, saying, "You've been such a blessing to our family, and I felt led to give you this."

Inside was more than enough to cover the repairs. My eyes welled with tears, not just from the amount but from the reminder that God meets us in our needs.

That moment stayed with me as a testament to His power and provision in even the most everyday struggles. Whenever challenges come, I think back to that rainy afternoon and am reminded that God sees, God cares, and God provides.

...

Lord,

Thank You for providing in my need, showing Your power, and leading me to trust fully in Your salvation.

Amen.

...

# Celebrating The Favor of Breakthrough

*Breakthrough moments are divine interventions, where God shatters barriers and unveils new possibilities. Trust in His timing and power, knowing each breakthrough is a testament to His favor and your faithfulness.*

**Now it's your turn to write your story of celebrating The Favor of Breakthrough.**

Reflect on a breakthrough moment in your life when God opened doors you thought were closed. How did this experience change your perspective and deepen your faith? Describe how His favor was evident through this breakthrough and how it continues to inspire your journey and trust in Him.

_____

_____

_____

_____

_____

_____

_____

_____

_____

_____

_____

_____

_____

_____

_____

_____

_____

_____

# THE FAVOR OF *Mercy*

God's mercy renews us daily and showers us with favor. His compassion never fails.

# Renewed Grace

...

## Lamentations 3:22

Because of the Lord's great love we are not consumed, for his compassions never fail.

...

Your life may be filled with ups and downs, and sometimes we stumble. But there's something profoundly comforting in knowing that God's mercy is ever-present, renewing us every single day.

This mercy is a continual blessing that meets us in our weaknesses and lifts us into new beginnings.

Lamentations 3:22 tells us that it is because of God's great love that we are not consumed. His compassion is unfailing, a constant source of hope and renewal.

In those moments when you feel overwhelmed by your mistakes or shortcomings, it's easy to let guilt and regret cloud your vision. Yet, God's mercy brings forgiveness and a fresh start. His favor is not dependent on our perfection but on His perfect love and compassion.

Each day is an opportunity to experience His mercy anew. Whether it's forgiving someone who has wronged you or seeking forgiveness for your own missteps, God's favor invites you to let go of past burdens and embrace the grace He offers. Reflect on the mercy you've received and think about how you can extend that same grace to others.

As you navigate through this week celebrating the Favor of Mercy, hold onto the promise of God's unwavering compassion. Let it be a reminder that no matter how far you stray, His mercy is there to guide you back, to renew your spirit, and to shower you with favor. Celebrate the gift of mercy, knowing it is a powerful force that transforms and uplifts.

...

## Merciful Father,

Thank You for Your endless compassion and the favor of mercy in our lives. Help us receive Your grace with open hearts, and teach us to extend it to others. May Your renewing love guide us each day, reminding us of the new beginnings You offer.

Amen.

...

# Divine Do-Overs

Benecia Ponder

...

## Psalm 23:6 (KJV)

Surely goodness and mercy shall follow me all the days of my
life: and I will dwell in the house of the Lord for ever.

...

Each year, my heart swells with joy as I volunteer at a golf tournament, a spirited event supporting Antioch Urban Ministries, Inc. This incredible organization brings hope and a fresh start to many, offering housing and rehabilitation for those recovering from substance abuse, sheltering and providing social services for individuals with AIDS and TB, and nurturing at-risk youth. They even run a bustling food pantry and clothing bank, serving thousands monthly.

One of my cherished roles during the event is at the registration desk, where golfers eagerly purchase raffle tickets and something intriguingly called "Mulligans." As a novice, I was puzzled by the term until a seasoned golfer kindly explained.

"A Mulligan," he said, "is a do-over—a chance to retry a swing without penalty if our ball lands poorly."

His words resonated deeply within me, unveiling a profound parallel to our lives as believers.

Just like in golf, where Mulligans offer players a chance to redeem themselves, God's mercy showers us with endless opportunities to start anew. Whether it's a second, third, or fourth chance, His grace abounds relentlessly. The beauty of His mercy lies in its price—already paid in full by His Son, Jesus Christ.

What a humbling and transformative gift this is, empowering us to learn, grow, and strive toward our best selves.
In every Mulligan, I see God's boundless love and favor, reminding me that no swing, no matter how misguided, is beyond redemption. His mercy offers the do-over we need to truly thrive.

...

## Merciful God,

I thank You for Your boundless mercy and the countless chances to start anew.
Guide me to embrace Your grace daily.
Amen.

...

# Rearview Reflections

Cynthia Beckles

...

## Psalm 121:7-8 (NIV)

The Lord will keep you from all harm— he will watch over your life; the Lord will watch over your coming and going both now and forevermore.

...

When I saw the flashing blue lights in my rearview mirror, I panicked. I had been driving within the speed limit. My heart raced as I pulled over to the side of the road. Tears blurred my vision, and the weight of the situation felt overwhelming.

I rested my head on the steering wheel and began to cry. It reminded me of a time years ago when a police officer tailgated me along a dark, desolate road. The emptiness stretched for miles—no streetlights, no signs of life, just the hum of my car and the harsh glare of his headlights in my rearview mirror. The tension was unbearable. When he finally pulled me over, I was still under the speed limit. There was no valid explanation given, and he eventually let me go. His commanding officer later apologized, but the fear lingered. What could have happened if things had gone differently?

Flashing back to the present, I lifted my head as the police car passed me and continued down the road. With a deep exhale, I felt my fists unclench and the tension ease. I was grateful for God's mercy.

I realized how often we overlook God's unseen protection—sparing us from dangers we'll never know. The detours and delays we question may be the very moments when His hand shields us from harm. In that moment, I understood that even in fear, God's care is constant, guiding us through the unseen. I whispered a prayer: "Thank You, Lord, for Your protection."

...

Lord,
Thank You for Your unseen protection and constant
care, guiding us safely through life's unknown paths.
Amen.

...

# Hidden Faith

Vanessa Fortenberry

...

## Matthew 15:28 (NIV)

"Dear woman," Jesus said to her, "your faith is great! Your request is granted."

...

Fear is often described as "False Evidence Appearing Real." Whether illusion or reality, fear wields immense power to shape emotions and actions.

A few years ago, health challenges tested my faith. My doctor's calls with lab results filled me with dread. One evening, after Googling my condition, I convinced myself of impending surgery and weeks off work. The next day, I shared my dire assumptions with my daughter. She gently rebuked me, saying, "At most, you might need physical therapy." Her words reminded me I hadn't even consulted the specialist yet. I realized I had surrendered to fear, imagining the worst without facts.

This sparked two questions in my heart. First, Do I know Jesus? Like Peter in Mark 8:29, who recognized Jesus as the Messiah, I, too, know Him as Immanuel, Way Maker, and more. The second question cut deeper—If I know Jesus, where did I hide my faith?

Life's challenges can weaken faith, but God's mercy remains steadfast. Reflecting on His works and goodness shifts fear to faith, reminding us He is always making a way.

We all falter, but God's mercy invites us to grow stronger. To keep faith flourishing, we can:

Begin each day with prayer and praise.

Stay in constant conversation with God.

Seek Him first during hardships.

Trust Him above our fears and doubts.

Fear loses its grip when we anchor ourselves in God's mercy. Strengthen your faith and trust His unfailing love.

...

Lord,
Thank You for Jesus' sacrifice. Help us follow His
example, serve others, and live in devotion to You.
Amen.

...

# Not What I Deserve

L. Marie

...

### Titus 3:5 (NIV)

He saved us, not because of righteous things we had done, but because of his mercy.
He saved us through the washing of rebirth and renewal by the Holy Spirit.

...

Mercy has been the heartbeat of my life—both as a nurse and as a believer. I remember one particular night on the ward, decades ago. A young man came into the ER after a terrible accident. His injuries were severe, and his blood-alcohol level made it painfully clear he'd been at fault. Many of my colleagues looked at him with judgment; I could see it in their eyes. But all I could think was how small the line is between us and a single misstep. Mercy doesn't look at the mistake—it looks at the person.

I stayed by his side, tending to him, speaking words of comfort, and praying quietly as the doctors worked. He survived, though he carried the scars of that night. A year later, he returned to the hospital—a changed man—looking for me. Through tears, he thanked me for the compassion I gave when he felt he deserved none.

That mirrors what Christ has done for me. Time and again, He's met me with mercy when I least deserved it. Being a nurse taught me that we're all broken in our own ways, and mercy is the balm that helps us heal, both physically and spiritually. It's the fullest reflection of God's love.

...

### Lord,

Thank You for Your mercy that heals and restores. May
we reflect Your compassion and grace in all we do.
Amen.

...

# Teaching Me Mercy

Veronica Washington

...

**Isaiah 30:18 (ESV)**

Therefore the Lord waits to be gracious to you, and therefore he exalts himself to show mercy to you. For the Lord is a God of justice; blessed are all those who wait for him.

...

When I was a young teacher fresh out of college, I had a student named Marcus. He was often late, rarely turned in assignments, and sometimes fell asleep in class. I saw him as a troublemaker.

One day, after keeping him after school to lecture him yet again, he quietly said, "Miss Washington, I'm sorry. My mom's been sick, and I've been taking care of my little sisters. I'm just tired." That moment cracked something in me. I had been so quick to judge him without knowing his struggle. I remember going home that evening and praying, asking God to teach me how to temper my judgment with mercy.

The next day, instead of scolding Marcus, I asked how I could help. I started giving him quieter spaces to nap during lunch and broke assignments into manageable parts. His grades improved, but what truly changed was my heart. I learned mercy wasn't about excusing behavior—it was about understanding it.

That lesson stayed with me long after Marcus graduated. Mercy shaped my faith, softening my edges and showing me how closely it's tied to love. It reminds me daily that we're not here to criticize each other but to offer what God so freely gives—grace.

...

**Lord,**

Soften my heart with mercy, guide me in compassion, and grant me the grace of salvation through Your love.

Amen.

...

# Celebrating The Favor of Mercy

*Mercy is God's limitless compassion, a constant reminder of His love and forgiveness. Embrace His mercy, allowing it to renew your spirit and guide your actions, transforming your life with His boundless favor and grace.*

**Now it's your turn to write your story of celebrating The Favor of Mercy.**

Reflect on a time when you experienced God's mercy in a profound way. How did this mercy impact your life and relationships? Describe how His favor was evident through this experience and how it has influenced your understanding of His love and forgiveness.

_____

_____

_____

_____

_____

_____

_____

_____

_____

_____

_____

_____

_____

_____

_____

_____

_____

_____

_____

_____

**WEEK 51**

# THE

# FAVOR

## OF

## *Encouragement*

Encouragement lifts others and invites God's favor. Through uplifting words and actions, we share hope and strengthen community.

# Uplifting Words

...

## 1 Thessalonians 5:11

Therefore encourage one another and build each other up, just as in fact you are doing.

...

Encouragement is a powerful gift we can offer one another. It has the ability to uplift spirits, transform perspectives, and build strong communities. In a world that often focuses on the negative, encouraging words are like a refreshing breeze that brings newfound strength and hope. God's favor shines brightly when we commit to uplifting each other, creating an environment filled with love and support.

1 Thessalonians 5:11 reminds us of the importance of encouraging one another. This simple act can change the course of someone's day or even their life. When we offer encouragement, we not only affirm others, but we also invite God's favor into our interactions. Our words and actions become vessels of His grace, spreading His love to those around us.

Think about a time when someone's kind words or supportive gesture made a difference in your life. It could have been a note of appreciation, a helping hand, or a heartfelt compliment. These moments remind us of the profound impact encouragement can have, sparking joy and strength within us.

This week, take the opportunity to be a source of encouragement. Whether it's sending a thoughtful message, offering a listening ear, or acknowledging someone's efforts, your actions can make an enormous difference. As you encourage others, you'll find that God's favor flows through you, creating a ripple effect of positivity and hope.

...

Gracious Lord,

Thank You for the gift of encouragement. Help us to be mindful of the ways we can uplift those around us. May our words and actions shine with Your love, building a community filled with hope and strength. Guide us to share Your favor through simple acts of kindness.

Amen.

...

# When Words Save

Alethia Saunders

...

## 1 Thessalonians 5:11 (NIV)

Therefore encourage one another and build each other up, just as in fact you are doing.

...

She called me from the closet. I wasn't sure at the moment why she called, but I'm glad I picked up. She was a client who vented to me at times, and I knew a little bit about her—her past, her struggles, her pain. So when she called me from the closet, I knew it wasn't good, and I knew if I didn't move fast, there wouldn't be time left. I got her help immediately but kept her on the phone. I let her know that God loved her, I loved her, and this wasn't the way.

A few months later, she called me back. She had been sent to rehabilitation and got the help she needed so that she could live. I was just happy that she dialed my number and that God gave me the right words for her because she deserved another chance to truly be happy. I'm so glad that I can say we are friends to this day! She brings this memory up to me every year or so, and I shrug it off as if it's no big deal. Deep down, though, I'm grateful I was able to encourage her to keep fighting the good fight!

...

**Lord,**

Thank You for empowering me to encourage others.

Guide me to continue offering hope and support.

Amen.

...

# Speak Life

Benecia Ponder

...

### James 3:9–10 (MSG)

With our tongues we bless God our Father; with the same tongues we curse the very men and women he made in his image. Curses and blessings out of the same mouth! My friends, this can't go on.

...

I decided to head to Starbucks for a change of scenery. Sometimes, the buzz of people helps spark my creativity. I ordered a hot chocolate and settled into a corner seat. As I opened my laptop, a conversation at the next table caught my attention. A young woman was speaking softly, "I'm just not good enough," she said, clearly fighting back tears. Her friend tried to console her, but she seemed trapped in her self-doubt.

Her words struck a chord in me. I remembered all the times I had spoken to myself that way. Times when I felt inadequate, letting negative thoughts dictate my day. But I also remembered the moment I realized those words had power. They could either build me up or tear me down.

As they gathered their things to leave, I felt a nudge within me. I leaned over and gently said, "Excuse me, I couldn't help but overhear. I just want to say, you are more capable than you believe. You're stronger than you know." She nodded and thanked me for my kind words.

It was a small gesture, but I hoped it planted a seed of encouragement.

...

### Father,

Guide my words to bless and uplift, speaking victory and favor over my life and others.

Amen.

...

# The Power of 5 AM

Dr. Katherine E. James

...

## Hebrews 10:24-25 (NIV)

And let us consider how we may spur one another on toward love and good deeds, not giving up meeting together, as some are in the habit of doing, but encouraging one another—and all the more as you see the Day approaching.

...

COVID-19.

Not much needs to be said. It was a terrifying time for many of us. A dear sister/friend of mine was struggling badly. She had recently lost the grandmother who raised her. She and her husband had a severe case of COVID. Few of us understood what was going on, and most were in abject fear.

She was significantly depressed, severely ill, and no longer wanted to live.

I, on the other hand, was having a different experience, desperately seeking a way to serve others. Thankfully, I did what I have been created to do, using my gifts and talents to add more love to the world with life-giving conversations. I began a weekday 5:40 am social media live show on February 20, 2020. My sister/friend, who I didn't know was suffering, credits the love and life that came from the "Why 5 AM" live for saving her life.

The show was developed from a challenge to go live for 30 days. Unbeknownst to me, God used this to get me to serve encouragement to His beloved daughter, providing her with hope to live. Four years later, the live continues, and many experience encouragement in the way they need it.

Many have been encouraged by Poppa's use of me.

How about you? Did you know that serving from your soul is an encouragement? I invite you to be sure you are honoring your soul's cry and serving encouragement to others from that deep well of hope.

...

Lord,

Thank You for the strength to serve and the love to uplift others. Use me to encourage and bring hope where it's needed most.

Amen.

...

# Be Blessed, Encourage People

Makini Theresa L. Harvey

...

Acts 20:2 (NIV)

He traveled through that area, speaking many words of encouragement to the people, and finally arrived in Greece.

...

One of my favorite spiritual gifts is the Gift of Encouragement. I love it because it is so easy, and it always blesses me when I can encourage others. Here are two encouraging instances:

From Women's Jail to Executive Chef

During a career workshop that I facilitated for women at the county jail, "Martha" sat with her back turned all day and didn't participate, while the others loved it. A year later, Martha stopped me in the mall, apologized for her rudeness, thanked and hugged me, saying she heard what I said that day and used the strategies to win a job as an executive chef at Nordstrom.

From Suicidal Thoughts to Wanting to Live Again

"Mary" was at the transit center waiting for the bus, crying. I asked if I could help her. She said her husband was dying because he refused to take his medicine. I immediately prayed for both of them. Days later, she and her husband thanked me.

...

**Compassionate and Merciful God, Abba,**

I thank Your Holy Spirit for filling me with the gift of encouragement, in the Holy Name of Jesus Christ;
Hallelujah and Amen.

...

# Doubt Didn't Win

Amber Rainsberry

...

Ephesians 4:29 (NIV)
Do not let any unwholesome talk come out of your mouths, but only what is helpful for building others up according to their needs, that it may benefit those who listen.

...

This was the day—my dream job interview! I'd had a great phone screening with Marcy a few days earlier. We'd connected over shared experiences, from attending the same college to having daughters the same age. I felt hopeful but had the usual interview jitters.

The interview was at 1:30, forty minutes away, and I planned to arrive early. That morning, I prepared a "brag book" of my sales accomplishments, even though Marcy had said it wasn't necessary. I liked the idea of being fully prepared.

Then, I remembered my coworker Kathy had interviewed with Marcy weeks earlier but didn't get the job. I called her, and she warned me that Marcy was "impossible" and claimed I had no chance since her sales numbers were better than mine. Her words got to me. By 12:45, I had taken off my suit, stopped preparing, and resigned myself to not going.

At 1 p.m., another friend called and asked if I was on my way. I explained what had happened, and she firmly encouraged me to go. She reminded me of the great connection I'd had with Marcy. Her words jolted me—I threw my suit back on, grabbed my brag book, and sped to the interview.

Though I arrived late, the interview went well, and I got the job. That role transformed my life, both financially and spiritually, over the next 10 years. I learned that discouragement can derail us, but the right encouragement can realign us with our destiny.

...

**Lord,**
Thank You for sending encouragement when I need it most. Help me trust Your plan and silence doubt.
Amen.

...

# Celebrating The Favor of Encouragement

*Encouragement is a powerful gift, uplifting spirits and igniting hope. Through kind words and actions, we become vessels of God's favor, spreading His love and building a supportive community that reflects His grace and compassion.*

**Now it's your turn to write your story of celebrating The Favor of Encouragement.**

Reflect on a time when encouragement made a significant impact on your life or someone else's. How did this uplifting experience change your perspective and relationships? Describe the ways God's favor was revealed through acts of encouragement and how it continues to inspire your journey and connections.

_____

_____

_____

_____

_____

_____

_____

_____

_____

_____

_____

_____

_____

_____

_____

_____

_____

_____

_____

# THE
# FAVOR
## OF
# *Celebration*

Celebrate every blessing as a testament to God's favor. Every day is a day to celebrate.

# Joyful Praise

...

Psalm 118:24
The Lord has done it this very day; let us rejoice today and be glad.

...

As we reach the end of this year-long journey, it's time to focus on the power of celebration. Life is filled with moments that deserve recognition, and each blessing is a testament to God's abundant favor. Psalm 118:24 reminds us that every day is a gift from the Lord, a reason to rejoice and be glad.

Celebration isn't just about the big milestones; it's about finding joy in the small victories and everyday blessings. Whether it's a morning sunrise, a kind word from a friend, or the sense of peace that fills your heart, these moments are worthy of joyful praise. When we celebrate, we acknowledge God's presence in our lives and invite His favor to continue working within us.

Reflect on the year that has passed and the countless ways God has shown up for you. Maybe it was through a new opportunity, a relationship that brought joy, or a challenge that made you stronger. Each of these is a reason to celebrate, a reminder of His faithfulness and love.

This week, make it a point to celebrate intentionally. Create a gratitude list, share your joy with others, or simply take a moment to thank God for His favor. As you do, you'll find that your heart fills with gratitude and your spirit is refreshed, ready to embrace whatever comes next.

...

Loving Father,
Thank You for the blessings You have poured into our lives. Help us to recognize and celebrate every moment of Your favor. May our hearts be filled with gratitude and our days with joyful praise. Guide us to share our joy with others, spreading Your light and love wherever we go.
Amen.

...

# Redeemed in Resilience

Rochelle D. Jacobs

...

Psalm 145:7 (NIV)
They will celebrate your abundant goodness
and joyfully sing of your righteousness.

...

This world has been full of sorrow, and life hasn't been easy. Financial struggles, grief, childhood trauma, broken relationships with my spouse and family, health scares, and roadblocks have tested my faith over the years. But through every hardship, the favor of celebration has been my spiritual weapon!

As I reflect on my faith journey, this space and season mark many milestones to celebrate my growth, transformation, and the power of God's unwavering faithfulness and favor.

I have shared in this powerful devotion how God has provided for me and my family during our leanest times, when nothing but faith and prayer sustained us. In this season of favor, let's pause to celebrate God's faithfulness. Every transformation in life—mind, body, and spirit—is a testament to His love, grace, and the work He is doing within. God's favor is evident as we walk in renewed purpose, wisdom, and strength. Through my faith journey, I have left behind the pain of the past, stepping into God's promises in His Word and a destiny full of hope, joy, and peace.

Beloved, I invite you to take a moment to reflect on how far you've come and celebrate what God has delighted in you, rejoiced over you, and know without any doubt that He is the source of every blessing in your life.

...

Lord,
Thank You for this season of celebration of favor. We celebrate the transformation you've brought to our mind, body, and spirit, and we stand in awe of the plans you have for us. Help us continue to walk in your strength, grace, and wisdom. May our life be a testimony of your goodness and love.
Amen.

...

# 60 Gifts of Love

Dr. Katherine E. James

...

Psalm 139:14 (NIV)

I praise you because I am fearfully and wonderfully made; your works are wonderful, I know that full well.

...

The Year of our Lord Twenty Twenty-Three, March 9th, marked my 60th birthday. What a blessing to live for six decades. I love this life of mine, where I get to use all that Poppa has imparted to serve His beloved with love.

On that day, I determined to gift at least 60 others with a specially curated love package. Per usual, there was a caravan that convened at my home around 10 am (my friends/sisters). They were among the first to receive the love packages. Then we traveled about an hour for our yearly birthday lunch, where I gifted many staff, servers, and fellow lunch-goers with the love packages (oh, the delight). Next, we went to a local mall where I cold-called, announcing to each mall passerby that it was my birthday, and I wanted to give them a present on my birthday. As you might imagine, there were mixed reviews—some suspicious. Mostly, it was well received. Finally, we ended with dancing. Yes, there too, I gave love packages. This birthday girl met and exceeded her goal to give out 60 gifts on my 60th birthday.

It is my life's purpose to add more love to the world. On my 60th birthday, I demonstratively honored my purpose.

Each year, I look forward to co-creating my birthday celebration with Poppa. How might you use the celebration of your birth to co-create with Poppa and honor your life's purpose?

...

Lord,

Thank You for the gift of life and the joy of sharing love. May every celebration honor You, spreading kindness and purpose to all I encounter.

Amen.

...

# 90th Birthday

Sibyl F. Cole

...

Psalm 16:11 (CEB)

You teach me the way of life. In your presence is total celebration. Beautiful things are always in your right hand.

...

It was a pleasant summer evening in August 2018, and our family gathered at a local restaurant to celebrate a momentous occasion: our mother's 90th birthday. She didn't like having a fuss made over her and fought me and my siblings at every turn about having the party; well, she lost that battle.

The private party room was adorned with beautiful flowers and colorful balloons, with soft music playing in the background. As guests arrived, each person stopped at Mom's chair to hug her, and as much as she protested, I know she enjoyed the love-filled attention.

Family and friends were asked to recount their favorite "mom memories." A close family friend shared how Mom helped her find room and board her junior year of college to attend summer school, while my nephew had us rolling on the floor laughing about the time Mom caught him skipping school at a local mall. She told him his secret was safe with her, then promptly drove him back to school!

As the evening wound down, everyone gathered around the beautifully decorated pink and green cake and sang, "Happy Birthday." Mom made her wish and blew out the candles, and we cheered, not just celebrating her age, but the incredible person she was and the many lives she'd touched.

After I was home and settled, I reflected on the evening's events and realized this celebration was a tribute to a life well-lived and a testament to God's love exuded through our beautiful mother.

...

Gracious God,

We thank You for the gift of celebration, the joy in milestones, and the blessings of togetherness.

Amen.

...

413

# Celebrating Christ In Me

Makini Theresa L. Harvey

...

Ezra 6:16 (NIV)

Then the children of Israel, the priests and the Levites and the rest of the descendants of the captivity, celebrated the dedication of this house of God with joy.

...

My youngest daughter was getting married, establishing her family and her home! I was truly honored and filled with joy to celebrate her big day. However, there was also a heavy dread because I knew her father, ex-husband #2, would be there with his fiancée. Praying fervently, I asked God for wisdom, protection, strength, courage, and His peace.

Our youngest son called, saying he "was elected by his siblings to tell me something." Already knowing, I said, "What?" He replied, "Dad is coming to the wedding with his fiancée." Smiling, I said, "Your dad is grown."

Praying daily, God's peace came over me. The Holy Spirit of God inspired me to write a marriage poem that I read at the wedding. It was well-received by the couple, my grandson, and guests.

When I look back on that day, I can't help but marvel at the favor of celebration God poured out on all of us. Despite every fear, every uncertainty, and every potential tension, the atmosphere overflowed with joy, love, and unity. It was so much more than a wedding; it was a glimpse of God's grace at work, stitching together hearts and creating harmony where division once lived. Only God could have orchestrated something so beautiful.

The favor of God was evident in every small detail—the calmness in my spirit, the peace among the guests, and the overflowing love that saturated the entire day. It was as though the Lord Himself smiled down on this celebration, uniting us all in a moment of pure joy and shared purpose. That favor allowed us to honor my daughter and her husband as they began their new life together, free of strife and full of blessings.

...

God,

My Shield, thank You for Your favor in our celebrations, uniting us in love and peace. Bless our gatherings with Your presence, in the Holy Name of Jesus Christ, Hallelujah and

Amen.

...

# God's Love in Every Hug

### Alethia Saunders

...

Ecclesiastes 2:24-25 (NIV)
A person can do nothing better than to eat and drink and find satisfaction in their own toil. This too, I see, is from the hand of God, for without him, who can eat or find enjoyment?

...

At just twenty years old, I was leaving home, embarking on a new chapter of my life. The years leading up to that moment had been tough—my parents had divorced, my mother was struggling and frail, and my relationship with my father had grown distant. In the midst of it all, my spiritual family became my anchor, holding me together when everything else seemed to be falling apart.

Determined to start over, I decided to move from Florida to Georgia. To mark this new beginning, I planned a going-away party, hoping it would be a chance to gather the people I loved most. Little did I know how much love I was about to experience.

The day of the party arrived, and it was beyond anything I had imagined. Over 250 people came to celebrate with me, filling the room with laughter, hugs, and well-wishes. There was a talent show, two cakes with my name and picture, heartfelt song dedications, and more hugs and kisses than I could count. Joy overwhelmed me as I realized the depth of care and support surrounding me.

In that moment, God reminded me that even in the midst of heartache, I was deeply loved. The people in that room wanted me to succeed and were cheering for my journey ahead. I'll never forget the joy that filled the space that day or the tears of gratitude I shed. It was more than a send-off; it was a celebration of God's provision, showing me that I was never alone.

...

Dear God,
Thank You for the celebration of love and support that surrounds me. May Your provision continue to guide me, and may I always cherish these moments of joy.
Amen.

...

# Celebrating The Favor of Celebration

*Celebration is a joyful acknowledgment of God's abundant blessings and love in our lives. Embrace each moment of joy with gratitude and let your heart overflow with His favor, turning simple moments into cherished memories of His goodness.*

**Now it's your turn to write your story of celebrating The Favor of Celebration.**

Reflect on a recent celebration that highlighted God's blessings in your life. How did this event deepen your gratitude and awareness of His favor? Describe the ways in which celebrating His goodness has enriched your relationships and faith journey, inspiring joy and thanksgiving.

# Gratitude and Hallelujah

Bonita L. Williams

...

## Philippians 4:4 (NIV)
Always be full of joy in the Lord. I say it again—rejoice!

...

As I reflect on my years, all I can say is thank You, Lord. The hymn Amazing Grace resonates deeply with me because it tells my life story. God's grace has carried me through trials and challenges on my journey. Every day, I am reminded of His goodness. As Lamentations 3:22-23 says, "His mercies are new every morning."

Though I've sometimes failed to recognize the blessings in my life, God never stopped sending them. His love and mercy amaze me. To think that someone like me—ordinary and flawed—is cherished by God fills my heart with gratitude and joy. It makes me want to shout, "Hallelujah!"

I encourage you to celebrate life. Each breath is a gift from God. Thank Him for loving you, not only when you do well but also when you fall short. Rejoice today. Thank God through your tears, frustration, heartache, and pain. Thank Him in your abundance and in your struggles. Whatever situation you're in right now, shout and celebrate the amazing grace of God.

Don't allow Satan to steal your joy. Pray, as Psalm 51:12 says, for God to restore the joy of your salvation. Stand firm on His promises. Right now, make a joyful noise to the Lord, our Rock, Redeemer, Help, and Savior. Rejoice and praise His name, for His grace is truly amazing. CELEBRATE!

...

**Lord,**
We celebrate Your grace and unending mercy. Fill our hearts with gratitude,
joy, and strength to praise You in every moment.
Amen.

# Meet the Authors

Dr. Nina M. Addison, Ph.D., the You Can Coach, empowers self-love, dream fulfillment, and self-publishing success. Passionate about youth, she inspires others to achieve their goals. Learn more at www.ninaaddison.com.

Beverley Anderson is the founder of "Flourish You!" As a Burnout Prevention & Executive Coach, she helps women leaders and pastors apply biblical self-care principles to reach their God-given potential in their careers, ministries, or businesses through her B.A.L.A.N.C.E Method.  https://www.flourish-you.com

Autumn Anesi is a loving wife, boy mom, and business coach who helps entrepreneurs build successful online businesses. She is passionate about studying God's Word and guiding others in both faith and entrepreneurship through Christ-centered principles. https://www.passivewealthpath.com/

Cynthia Beckles is a marketing professional and 12-time best-selling co-author. She specializes in helping business owners overcome challenges by selecting effective marketing strategies to elevate their brands and increase clientele. In November 2023, she released her first journal, "Overwhelm Rewired." Find out more: https://bit.ly/maximizingmarketing

Dr. Theresa Billingsley is an author, coach, entrepreneur and minister. Connect with her at drtheresabillingsley@gmail.com

Kimberly Brown, an executive assistant, is passionately pursuing certification as a spiritual health and wellness coach, dedicated to personal growth and empowering others on their wellness journeys.

Sibyl F. Cole lives in Atlanta, GA, and enjoys spending time with her family, especially her two grandsons, Matthew Jr. "M.J." and Kaycen. She cherishes her friendships and is a dedicated member of Alpha Kappa Alpha Sorority, Inc.

Stacey Collins is a heart visionary coach, worshiper, and author empowering women to rediscover their God-given purpose. With a passion for faith, creativity, and transformation, she inspires others to dream, heal, and create a legacy. Connect: @themommacollins.

Elvetra Cossie is a creative, multi-talented soul embracing greatness in the second half of life. A lover of words and oratory endeavors, Vetra is known for her moving prayers and seeks all things nourishing for the mind, body, and spirit.

Ebony Marie Cottman is a devotional writer from Baltimore, Maryland. Her first project, a devotional planner, debuts in January 2025. Visit EbonyMCottman.com to explore her faith journey, teachings, and revelations as she shares God's word and disciples others.

Rosie Davis, children's advocate and tutor, empowers young learners to succeed. Passionate about inspiring young minds, she champions every child's potential.

Ishaq Edwards is a 9-year-old author of four books and creator of The Great Adventures of Ishaq and Kadeedee. He loves cooking, making videos, teaching, and is active in both his church and school community.

Dr. Vanessa D. English is a licensed professional counselor and founder of A New Normal Counseling Services, LLC, serving the Atlanta metro area. With 30+ years in education, she now empowers clients to transform their lives. Learn more at anewnormalcounseling.com.

Vanessa Fortenberry provides relatable and memorable stories. She uses her writing as a tool to communicate inspirational messages for children and adults. Vanessa is an award-winning author of the children's book series, Families Growing in Faith. To learn more, visit: www.vanessafortenberry.com

Makini Theresa L. Harvey is a devoted follower of Jesus, Certified Professional Résumé Writer, and Career Coach, helping professionals land ideal jobs with great benefits and salaries. Contact her at makini@careerabundance.com

Carol Holesak, born into a Jewish family in Brooklyn, New York, discovered faith in Jesus after receiving a Bible in 1978. Her book, Jesus: The Life Journey of a Jewish Girl, is available on Amazon. Visit her at frommyheart2yours.org.

Mrs. Karen McKinney Holley is a Christian. Her belief in the Lord Jesus Christ guides her entire life as she tries to embrace others with love (John 13:35) and serve in whatever capacity she's called to with excellence (Colossians 3:23).

Rochelle D. Jacobs, Amazon Best Selling author and speaker, empowers women through coaching and her podcast, "Free Yourself Friyah," promoting healing and self-care with inspiring dedication.

Dr. Katherine E. James loves loving God, loving others and loving herself. Amongst other roles, she serves as a Self-Love Coach and treasures healthy relationships. Dr. James is especially grateful for her husband, son, and daughter in-love. Connect at drkatherineejames.com

Ashley Jenkins, a work-from-home customer service rep and IT student, is passionate about problem-solving, lifelong learning, and turning everyday challenges into growth opportunities.

Rev. Joyce S. Mallory, PhD, is an accomplished author, speaker, and educator with five decades of experience. As founder of joycemallorybooks, she empowers others to achieve their goals through her writing, teaching, and impactful storytelling.

L. Marie, a widow and proud grandmother of six in Stuart, Florida, is a retired nurse who now enjoys writing and gardening.

Lori Ellen Miller, a Spiritual Empowerment Pathfinder and Speaker, guides women through personal transformation and authenticity. She shares her wisdom to inspire healing, growth, and alignment with their true selves, fostering courage and integrity for a fulfilled, purposeful life journey.

Miya Mills is a mathematics education specialist with 20 years of expertise in teaching, curriculum development, and educational leadership, transforming learning experiences and inspiring future educators.

Adrienne Murphy is a woman of strong faith and resilience. She is the mother of four adult children and grandmother to five grandchildren. In 2021, she became a caregiver to her husband of over 23 years until he succumbed to his illness.

Cody Persell is the Founding Partner of Red Cord Publishing, a minister, author, and speaker passionate about equipping believers in prophetic, healing, and deliverance ministries, helping them experience freedom and walk boldly in their faith.

Felicia Pichon, Houstonian, wife, mother of five, Army veteran, educator turned social entrepreneur. Founder of Sisters Thrive, championing BIWOC health equity and amplifying voices for impactful change. Advocate for thriving, not just surviving.

Kim Porter is a dynamic women's empowerment coach, inspiring women nationwide to embrace their potential and live out God's best for their lives.

Ebonie Pritchett, a doctoral student in Strategic Leadership at Regent University, is an author, former police officer, and leader in women's law enforcement organizations, holding advanced degrees in Cybersecurity and Sociology and inspiring others through her professional and written work.

Mary Riley is an avid reader and aspiring author of Christian romance and women's fiction, devoted to sharing her faith in a genuine and relatable way.

Alethia Saunders, a committed Career Development Coach and Ghostwriter, empowers others to reach their fullest potential, dedicating herself to supporting personal and professional growth in those she serves.

Sheryl Simms is a librarian and loving wife, passionate about spreading God's love and uplifting others in her community.

Mary Haney Underwood writes from her home in Northern Virgina. You can contact her at mary@whatemptynest.com. Her book, Adopted Twice, the story of God's faithfulness through her adoption, comes out in spring 2025.

Veronica Washington is a retired teacher who cherishes her grandkids and uplifts her community through volunteering, mentoring, and spreading kindness every day.

Janice White is a Faith-Based Life Coach and Entrepreneur specializing in helping others navigate life's challenges with trust and resilience rooted in God's promises. With a background in financial consulting, she uses her own powerful testimonies of divine provision and perseverance to inspire others to lean on faith during their toughest seasons.

Bonita L. Williams, devoted to spreading the Gospel, inspires women as an author, speaker, and founder of Faithful Sisters Movement Ministry, uplifting Jesus Christ and nurturing God-given gifts.

Melanie Winters is a dedicated Personal Self-Care Strategist with a passion for helping others achieve balance and wellness. With her expertise in self-care strategies, she empowers individuals to prioritize their well-being and lead fulfilling, healthier lives.

www.ingramcontent.com/pod-product-compliance
Lightning Source LLC
Chambersburg PA
CBHW070548100426
42744CB00006B/246